Books by Michael Rossman

THE WEDDING WITHIN THE WAR

ON LEARNING AND SOCIAL CHANGE

On Learning and Social Change

ON LEARNING AND SOCIAL CHANGE

Michael Rossman

RANDOM HOUSE
NEW YORK

Grateful acknowledgment is made to the Regents
of the University of California for permission to
reprint material from *The Teachings of Don Juan,*
by Carlos Castaneda, University of California Press.

Library of Congress Cataloging in Publication Data

Rossman, Michael.
  On learning and social change.

  Includes bibliographical references.
  1. Education, Higher—1965–   . 2. Learning,
Psychology of. 3. Social change. I. Title.
LB2322.R67   378   72–621

ISBN:0–394–48082–1

Manufactured in the United States of America by
American Book–Stratford Press, N.Y.

98765432

First Edition

Acknowledgments

After "private" circulation and informal printing by student groups at Antioch, Dayton, Urbana, San Diego, and the National Student Association, versions of these chapters were published as follows: (1) *Change Magazine,* January 1970; *Glamour,* August 1970; (3) *Here And Now,* May 1970; *The Changing College Classroom,* Runkel *et al.,* eds. (Jossey-Bass, 1970); *Thought from the Educational Reform Movement,* Kean, ed. (NSA, 1970); (4) *Summerhill: For and Against,* Hart, ed. (Hart Publishing Co., 1970); (5) *Sunrise,* April 20, 27, 1970; *The L.A. Free Press,* September 11, 1970; (7) *New American Review* #12; *Ecology: Crisis and New Vision,* Sherrell, ed. (John Knox Press, 1972); (8) *The Ed Reform Papers,* Linney, ed. (NSA, 1969); (10) *New Schools Exchange Newsletter* #s 51, 52, 70. I thank them each and all for helping this work to circulate, and also for the permissions that enable its present publication.

In addition, certain special thanks: to Len Stevens for encouraging me to write dialogue: to Tom Morrey for rekindling technological romance; to Heinz von Foerster for cultured hustling to support self-organizing systems; to Sarah Hartley for the same; to Harold Taylor for five years of encouragement and the last-minute consultation that nerved me to include Chapters 2 and 6; to Michael Kinney and Anne Freedgood for their deep involvement with the material itself as well as the process of bringing it to its present form; and to Karen McLellan for sharing in some of the thought about the Tao as well as with some of the shitwork.

The chapters, as they were written:

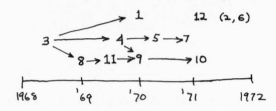

1   12   (2,6)

3 → 4 → 5 → 7

8 → 11 → 9 ————→ 10

1968   '69   '70   '71   1972

INSCRIPTION FOUND
IN THE HOUSEBOOK OF
A SECRET ACADEMIC SOCIETY,
HIGH IN THE SIERRAS:

Love your laity

in this time of doubt, look beyond

the Keepers of the Tablets,

do not take their Word

for granite, do you, du?

there are common

deeper voices, find them

in your own.

Contents

METAPHORS

METAPHORS

I.

A Curtain Raiser: Transcending the Totalitarian Classroom

SETTING THE STAGE

THEY DON'T KNOW ME from a Professor—and neither do you, though I look like the freak from down the block—when I walk into this classroom of college kids, tell them my name, and say:

"I want to lead you through a learning game called the Totalitarian Classroom. Whoever plays must agree to a few rules and roles. These create a stage. Upon it, we'll hold a real discussion of a critical subject: how people act out their parts as *good students* in the classroom game. Maybe we can go on to consider what, if anything, this game has to do with good learning."

I think they expect a lecture. What else, from the Education Department? All they've been told is that I'm a resource in educational reform who's worked with many student groups around the country and wants to talk about the way students and teachers alike have been conditioned to play the social games that dominate education. But I want to do more, especially since some of them are organizing a Free University off-campus and looking for new ways to think about learning.

So I decide to take us through a *de*conditioning game, make a theater of our experience to give a new perspective on the roles we normally play in the learning game.

"I start by assuming you're each a *good student*. I take this to mean you're independent, critical, you have your own unique viewpoint. So I'm always free to ask you to express a view that *differs* from one someone else gives—say, by extending or contradicting his. Likewise, I assume you're in command of the material and can make connections between its parts. So I can call on you to explain the *connection* between any two points other people make. These are the only rules. And they're reasonable, right?"

I think of how they'll feel when I indicate that the connection between A and B is quite clear and ask by words or a look why they can't see it. I don't need much idea of it myself—no one will challenge me to describe it. Who wants to beg for a lecture and see his ignorance further displayed? But for now they are eager to play. So I ask for volunteers for the three formal roles of the Game.

"One way to present yourself as *good student* is to display your command of the material. So we'll want a Scribe, to take absolutely verbatim notes. Another way is to brown-nose, to agree with the teacher. So we want a Yes man. When I ask him about anything, 'Is that right, Mr. Yes?' his job will be to say, 'Yes, that's right,' and then *explain why*. Likewise, since you also win points for creative disagreement in the classroom game, we'll want a No man, whose job will be to answer, 'No, that's wrong,' and then explain why. Is all this clear?"

"Are the rest of us supposed to play roles?" asks someone.

"No, no one else should be trying to play-act a role. Everyone should respond as who they are—even the three volunteers, except when they're called on in role. So let's be our natural selves and try to make the discussion as real and substantive as we can."

I too will be natural, though they'll find this hard to believe afterward. They'll point out the way I use the rules to punctuate or speed the game and advance the discussion. But these are only the formal traces of the control the group grants to the role of Authority. Like a grading system, they create a stage for totalitarian theater. Simply establishing their power is enough; I can run the classroom game to my desire while calling them rarely into play.

As I ask for volunteers for Yes man and No man, I can tell by the way people shift in their seats who depends on these strategies in everyday games. I do not pick the most promising candidates. Later I will use them unofficially to shape the discussion, for their responses are keyed to me; and then lead them to recognize their unconscious roles.

But no one wants to be Scribe, it's an enormous dirty job. I state that the richest examples of *good student* behavior lie in the precise words people choose for their responses, which is true; and then drive the group into a "democratic" election to stick someone with the role. They spring gladly to pinning the tail on a donkey; I can see all sorts of trivial antagonisms surface in joking nominations. They choose a girl, of course. Later she'll cry when I press her with questions and she tries to explain how impossible it is to think or respond while she's recording material for playback. But she'll go back to taking notes when I demonstrate, by calling on people, that no one can remember accurately *anything* anyone else has said.

ACT I: THE CLASSROOM

Already, as discussion begins, I'm in total control. Marked as the Expert, bankrolled with special Knowledge, I'm the Man Who Knows What Should Happen. I ride with the illusion as I lead our theater through its acts. In the first, I get them to describe in detail ways in which *good students* act out their roles.

"Okay. What are some ways in which people project themselves as *good students* in the classroom theater?"

"They come to class on time."

Someone else: "They hand in their homework."

"Yes. Yes. Some other ways?"

"Eye contact with the teacher is very important, so is volunteering information."

"So is coming up to him after class to talk about anything."

"And if you dress neat."

Too many people are trying to talk all at once, they start raising their hands. I call on the girl who puts hers up first. "Good students sit in the front row," she says primly.

"But you can also use *not* sitting in front to show you're a *good student,* don't you think?"

She looks worried. "Well, I guess so . . ."

Toward the back of the room I see Mr. No twitching in his seat. I shift my eyes to him. "It's because sitting in front looks too phony," he says. "That makes sense, doesn't it?" I ask her. She nods uncertainly.

"What about the way people look?" I ask the fullback type hunched in his chair. "How do you look when you've just been asked a question you can't answer, but you don't want the teacher to know you haven't thought about it?"

"I sit up straight and wrinkle my forehead, searching. Maybe he'll speak first."

"And you?"

"I lean forward a little and look earnest and try to talk about something else."

"And you . . . ?"

Soon our discussion reveals that different choices of where to sit, of posture, dress and expression, of docile or cocksure attitude, etc., are rich elements in a variety of styles of projecting oneself as a *good student* in the classroom. I lead us on to recognize complete strategies.

"What might go with sitting in the back row and looking out the window, to project a whole *good student* image?"

"Missing a lot of classes, but seeing the man in his office, maybe not during regular hours."

"You, can you give me an independent opinion? No? Well, you, then?"

"Being casual with your homework, but sparkling on the final."

"What's the connection between the last two answers?" I ask the one who seems to be class Cynic.

"Both times you're showing that you know what's important."

"Very good!" Actually, it isn't, but I like to give praise. It makes them feel appreciated. "This strategy will work with every teacher. Is that so, Mr. No?"

"No, that's wrong, it'll only work with some."

"Because?"

"Because some teachers are uptight about petty detail."

"In other words," I say, reading his reply to suit my prejudice, "what's important is what *they* think's important. I take it you use this strategy yourself?"

"Something like it," he admits.

"All right. So it's clear, different strategies work with different teachers—and different classes, they're part of the audience too. Now the question is, why? What determines whether a particular projection of yourself as *good student* will be successful, besides your skill in acting it out?"

"If it helps the teacher play his own role well, if your role complements his."

"Hmmm. Is that right, Mr. Yes?"

"Yes, that's right. Because then it satisfies his image of himself, it feeds his ego."

"Is that your real opinion, or your role speaking?"

He hesitates and then says, "Yes."

"Then does the image or role of a *good student* necessarily resemble that of the *good teacher* he's facing?"

"No."

"Can anyone give an example?"

"What about the acid-freak in class, and the scholarly prof who translates the freak's occasional insights—which of course *he* recognizes—so the rest of the dull class can understand them?"

ACT II: WE LOOK AT US IN THE CLASSROOM

Now we are caught up fully in the roles and rhythms of the classroom. I respond to each person, each thought, with genuine interest, and by this incessant validation keep the group's energy always focused on me. I am overdoing it, of course—I only need react to every fifth interesting thought, and grunt or smile in between, to control the space.

From here I take the Totalitarian Classroom into its second act, in which it becomes *reflexive* theater, play that begins to comment upon its own performance.

"How long does it take to figure out what a teacher expects and what *good student* strategy you can play with him?"

An indistinct buzz. The lowest estimate: "Maybe like three weeks."

"Anyone think the time is shorter?"

"You can tell where most teachers are at inside the first hour or so," says the fullback.

"Can you tell him why you think it doesn't take three weeks?"

"The way he talks about midterms and homework, how he's dressed, whether he wants to bullshit a bit or get right down to it, things like that."

"Why did you say that looking at *me*, when I asked if you could explain it to *him?*"

"Because . . . I don't know."

I ask the other one: "Did his explanation make sense? Do you see why three weeks is too long an estimate?"

"Yes, I can see that it starts right at the beginning, like whether he asks the class questions about themselves."

"Wait." I ask the group, "What is there about what he just said that presents him as a *good student?*"

"He admits his mistake."

"Anyone have a sharper answer?"

"He not only admits it, he shows he's learned by adding something new."

"Right on! Now go back. When I asked how you look when trying not to show you don't know the answer, five people gave me different answers—showing they were individuals, that's fine. But everyone answered in words. No one demonstrated their look itself, even though we all know how many words a picture's worth. How come?"

"You wanted us to answer in words."

"How do you know? As a matter of fact, I hoped someone wouldn't."

"It's because you're articulate. I think."

"How is that a *good student* response?"

"He was uncertain and afraid you'd tell him he was wrong, so he took care to qualify it."

"Right. But I think he's right. Can you go on? I mean, how does my being articulate work?"

No one follows me. "Let's get at this differently," I say.

I can change ground whenever I want. On the familiar territory of my specialty, I need never appear at a loss for words. "The other side of the *good student* game is the *good teacher* game. So: in what ways have I been presenting myself as a *good teacher* here?"

"You're confident, you seem to know what you're doing," says a natural Yes man. "You care what people say and try to draw them out."

"Thanks for feeding my ego. Something more impersonal?" Or personal?

"Well, first, you stand at the front and you're always moving," says someone, "that way we have to focus on you. Secondly, you look people in the eye—that's how you call on them to speak too. Third, you keep trying to probe deeper for answers. Fourth . . ."

"Stop right there. Can someone say: how is he projecting himself as a *good student?*"

"I'm not playing *good student,*" he protests.

"I don't think you're trying to. But I'm not asking you. Someone else?"

They guess. He volunteered, he's observant, he's original. I ask for something more original.

"He said, 'first, second, third . . .'," says a blonde.

"Right. How does that present him as a *good student?*"

"It shows he has an orderly mind."

"Do you always say, 'first, second, third . . .'?" I ask him.

"No."

"Why do you say it here, how do I cue that response?"

"You speak like that yourself, even though you don't say the numbers."

Hmmmmmm. . . . "How was that a presentation-of-self-as-good-student?"

"He gave you a sharp answer," says Mr. No, "even though it might have offended you."

"How do you know that strategy's a good one to choose with me?"

"Because of how long your hair is."

"Yes, I pride myself on my tolerance. But I talk like a pedant still, so you know to give a pedantic answer. Right?"

Ah, we are all so deeply conditioned! We cannot discuss the classroom game without at the same time playing it. I am acting out the role I was trained to assume in a context of directed and goal-oriented learning, and so is everyone else. But here with a difference, for I call our attention constantly to this. Unlike the theater of the standard classroom, here the rules of the play are on stage as a focus of the play, not politely unmentioned. And we are thus forced to a doubled consciousness, within the play and of the play *as play,* simultaneously, which painfully opens a new way of seeing.[1]

(You might notice the family resemblance to Brecht's notions of *alienation* in the theater. It's not accidental. Totalitarian Classroom Game was first designed by a young professor of English, Neil Kleinman, who was deeply involved in the study of modern theater and reflexive form.)

By now, late in the second act, the pressures and pain of this new consciousness are mounting. The players become confused and frustrated as they struggle to keep going on by responses whose conditioned character someone may at any time point out, eagerly and accurately. I ask someone again whether it's he himself speaking, or a role. He complains in anguish that he *doesn't know.* Not even the Teacher's Pet is at ease.

I've never seen a classroom game without a Pet relationship, if not two. This time the Pet is the willow blonde with quick eyes, though it takes me almost an hour to figure this out. Now I understand what happened to the brief sexual flash which passed between us as our eyes met when I entered the room and continues to echo. But I'm still surprised to recognize how the fact that we respond to each other as man and woman has acted below the surface of our awareness to make her a protected person, keep her

[1] For more on this, see pp. 119–20.

warm in the cold classroom climate, and leave her free to play with her mind. And be my Teaching Assistant, in effect —of course, that's part of the bargain.

"Oh, I see how it happens," she says now, without even raising her hand. "The 'first, second . . .' business, I mean, it's a closed system. The men who run the School of Ed happen to be good at explaining things analytically. So they teach us that's the way to deal with teaching. If you can't fit to their style, too bad. But I'll get my credential and super recommendations, because I've learned to understand things their way and forgotten other ways. And then I'll go teach little kids. I'll smile when they explain in a way I can understand, and I won't smile when I can't understand them. And they'll grow up to be like me. Or Professors of Education."

"That's the way it goes," I agree. "That's why two million kids have dropped acid; it's one of the ways to learn that there are many ways of knowing other than the ones they teach us in the schools."

I look at her again. Our eyes merge. I pull away, switch into reflexive mode, and ask around the room for people to comment on what they observe here of my relation to her, hers to me. No one feels like volunteering much by now, even on safer topics. So I spell it out, about the sexual dynamics and her being my T.A. and all. She colors. The room is eager and fearful. No one feels comfortable, talking about the rules or about the processes they mask.

"I don't like what's going on!" someone bursts out. "I can see we're learning, but the way of it's messing over my mind."

"Can you see another way to learn about classroom process?" I ask him. "This is the only way I know that's not simply rhetorical."

He is silent. "Oh, he's just playing the rebel role again," someone informs me in eager support. The rebel retreats in indecision, slinks down in his chair.

I marvel again at how instantly ready they are to tear each other down after 15,000 hours of conditioning in the competitive classroom, worshipping the gods of Success and Failure. I call on a girl who has been watching in shrinking terror to tell us what kind of game the rebel-*watcher* is playing. She starts to stammer out an accurate indictment. Then she realizes that in this context she is simply compounding the violence. She breaks down crying. The rebel jumps up and slams out of the room.

Either way, an act of defeat. But also the blind start of an act of liberation, saying in angry pain, "I won't play your game any longer." At last someone moves to comfort the girl, and I announce that the Totalitarian Classroom Game is ended.

And just in time: the invisible bells ring, another group of inmates has to use this cell. I ask whoever cares to continue to come on over to the cafeteria.

ACT III: DEALINGS WITH THE FEELINGS

Scene 1

Late afternoon, the tables are almost empty. We gather over coffee in the formica desert. And Act III begins, the one without a program. I ask people to say what they were feeling in the classroom, read out their emotions instead of their thoughts. There is a long silence.

"At first I was open and curious," says a guy who sat near the front, "and excited by what you were driving at. Then I don't know, it was like I just got bored somehow, and my mind quit following, and I started looking out the window."

"I was so frustrated!" exclaims the girl beside him.

"Every time I thought of something you called on someone else, or on me only to follow up some point you were making."

"It was suffocating," he agrees. "You never let the talk get very far off the subject, and you kept it moving along. There was no place for me."

"But he had something to teach us," someone objects, "and only the time of the class. I think what he pointed out is useful."

"Emotions, emotions," I say. "What were you feeling?"

Finally the girl who cried says, "I was afraid of you. Right from when we started I was scared to volunteer. You were so quick, you knew just what you wanted. I felt stupid, if I gave an answer you got someone to give a better one, or took mine and twisted it."

"He helped us take what we see every day and put it together to see in a new way. I don't think I'll ever see the classroom the old way again, as if it were some benevolent paradise."

Emotions, emotions. We go around the table. Now that Fear is named, many confess to it. Early on our classroom became for most a place where reward is to be left alone; and punishment, to be called upon to answer by the finger of Authority. They argue: was our last hour a parody, or did it simply expose the main features of the classroom process in high relief? How we hide our feelings!

"What about anger?" I ask. Silence. "Surely the guy who slammed out was angry. No one else?"

"Well, I was very frustrated," says someone. "But I wasn't what I'd call angry." Some nod in agreement. Most sit in their chairs rigid with hostility.

"Is thaaaat so?" I drawl mockingly, sorry to have to go through it again. "Well, I think there's so much anger here with the fear that people are afraid to show it. Because I've been doing a lot of violence. And everyone has been help-ing me do it. You're eager to give a better answer than the next guy. You believe me, or at least back down, when I tell you you're wrong and give you any old quick argument. You don't address each other, and you meet only my eyes. I attack people, and no one defends them. No one touches any one. Someone has to break down crying to get a little support. And you're still choked with anger. Clearly."

Learning is mostly silence—but this live kind, not the other. Finally Willow Blonde says, "It makes me think of Kitty Genovese. The girl who was stabbed to death on a New York streetcorner while thirty-two people watched. And no one did anything."

"And it's like the Milgram Experiment," I remind her, "that you read about in Psychology, where they took people off the street and had them give electric shocks to strangers to punish them for getting wrong answers to a test. One in three would shock someone into unconsciousness. Just because the researcher told them to. All that obedience conditioning, it gets to be a habit."

The Free U kids wear anti-War buttons. I can feel the guilt rise in the room. Then Willow breaks out in confusion. "But I've done it again! The same behavior. Haven't I?"

"I don't know," I tell her honestly, "it's a hard game to break. I think we need to behave differently to break it."

"It goes on and on like a nightmare," says the ex-Scribe.

"This is unreal!" says the fullback, now openly angry. "I think it's you that's playing the game. You're faking the situation, you want to keep control of everything. But we aren't in class any more."

Scene 2

"We may have changed the way we sit to a circle, but it takes more to change the game," I tell him. "Even more than my not wanting control. Your body wants to hit me now, but it half-raised an arm for permission before you

spoke. You're still making me the focus of attention, reacting to me. You give me the control.

"And do I want it?" I go on, enjoying it. "Damn right!
Because I'm using it for something. You see me playing a
destructive game. I think I'm trying to drive an old form
past its limits and into something new. Maybe we're both
right. But I wish you'd recognize how real our situation is
and believe that I'm not faking.

"For you're here freely to learn, so am I, to help you.
I come in with some specialized knowledge I've worked to
help generate. I know some find it useful. You know about
this, but don't know quite what it is or really what you want
to know. So you treat me as an Expert. And I share what I
have the best way I'm able, by sharing the experience instead of just describing it.

"For what we're doing here, reflexive theater—though it
feels like torture more than we can put in words—is really
two tools pushed to extremes. One is our awareness of the
process of our learning."

Do you sort back, watch yourself reading this, to think of
how that has been, of how you display yourself as the
learner you are?

"Paying attention to process is a consciousness, there are
ways to develop it. It's the strongest tool I know for creating
a different and healthier way of learning. The other tool
is theater itself, which leads into many new learning-forms.

"But my helpfulness in pointing this out doesn't change
the fact that our experience in this new form is an old game:
I'm still running you through my program. And your anger
is still unaddressed. And the pain is still happening. I know
because I am in pain, because I too am forced to see by the
theater we create.

"I see that to teach you tools that empower, in the best
way I know, involves putting you through painful changes."
Is this better than the lecture's safe tedium? "And that I
also am willing to do this, to give you a little pain with your

illumination—for your own good, of course." Sometimes it terrifies me, how naturally I can play the Professor, cop to all those hallowed liberal rationalizations.

"And I see the part of me that always wants to lecture, to cram in some more information, get it all said now, instead of waiting for people to develop in their own time and ways." But do you have the patience? "And the part that needs constantly to be proving, in your eyes and mine, that I am a 'good teacher.' " And what is the style of your need for proof? "And the part that loses patience when you do not see what I see, and by informing you steals your discovery. And the part that rises up angry when you see something that matters differently than I do and threaten my view of myself and the world's order."

For I see my soft fascist, who believes he must control all and tries even now with the power of my words to coerce you into agreement.

"Because I too am afraid of the dark and the Chaos beyond the mirrors we make. And I see also the part that fears what you will think of me for all this and struggles in me not to meet your eyes."

Late afternoon, in the wilderness of the cafeteria. "We're paralyzed as much by your confession as by your reasoning," says Willow wonderingly.

The fullback is growing angrier. "You're still playing the game!"

"No, *you* are," accuses someone.

And then Mr. No stands up, his hands behind his back, and announces, "I think I know how to break the game." Laughter and anger struggle on his face, triumph and fear, as his hands whip into sight: one with a fistful of sugar packets from the table container, the other throwing one that stings my ear with a soft *spat!*, and another that misses as I duck down by my chair.

In a minute the air is busy with flung missiles. I get my appropriate share of attack, most thrown with real feeling.

And so does everyone else; an indiscriminate bombardment forces even the reluctant to join in self-defense. You wouldn't believe how much sugar they set out for dinner. For ten minutes we go at full tilt, tipping tables and hoarding our stockpiles behind their barricades. Packets are splitting on the ceiling fixtures and showering sugar in our hair, and finally we all collapse in general laughter and shouting.

Scene 3

We are tidying up when the building manager arrives, huffing and puffing. He's outraged, he wants to know who's in charge, we can't do this here, etc. I set my Responsibility instinct to work counting packets, and wait. "There's no one in charge," Mr. No informs him. "We're a class in experimental theater, we're rehearsing. And you can relax, we'll clean it up. Do you think you could find us a broom?"

Could he have apoplexy? His assistant arrives. Someone warns him: "Careful, man, this is liberated space."

"That's right," says the girl who was Scribe, tossing him a handful of sugar. "If you stay, you got to play." Two or three kids get set to throw at him. In jest?

They have no program for even a sugar rebellion. Jealous of their dignity, they retreat, warning us to clean it up and threatening us with their return. As they leave the manager is asking his man who the Chairman of the Drama Department is now.

"For a moment there," says the fullback, "I saw a flash of pure hate cross that guy's face. He's even worse than he is"—pointing at me—"about giving up control. Or maybe just more transparent."

Heady with disobedience, we straighten the tables for our own comfort. "That's really the problem," says Willow. "He controls all the space. We're always forced to deal in his terms, whether or not he's the one talking. I think we need to learn how to share space. As well as take it over."

Another silence. We are easier with them by now.

The girl who always sits on the outside breaks it. "I don't think it's by having no leader," she says. "It's by each of us leading in his own way when he should. Like me, I watch people. I see lots who relate differently to books than the ones who talk easily in class do. Sometimes I hear what the teacher and talkers don't. I could translate it for them or tell them something about how they see differently. I don't because there is no support. But I should."

"I'm curious," says the Cynic. "That's the first thing I've ever heard you say. Why did you start talking now?"

"I guess being in the sugar fight opened things up. Inside me, as well as between us. It was partly just moving. I think it's sick to sit in a room and hear things that make you angry or sad or happy and not be able to move your body or yell."

"I can dig lettin' it out," he agrees. "But it doesn't help change whatever messed us up in the first place."

"Well, it does," she says. "I threw sugar at you because I like how you think but not the way you cut people down in class. Next time you do that, I think maybe I trust this group enough to throw at you again. And now that I've gotten angry, I don't feel so choked up. It's like I have energy, maybe to do something different."

"There's so much anger," says someone in wonderment, looking at the mound of packets we have piled up. "If it's getting built up like that all the time, I can see why more and more campuses are exploding."

"Sure, people don't like having nothing to say about what they have to do," says the fullback. "In the army I heard of whole battalions refusing orders. They try to hush it up. When I got out I went into business. But it was all the same. So here I am now. Whaddaya know, it's like high school was."

"Maybe we should all be in encounter groups," suggests the Scribe. "Like this one."

"But that doesn't change who has the power and who's in control," says the Cynic. "I see people using groups and 'sensitivity' to avoid dealing with real issues."

Willow agrees. "I feel groups are like a playground for the emotions, where they're isolated, just like class is an isolated playground for my mind. But I want to bring them together—that's part of the power and control I want. And I don't think this is an encounter group. What excites me here is that we keep working with our ideas and our emotions at the same time."

What excites me here is you, my dear, plus about seven other people so far. And the notion that, unlike encounter groups, this game doesn't work to adjust people to the established power structure.

ACT IV: MOVING ON

"The idea in this that gets me is theater," says Mr. No. "Like, I knew when I threw the first packet that I was picking a way to *act out* my anger. Like it felt very theatrical. But it gave us something we could all do together, to focus on what we were dealing with and then talk about afterward. *That* kind of sequence excites me. I'm not used to learning that way. I can see that it's a strong tool. What I want to know is, what else can we use it for? Someone said we need to learn how to share space. That's true in the Free U too, we're free of a lot of the old restrictions but we still need to learn how to cooperate. Is there some kind of theater we could do around that? Would anyone like to try something like that?"

A murmur of general agreement. Now that the lead is flexible, I can share it if I'm careful. Grateful for the chance to make what I know useful instead of paralyzing, I say, "The people I share work with call that sort of thing a learning game. It's not hard to get the hang of making them. One way to start is, you divide into teams on some basis, and then pick a tangible way to represent what you're trying to think about."

They ponder that. "Each team could dance together, to act out cooperation," says the outside girl. "Or maybe build something together, like we could build it here, with these tables and chairs. Each team could have half the space."

"Yes, but they should have to compete for materials," says Mr. Yes. "Because that's how it is."

The fullback digs that. "When we get done building, each team could take turns attacking while the other defends what it's built."

People object, "That'd be dangerous." Someone says, "Maybe we could do it in slow motion, to make it safe?"

"Hold it, hold it," I urge. "Already we've got a very rich game. See, when we construct something, we're also building a team society at the same time, with some balance of competition and cooperation; and it'll go through a lot of changes in attack and defense. We've got to force ourselves to make the theater slow. Slow motion's a beginning."

"What about doing everything without words, only noises and gestures?"

"And we could do it in a time-jam. Like give ourselves twenty minutes to build, and maybe some time to plan strategy, and then ten minutes each for attack and defense."

"What about we have one team women and the other men?" says Willow. I notice for the first time her Women's Liberation button.

"What about we get some dinner first," I suggest. "We need a change of rhythm. And it looks like it's going to be a long night."

Later this evening we play our game and study how men and women tend to build, compete and cooperate in different styles. In slow-motion conflict the subterranean tangle of hate and love borne by the sexes for each other reveals itself in brief violent tableaux among symbolic architecture. Talking this over among themselves, some more of the women realize with delight and some fear that they like each other, that they find what they have to say to each other interesting—more interesting now than the men.

The men talk about politics. The activists start to see how, despite the partial liberation of its anger, their campus movement is still shaped by the classroom conditioning; how people paralyze their energies by re-creating old Authorities to make their decisions. Together we talk of how political meetings display the aggressive ego-struggle of the seminar stripped of its velvet gloves, of how even the women's team in our game fell back to this behavior under the pressures of time and attack. And then it is midnight.

In the morning I type out Sylvia Plath's incredible poem "Daddy" with its brilliant imagery about teaching and the *macho* figure.

And I leave it on the stove for Willow to find, with a note: "To let you know who else has been leading my learning. Love, Michael."

By the time she wakes I'm sharing a ride to another campus some hours away, to be with friends who have moved along one of the roads Willow and her friends may follow up if they choose to keep working together. They organized a collective, to learn to share space and work. My sisters there used the faculty to force the administration to establish a Women's Studies Program. (Sometimes they took their brothers' aid.) The men are setting up new media for the unheard voices.

Together we want to work out a series of learning games to probe the aspects of our sexuality and connect them up with our political behavior. The sisters are starting a Free School for community children. Its staff will be a learning group of the Free U; they will work on the problem of reformulating education, of freeing its perspectives and methods from the dominant style of the exploitive male ego.

I don't think higher education as we know it will survive. It is designed around one way of knowing and learning. But each group of young people I see work seriously to figure out what they want to learn and then how to learn it, come to share a common experience. To learn together they have to reverse just everything about the totalitarian classroom. Instead of meeting as strangers at arbitrary times to touch only minds, mutual interests draw them deeply into each other for long open periods. Instead of a society centered on Authority and its punishments/rewards, they work for a democratic peer society that generates its own motivations. They grow toward becoming a family, an intimate collective of learning and action. I don't think such a learning family can survive inside a classroom, however the walls be redecorated.

The liberation of education is only now beginning. In headlines and in secret, on a thousand campuses and in many ways, people are figuring out what to do next. So was I, in 1968, when I had to speak at a conference on educational reform, and remembered Neil's Totalitarian Classroom Game. Now on strange campuses I meet students who learned it from someone who learned it from someone who learned it from someone who was there, and they explain how they're designing the freshman orientation program around it. Thus our learning games spread.

If you're still in the classroom you can close this up, treat it just like another book, thinking, "Pity he talks so much." But if you're looking for something to start with, you might consider the T.C.G. In this theater we share right now, you watch me watch you reading what I'm writing. You try to understand whether this play of our interaction has been *reflexive* all along, and whether this would make sense of my odd awkward phrasings and redundancy. What are we doing here? Is this the old Totalitarian Essay game again, where I exhort and you uh-huh? But we see that you have the option to open another act, if you're tired of all this repetition and you want to provoke a new experience. Take it from me: reflexive theater is a form, not a specific program, and anyone can lead it. We've all been well trained, all it takes is figuring out the style in which your own soft fascist works, and being willing to meet him or her in public, if you haven't already. For you know how to introduce it after that: you walk into class, and begin,

"I want to lead you in a learning game. . . ."

II.

Context

THIS BOOK STARTED COOKING in 1964, during the Berkeley Free Speech Movement, the first open revolt against the institution of American higher education.

Though I had been active six years in the young New Left, up to then we had attempted few organized alternatives to anything. So I was a Teaching Assistant in Mathematics, as alienated from the university as everyone I knew, doing acid and going through personal changes. I'd thought some about my schooling, but never deeply about learning in general. The FSM changed all that. What began as a political movement led many of us to reconsider our education itself. For the first time, we began collectively to articulate our discontent and to move to build new forms.[1]

The year after FSM was my last in school. I taught in an experimental undergraduate program. Its head doubled as Chairman of the Philosophy Department and was proud to share a birthday with Thomas Hobbes. We differed strongly over educational policy. He cursed me all over campus for being a mindless anti-authoritarian, an inciter of barbarian hordes who would destroy Western Civilization. I thought he was mostly right, except about the mindless part. Even there he had a point, for I was pretty inarticulate then. Battered by encounter and confrontation, my frameworks were breaking down, and the new ones forming were still all scraps and partial, raw energy unformed. I could hardly find words to tell him why it should be destroyed, let alone to describe what might be born from its death.

I had been marking time as a mathematician and student activist while looking for a way to invest my long-term energy. I'd long since lost faith in electoral politics as a technology for significant social change, and the Vietnam Day Committee experiences of October 1965 clearly foreshadowed the limits of confrontation politics. Now I began to think that educational change is a more basic technology —that systematic root-reconstruction of education is a key lever for freeing human energy for the radical potentials of this time.

Watching the way the scholars and bureaucrats responded to the issues raised by the FSM made me realize how pernicious to thought and action the academic atmosphere really was. Teaching in a System-sponsored "innova-

[1] As I was one of the more visible figures of the FSM, the media have ever since been after me with the burning question, *What happens to student radicals as they grow up; are they still as crazy seven years later?* How can I tell them, it is a process, not a state? But you might take my sketchy account here as being, beneath its personal particulars, somewhat representative of the committed activists I've known—for almost all still continue to seek ways to move on.

tion" raised hopes only to frustrate them and convinced me that if I wanted some leverage to transform education, inside-the-System wasn't where to stand to get it. I would have to go outside, to find or help form some independent base from which to deal with this institution in my own terms. To reinforce my decision I was fired from the program—"for grooving with the students," as Hobbes put it—and then literally kicked out of graduate school for finally getting up nerve enough not to pay a library fine immediately.

"So I dropped out of school and drifted for a time." How many people have told me that in their tales of changes? For five seasons I drifted through the confusion of changes that comes when you leave the context in which you have grown to define your work and your skills and set out to re-create them in new social space. Even if you are in touch with your secret processes, you endure this period of deep reorganization during which thought won't focus and your powers are scattered.

I felt as tender as a crab freshly moulted of his shell. Karen shouldered the money-hassle during this time, freeing me from the need to harden too soon—we have been able to take turns doing this sort of timely thing for each other—and, thus protected, I had only my own yammering need to "be productive" to fight against in yielding to change. As I poked around, new thoughts and new arrangements of skill slowly came together in me, and I began to learn ways to connect my energy into the common pool.

I spent the summer of 1966 aimless, save for writing down what I understood about the relation between the New Left and education in pretty chaotic prose.[2] That fall I hung out at the San Francisco State Experimental College,

[2] The coherent part you will find in *The Wedding Within the War* under the title "The Movement and Educational Reform." Besides several other essays on the outer politics of educational change, *WWW* also goes more deeply into some examples and themes of this book as they appeared in historical context (particularly those of Chapter IV below).

then in its first flush of success as the prototype campus-based "free university," absorbing some perspectives and skills from its founders. That winter Harold Taylor invited me to New York to work with him. We fed each other's minds delightfully. He was marvelously supportive and gave me the freedom to do what I wanted to at a pregnant time: I spent three months traveling to Eastern campuses, studying the political movement and the newly sprouting student-based movement for educational change. I met many people in many places beginning the struggle to organize themselves into power and clarity; and I learned to play a useful role by asking sharp questions and helping information circulate.

I came back West to wander around the Haight and dig its lessons in the spring of its unveiling and destruction. I was still waiting to go to jail for the FSM, for my part in that signal rejection of our parent institutions; here, barely two years later, the first of our counter-communities was sprung full-blown and struggling to survive, and a hundred more were budding in America.

That summer of 1967 I spent in another sort of school, Santa Rita Rehabilitation Center, learning what it had in common with conventional schools—in particular, learning about my own conditioning to be, as a teacher, an authoritarian control-figure—and brooding in rare peace upon what was signified by all the quick changes of the past few years. It was just then becoming clear that we were committing ourselves not simply to a movement of political liberation and social justice, but to a profound and comprehensive cultural transformation. In this light much traditional liberal wisdom about the progressive reform of education was overshadowed. What was needed was root reconception of education, the risk of searching out new ways.

After I warmed up from being in jail, I was finally ready to do serious work. For the next three years I spent almost half my time on the road, dealing with students on campuses and at conferences and later in freak communities as they grew. I was a tame sort of traveling organizer, working on the interface between politics and education, trying to link their new energies into feedback. In the late sixties many others started traveling, usually after some period of local organizing experience. I hitched and rode planes with guerrilla theater troupes, community organizers on OEO funds, Yippie! and White Panther and YSA spokesmen, underground press consultants, psychedelic and ecology gurus, and many impossible to categorize—all transformers of the awakened currents of a generation, valves for the flow of collective energy, cycling the spectrum of news and lore and perspective developing across the nation. We were a family of insects in a broad meadow of change, cross-pollinating the flowers opening awkwardly everywhere; the texture of our lives was a continuous many-toned buzz of information and heady vibration.

By 1969 I knew perhaps a hundred other travelers dealing in "education." Together we formed a loose national infrastructure for a movement of educational change. We rapped to large groups, trained small ones in organizing skills, held seminars on theoretical perspectives and strategies of institutional change, developed workshops and learning games to teach cooperative skills. And we got around a lot—I spent some 400 days going 150,000 miles to work on seventy campuses. It's a matter of pride, and of some sociological significance, that mostly we worked for students, at their invitation, and they paid our expenses and subsistence from their own funds—that is, we were ourselves, as an organizing network, an alternate educational institution developed and supported by the student movement.

By 1970 some 500,000 students were involved in various self-directed efforts to change higher education. This movement's infrastructure had generated a fairly well rationalized system of regional and national conferences; and campus visitations had grown more elaborate, sometimes involving a dozen travelers in week-long coordinated workshops. A few regional and national clearing houses for circulating skilled people and information were well-established enough to be able to seed frontier organizing projects. For example, there was Pennsylvania Project, an OEO-funded spinoff from the National Student Association. Its five organizers stirred and linked ed reform currents on forty-two campuses, mostly in rural areas of the state, during the eight months before FBI surveillance, dope busts, YAF pressure in Congress, blackmail by their grant supervisors, and general kickback from federal, state, town and college administrators cancelled out their funds and sent them for a time into anonymous dispersion.

These clearing houses depended for support upon major grants from foundations and the government. Though these were negotiated independently by their organizers, this dependence created major problems for operations so funded; and the lure of grants seduced the infrastructure's attention away from organizing the level of cooperation among students that would ensure a fully independent support-base for its growth. But that story belongs to a closer study of this movement, which, like all else, is changing so quickly and deeply that in recording even these sketchy notes about it I feel as though I am writing about some transient phenomenon, a wave rising and now gone, its energy passed on to other motions.[3]

Through our work we were developing a body of thought and skills to apply to the reconstruction of education—but a body whose nature was changing with each season. For, all the more so for being young, we were subject to a key law of social transformation: *whoever works with others to*

---

[3] For a bit more about the ed reform movement, see Chapter IX, and "The Context of Campus Violence" in *WWW*. A rich panorama of its upper inner workings during an early crisis is provided by *The Ed Reform Papers,* edited by Tom Linney, published and then suppressed by NSA's Center for Educational Reform late in 1968.

*create a context of change is himself transformed by that
process, gains new consciousness and perspectives.* Involved
as we were with heavy change technologies—from acid to
sit-in, encounter to organizing—as we tried to direct ourselves through History the whole fabric and most intimate
textures of our lives kept changing.

In our sense of work, as in our private selves, these
changes unfolded in orderly progression. My case is somewhat typical. At first I was concerned mainly with the
formal rules, operations, and power distributions of the
bureaucratized institution, and with organizing skills and
strategies for changing them. This led toward action on
issues: the rules governing student political activity; language and breadth requirements; student representation
on committees and financial autonomy; interdisciplinary
studies and the adviser system; the composition of boards of
trustees; etc.

Slowly I grew equally concerned with the level of *process*
upon which learning occurs. Working with students to organize social action, I came to see that the efficacy of our
action groups is rooted in their nature as learning groups.
I saw how deeply our learning for our own uses is crippled
by our conditioning in the established system of education.
So I studied and experimented with the processes of group
learning, and helped develop some new forms and skills—
learning games, facilitation roles, deconditioning exercises,
energy rituals, and so on.[4]

Our work was all reflexive. As in the Totalitarian Classroom Game, we studied ourselves in play and sometimes
managed to apply our knowledge to ourselves. Working in
brief intensive cooperations in this nomad learning con-
spiracy, our consciousness became self-centered to a critical

---

[4] Of what new knowledge has developed in this movement, this is the
most valuable, and I wish this book offered more than a few scattered
examples. But neither I nor anyone I know who has practiced these
new arts has managed to write down more than a fragmentary account
of some one aspect.

degree. My spirit, like many, crossed a major divide. I lost interest not only in the old perspectives of institutional reform, but in the very prospect of re-forming the present institutions gradually. As I outgrew the role of teacher (and organizer) learned within them, I came to apply myself more to the process and society of my own learning, and it seemed less and less conceivable that these could be properly contained or nourished within even the most intelligent and humane reformation of the present system.

My priorities shifted to creating an intimate context for my own ongoing education, using what I'd learned while trying to reshape the System. My need grew urgent, to be involved in building a learning-family: a long cooperation in a democratic group, supportive and skill-sharing, flexible enough to be seminar, action-group, economic collective, playground and hospital—the undifferentiated core unit out of which a system and culture of revolutionary learning can evolve. I put it in these terms to accord with the pretensions of this book. But of course what I imagine is also a pride of mutual lovers, each father and mother and teacher to the children; a band of comrades working to survive and serve the highest interests we can conceive; and so much more.

And here is a remarkable fact about working to change education in white Amerika in the late sixties. Almost everyone I know who worked for more than a couple of years in this movement came to their version of this place, came to see the most important thrust of their work as being the creation of their own learning families (or whatever they called them). During the past couple of years I've been involved in two attempts, partial in their joys and heavy in their pains; now I'm ending a retreat into the privacy of writing books and, with Karen, gearing up for another try. Most of our brothers and sisters in work have gone through some such progression.

Though our road keeps changing, I think it will take us farther yet along this way. In time it will lead us back to the level of mass institutions, but from a very different perspective of experience. That for now we invest our energies on a more modest and personal scale is not a de-politicization but a radicalization, strengthening the roots of our change. For in a time in which change spreads by example, the strongest politics is to begin to live in the ways that our movements for liberation have opened to our imagination.

As for schools as they are now, from colleges on down, their present form serves two functions, to transmit information and skills and to impress a social conditioning in the interests of a certain social order. From within and without, that order is being challenged and rejected as leading to death. Revolution—in the means of communication, both material and social, and in our notion of how free people learn what they need to know—is leading us to serve these functions differently. Though the schools still seem intact as a social form, in fact they have begun to evaporate. Already masses of the young are fleeing them, and even before high school grow frantic to disengage. If humanity survives, in fifty or a hundred years the massive and endlessly duplicated architecture of educational institutions will be turned to unforeseen uses, or, more tastefully, razed.

I can't write you a scenario for the withering away of the State's schools; it won't be just another shift of academic fashion. We have no precedent for the depth of the cultural transformation we are entering. As one aspect of it, all the essential divisions that characterize our present version of education—teacher/student, learning/action, administrator/scholar, school/world, imitation/creation—will be melted down and reconfigured. To the extent that education may be distinguished from the other processes of society, it will of course occur through "institutions." But these will be radically different from present institutions, and we will need a new language to describe what happens within them.

In this book, then, you will find no recipes for changing colleges, no program of institutional reform. On such matters there is a sufficiency of common wisdom. Wherever students sit down seriously to figure out what's wrong with their current institutions, and how these might be changed for the better in the short run, they come up with roughly the same analysis. I have seen the same manifesto, comprehensive and intelligent, written independently at fifty campuses. What is lacking is the power, and to some extent the will, to implement its immediate conclusions.

But we are headed far beyond them. It is not my purpose here to summarize the conventional radical analysis, though mine shares many of its assumptions and values and should be understood as extending it. Rather, I want to pass on some scraps of understanding about the deeper transformation education is undergoing—some ideas to apply to our longer vision and to put the immediate changes of the present in perspective.

The heart of this book is a series of metaphors about learning: the Authority Complex, Open Space, the Tao of Learning, and Golem (Man-Machine). They are mindtools, lenses through which to view the unities that underlie broad ranges of our experience. They represent thinking I haven't discarded, deeper organizations of thought that accumulated as my terms kept evolving—such of them, anyway, as I managed to set down when ripe, in between the raw intensities of working and living.

The outer politics of education are well studied: they have to do with distributions of power, philosophies of production, and the sharing of scarce resources; inevitably their focus is institutional. The inner politics are not much spoken of. They have to do with the process and psychology of learning, especially as these reflect and complement the outer politics. My metaphors all deal with the inner politics of education, with basic perspectives on the struggle to remake the authoritarian learning systems we have inherited in more balanced, democratic, and liberating ways. (It is my fancy that they supplement three bodies of partial knowledge: what the system's scholarship has gathered about learning; the insights of radical study about the gross operations of power; and the social theory of a resurgent Marxism, which holds promise of flowering more strangely and fully.)

That my broad theme is political reflects my position on the thin political fringe of educational change. It was pretty lonely, having a political consciousness and working within that movement. For it's a sad fact that, during the last half of the sixties, the political and educational branches of the student movement grew mostly independent of each other. They overlapped some in their persons on campuses, and each indirectly nourished the other. But by the time you reached the level of organizer and national infrastructure, each movement's people rarely interacted with the other's; and overall there was little sharp interchange of thought or reinforcement of perspectives. I knew few organizers in education who were also committed to leading an active political life in campus and community struggle; and I found few SDS figures who understood the relevance of educational process to social action (though more in the Resistance did). Sometimes I felt kind of weird, doggedly rapping about how good politics must be grounded in good learning, and how educational change was empty without a political edge and aim.

My metaphors, then, come from where the direct investigations of learning and of social change reinforce each other. Our competence in the intersection of these domains is crucial to our being able to modulate human culture deliberately. That this area has not been well studied is due partly to the way the departments of education and the social sciences lie at opposite ends of the campus, are inhabited by academics, and function in the service of repressive social control; and partly to the newness of our urgent need for understandings here.

After the metaphors, I include a collection of movement studies. All these were written more or less spontaneously, during the years I was traveling, as natural expressions of the need to order my understanding and as tools to use on a modest scale in my work. Feeling uncomfortably like a fanatic, I Xeroxed them up by the hundreds on the local student corporation's new high-speed cheap machines, hauled them around to campuses, handed them out at conferences, burdened the mailman. They passed back into the common flow with little direct feedback. Here and there some kids on a campus I worked at would knock me out by scrambling together a dozen volunteers to spend their dear time typing stencils and cranking out a thousand or two mimeo copies of some core essay, giving me a hundred or so to take somewhere else.[5]

My writings bear the imprint of their development in this milieu of ephemeral information circulation, and I've chosen not to erase it. Rather than melted down and recast into a smooth piece, they are here essentially in the forms in which they were circulated among their original audiences —and so tell some indirect tale of a progression of consciousness and needs. On the Acknowledgments page you will find a diagram describing when these chapters were written. In particular, I beg your tolerance for the earliest chapter, which follows this one: it now seems somewhat fuzzy and dull, but its metaphor is still essential to begin with.

I can't tell you how strange it was to write them, let alone to make a book of them. For our school of thought was not

---

[5] Along the line of how metaphors spread, I must mention Jerry Farber's "The Student as Nigger," (Pocket Books, N.Y., 1970). For two years after its publication in an underground paper in 1967, on every campus I visited I found Jerry's tight gutty little essay—in the student paper, dittoed for English class, mimeographed by SDS or the student government or the local free university. It was reproduced spontaneously on a thousand campuses—those that later flared up at the time of Cambodia—and not only by students. If quickness and depth of popular response mean much, it was the most powerful single piece of writing about education of its time.

like that of the Academy in which I developed as an intellectual, with its book-dominated textures and endless empty writing practices. Though we digested a deep and eclectic array of texts, what circulated was not sanctified, but earned its value by its usefulness in our practice. Overall, books were for us a distinctly secondary source of knowledge.[6] Most of our thought developed and was transmitted in an oral tradition, a national conversation as continuous and intense as a telephone exchange. Its written reflection and support was ephemeral, impossible to summarize, a swirl of eddies in the vast circulation of underground media.

It is still borne this way. Little has passed into books—so much depends upon the quality of our conversation. That the counterculture has produced relatively few books of its own, among the flood of writing about it, is not due simply to the public's preference for having its insights predigested by the official agencies of cultural interpretation. Our capacities for writing in the old modes have eroded in our change. Even to write essays is becoming a rarer skill, save perhaps among the political movement, where traditional ways are strongest; and the dominant aesthetic governing such books as we do write has come to be *assemblage,* reflecting the flow of the surround.

So I think my difficulty in turning my part of a rich web of interchange into even such linearity as I have managed reflects more than the traditional private struggle of the writer. The old modes of writing seem to me increasingly inadequate to express the intricacy of even the technical aspects of experience; I find myself drawn toward richer

[6] Among authors on learning, I have found particularly helpful Carlos Castaneda, Harold Taylor, Judson Jerome, R. D. Laing, John R. Seeley, Aldous Huxley, Timothy Leary, Lao-tzu and Chuang-tzu, Black Elk, T. H. Kuhn, Kenneth Keniston, Herbert Marcuse, John Lilly, A. N. Whitehead, Mao Tse-tung, Norbert Wiener, A. S. Neill, Roger Harrison, Maxim Gorky, Cesar Vallejo.

media like videotape; the nomad necessities of a changed way of living militate against the kind of forced-march thesis discipline that goes into most serious books. In the context of my life, writing essays is coming to feel un-natural, and producing books is almost unbearable, it so absents my energy from the web of transformation, inner and outer, that goes on now all the time and needs tending.

I have undertaken this weird painful business not only for crass motives of personal ego, and in the hope of its social utility, but out of a sense of responsibility to the many co-producers of the thought I express. In deep ways these essays are not mine. They were written not from solitary inspiration (though any writer is often alone), but from engagement in the awakening of a broad popular struggle for liberation. They are a valve-off from a flow of collective thought. I don't know how many people I touched minds with, those four years traveling and in Berkeley; I hardly know what is "my own" now in mine, or in what I have written.

Of course I take some glad responsibility for the broad organization of Metaphor. But in the thought of this book I can see what was passed on to me directly by Vic Fein, Jim Kornibe, Lynn Kleinman, Adrian Mellott, Rich Adel-man, Joan McKenna, Sky Garner, Arthur Gladman, Norm Jacobsen, Patsy Engelhardt, Patsy Parker, Jim Goss, Heinz von Foerster, Neil Kleinman, Steve Crocker, Gayle Rubin, Dennis Church, John Judge, Alan Potter, Tom Morrey, Mark Cheren, Rick Kean, Doug Glasser, the game freaks at Denison, Ira Einhorn, Saralee Hamilton, Harold Taylor, Blair Hamilton, Robert Greenway, Harris Wofford, Roger Landrum, Chuck Hollander, Phillip Werdell, Michael Vozick, Bob Black, Linda Thurston, Bill Coughlan, Ray Mungo, Jim Nixon, Cynthia Nixon, David Harris, Russell Bass, Ken Margolis, Charlotte Margolis, Karen McLellan, Mario Savio, Jack Seeley, Carol Rowell, Tom Linney, Lonnie Rowell, Glen Lyons, Joe LaPenta, Peter Berg, Beth

Rimanoczy, Thamar Wherritt, Burt Kanegson, Jack London, Harold Rossman, Mark Messer, Richard Flacks, Jackie Perez Motion, Barbara Blackwell, Everett Gendler, Ann Siudmak, Frank Bardacke, Abbie Hoffman, Lorca Rossman, and I'm not sure how many others whose names escape me at the moment, during coffee table days and stoned nights late. To credit them all properly would take more than enough footnotes for a thesis.[7]

There are nine Ph.D.s on that list. Only one is younger than I. Of the forty-two other younger people, only five or so have much likelihood of going for their doctorates. That is, of the serious young workers and thinkers in educational change whom I've known, only a small minority will now even bother to credential themselves for high-level work in the established system. Are we simply ourselves, an impromptu deviant band; and if so how shall we survive? Or

[7] If you're saving raw data for the study of the sex- and age-based origins of thought, that's forty-nine men and seventeen women, with an age-distribution roughly like that in the diagram.

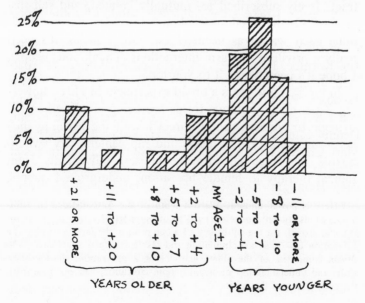

has something broken down decisively, do we represent in our exodus from the Academy a leading edge of the vital energy of an entire generation? Whichever, the departments of education, long slums, will languish further without us.

This book is a fragment of a collective thesis, for a floating college unchartered by the State. Its writing was supported not by the good offices of an institution, in return for certain service; nor by article sale or publisher's advance, in response to the winds of fashion and profit. As a scholar I was supported largely by *the people,* that mythic beast sometimes miraculously actualized—in this case by students, overall some thousands of brothers and sisters, who traded their own funds face-to-face for honest work trying for social consequence.[8] Their support was generous enough to free me from hustling during the forty or so weeks it took to write these essays, and flexible enough to enable me to write, teach, act, and learn whenever any of these seemed right, and as best I could. In what accredited multi-versity could I have had the honor of learning contracts freely subscribed to, mutually created, and self-sustaining? Or the freedom to change my roles and my discipline each season as needed? Far out! I mean, it's been really a privilege of warm interactions. Thank you, people, I hope it's been worth it to you too.

In the past few years a broad experiment has been flowering. Now many tentative forms are being employed in the struggle to connect people directly with the learning they need—free universities, crisis and rap centers, city switchboards and regional clearing houses, movements from radical therapy to female liberation, underground papers,

---

[8] Here is power unused: Were a tenth of the $150,000,000 in semi-autonomous student budgets turned to the support of a *free professoriat,* it could provide for the equivalent of 4,000 posts in the faculty of Floating Liberation U—— a vast circulation and residence, upon America's 2,500 prison campuses, of the ablest learners of a generation, sharing their skills and understandings of social action, education, art, earth-survival, the body, law and the spirit.

intercommunal need-exchange bulletins, speakers' bureaus, audio/video media collectives, army-base coffeeshops where revolution organizes in the military, overall thousands of groups touching the lives of millions of persons.[9]

To my sisters and brothers working in all such nexuses of our free learning system, I direct this archaic text—not for its immediate practical relevance, but because it attempts the depth of thinking that all whose work involves the re-creation of education must now share in. The image strongest on my mind, right before my child's first birthday, is of the free-school parent and teacher; but what I have to say to you is for the others as well. The metaphors that follow are as much a reflection on the education we experienced as they are an evocation of what might be. Though they're phrased mainly in terms of "higher" education, they have to do with the unities underlying all our experience of organized learning. To be able to remake education for our children, we need to understand our own deeply in the process, and better it for ourselves.

. . .

Undoubtedly this book will find some use as a text for good intentions in education classes and other sinks in which the written Word misfunctions to prison the Spirit. As a charm against this fate I intone the truth,

> What is in here writ
> I learned from your neighbor
> and the wandering stranger,

and urge you to conspire first with your brothers and sisters.

[9] The *Source* Catalogues (Source, 2115 S St. N.W., Washington, D.C., 20008) are the best present index to them.

III.

The Authority Complex

I. THE FAILURE OF THE UNIVERSITY

To PUT THE MATTER SIMPLY, the university does not equip us with the tools to begin to solve the critical social problems of our time. It does not produce the knowledge we need: designed to serve corporate power, its sociology and political science have not informed us usefully. It does not instill the skills we need: its graduates, taken all together, do not know how to control their government in a way that ensures the satisfaction of their needs within a healthy society. Indeed, few of them seem to have the sense that government is a thing to *be* controlled.

I don't mean to say that the university produces no useful knowledge and skills. But an historical judgment is clearly being made upon our educational system: too little, too slow.

What Is the University's Function?

Many good people, even some who recognize that we are flirting with genocide at home and abroad, still feel that the university should not serve as a tool to make the tools to solve our society's problems. They do not reply directly to the fact that our society has no other institution that fills this function. But they argue that the university's basic purpose is quite different: to preserve and transmit the intellectual heritage of our culture, and to train new workers in those vineyards. If you want results, go somewhere else.

Unfortunately, that ideal of the university was formed in an earlier, ivy era, when higher education served narrowly to train a narrow elite in a narrow spectrum of skills. Now it is the morning after a night of change in the Groves of Academe, and we are suffering from a cultural hangover. Suddenly America has become a technological culture deep into an experiment in universal higher liberal education. In this new time the university is a new institution, whose nature is hidden under the rhetorical cloak of an old purpose.

Those who try from scratch to analyze its present function find that it trains people in the skills a technological culture finds most immediately useful under a capitalist economy. Since the educational system is the society's central socializing mechanism, the university also functions as the last main segment of this mechanism, imparting a crucial conditioning to those it processes.

Beyond this, there is little useful discussion of what the university's function *ought* to be, or *might* be; of whether it serves its present functions well, or should serve them quite differently. We do not know what the institution is *good* for. All we know is that almost all of the young of the culture's main class spend a crucial part of their development within its context, and that, if education is the process that gives people the ability to meet their individual and social needs, then our education is not only inadequate, but disastrously so.

The University Fails on the Personal Level Too

On the personal level the disaster is more diffuse and less dramatic than on the social level, but no less massive. If you take our literature seriously as a barometer to the inner weathers of America, you will read that we mostly lead lives of uncertain frustration, vaguely and powerfully unsatisfied, not knowing why or how to go about changing. All the other guides to our condition, from the literature of social psychology through divorce statistics to the *Reader's Digest* tests, confirm this. This is your secret nightmare, if you are young, this sense of emptiness—and with good reason, for those instruments measure truly.

Is it appropriate, in a serious discussion of the function of the university, to include the topics of I A.M. bull sessions in the dorm? It sure is. For the university is an institution that embraces and penetrates our entire lives for a period, and so it has many aspects. Outside the classroom, but still in school, we speak and try to learn about the matters that are most important to us in our full personhood. Later, looking back on that constant delicate web of conversation, which forms what we might call our nighttime university, we recognize its importance and place it more accurately as part of our university education.

The tragedy is that we carry on that conversation so badly—though we seldom realize this, having few standards of comparison. We rarely connect this dimly grasped failure with our powerful sense of unsatisfaction. Nor do we realize how strongly the conversation of the nighttime university is influenced by what goes on in the daytime university. All that is clear is that the university's failure to provide us with the tools to meet our needs is much the same on the personal as on the social level. We have little sense of control over ourselves or our contexts; and we are not much good at talking with ourselves or each other. And all this is another sort of death.

II. TWO MODELS OF LEARNING

Against this background, I want to talk about learning: what it is, why we're not very good at it, and how to begin getting better. I want to talk at the same time about social change. So let me suggest a useful way of thinking about the connection between these two.

Learning and Social Change

How do we measure learning? By changes in behavior. Whether we are declining Spanish verbs or creating a non-violent society, this seems to be a useful description. And if we extend this to say that we are what we do, then changed behavior is equivalent to changed identity. So it makes sense to speak of learning, behavioral change, and identity change as alternate names for the same human process.

These terms are interchangeable on the social level also. To say that a society, or an institution, learns is to say that sub-institutions and processes behave differently; which is to say, in turn, that its identity changes, since this identity lies in the actions of its parts upon its persons. When this change is great enough, it is called a revolution. Later I will indicate a sense in which all learning, both personal and social, is revolutionary, and draw from this some conclusions about how to go about helping people and societies to learn.

Conjugate Levels of Learning

For the moment, I am concerned with the intimate connection between the two levels of learning, the individual and the social. Its importance is clear. We who numb ourselves to inner lives which we cannot control are also we who cannot feel the foreign flesh that chars beneath our napalm, or the pain that swells to riot bursting in our black ghettos.

The connection lies in the fact that the "individual" and the "social" are merely different perspectives on a single human complex. They are not *separate* but *conjugate,* in the sense that each prepares the shape of the other and carries this shape within itself. (The "personal" and the "cultural," the "private" and the "public" are parallel pairs of conjugate perspectives.) It makes sense, then, to say that individual learning and social change are two faces of a single coin. And it is not surprising that the skills of the learner are essentially the skills of the society that is able to learn; that the problems involved in changing private behavior mirror those involved in changing public behavior; or that the processes whereby individuals and cultures reconstruct their identities are closely similar.

Given all this, I think there is power in talking abstractly about the skills of learning and the problems of building change-environments. And I hope it will not seem disconcerting if the talk flashes back and forth between the

personal and social levels of learning, or between diffe
descriptions of the process of change. For it is all one th

The Skills of Autonomous Learning[1]

What is a good learner? It seems useful to think of him as
someone with a certain set of skills. He knows how to
formulate problems. He can identify the relevant resources,
of information or whatever, that are available in his environment. He is able to choose or create procedures and
to evaluate his results. Beyond this, there is a set of higher
skills, which we might call "meta-skills." Stated very
loosely, they include the ability to know what he wants (or
needs) to learn; the ability to see clearly the *process* of his
learning; and the ability to interact with others to help
learn these meta-skills. Out of all this, he is able to create
useful knowledge. Let us call him an autonomous learner,
for he directs himself.

These skills and meta-skills are somehow *natural:* little
children are wizards at accomplishing useful learning. And
if older children and their institutions were as skilled, we
would be less involved with death than we are. The problem, I think, is that we construct environments that stunt
and warp the development of these skills.

Authority-Centered Learning

Consider the university. By its very nature, it forms an environment that inhibits the development of autonomous
learners. For *teaching,* in higher education, is generally
taken to mean a particular way of conveying information

[1] For a more thorough treatment of this model, see the paper cited
on page 144.

that is already known. It is based on the assumption that the student must have a certain quantity of knowledge before he can question what is known or create new knowledge. (His arrival at graduate status is usually accepted as minimum preparation.) And so the creation of knowledge, usually conceived of as either "research" or "scholarship," becomes an expert's job. The teacher's task is to transmit it; the student's task is to learn it.

In this model of education, problems are identified for the student by authorities ("experts") who also define and supply problem-solving approaches. Relevant information is labeled as such by authorities; and methods and results are evaluated by them, in comparison with known solutions.

This model was more or less suited to the university's hallowed nominal purpose, the transmission of the culture's intellectual heritage. It served (and still somewhat serves) to train scholars in the ordering, preservation, and presentation of established knowledge.

The university's present main function is quite different; but this model of education still persists. It trains people in the styles of technical expertise and prepares them for pre-established social and technical roles. The man educated in this model makes himself useful in immediate, limited, and necessary ways. He is prepared to deal with problems whose nature is well defined, which can be approached from within already-formalized disciplines or styles of thought. *And training in this model generates a particular notion of the nature of useful change: it is conceived of as a linear, continuous advance within the existing organizations of knowledge, technology, and society. It is explicitly not revolutionary.*

Surely well-defined problems must be dealt with, and linear advance should be effected whenever it is appropriate. And surely any notion of education must include some version of expertise, which is to say some development of the indispensable sense of what it is to "know in depth."

But the authority-centered model at best equips its products to function well within the bounds of a discipline of some sort. The trouble is that all real human problems are transdisciplinary. Even designing a building requires the integration of a whole spectrum of skills, of which structural engineering is the least important. And the increasing unlivability of our cities testifies to how poorly we accomplish even this.

Its Failures

Authority-centered education is not particularly well suited to the university's present function of servicing a technological society. Not only are its products unable to cope well with the problems such a society generates—the inner problems, the social problems, the foreign problems—they are also less and less well prepared for those social and technical roles for which university education supposedly *is* designed.

There are two reasons for the growing failure of the authority-centered learning system to satisfy even its own goals. One is that the *kinds* of work it trains for are becoming more and more transdisciplinary. The other is that the nature of the society's jobs and roles is changing fundamentally. The increasing rapidity of social, technological, and intellectual change means that the traditional notion of a job as involving the application of fixed kinds of knowledge to fixed problems is becoming unreasonable. (This is reflected in a limited but striking way in some fields of engineering, in which a graduate's knowledge is outmoded within five years, unless he undergoes an almost continuous retraining.) Similarly, the social and personal roles people play are no longer fixed, defining rigid adulthoods, but are becoming fluid, in ever-more-rapid transformation.

Autonomous Learning Is Better

Taken together, these trends suggest an appropriate set of skills: those of the learner who must constantly be redefining and re-creating his competence to deal with problems that cannot be isolated from the social environment in such a way as to become targets for expertise attacks. He must develop information and resources from the entire social environment. He must define the problems themselves and generate relevant approaches to them. He is concerned, not with verifying established truths, but with a social process involving people's attitudes, irreconcilably conflicting information, and a search for imperfect but viable solutions with action consequences. Hence he must be able to establish his own criteria for success.

These skills are necessary not only to solve social problems, but also to direct personal learning as a continuous process of change to satisfy one's individual goals and needs. They are, in short, the skills of the autonomous learner. Ironically, they are precisely the skills that are inhibited by authority-centered learning, and by the system of education based on this model. So it makes sense to look at the pervasiveness of authority-centered learning before turning to the question of how we create healthy learning and change.

III. THE AUTHORITY COMPLEX

How to create limits to the expression of energy is always a problem. Ideally, the limits are flexibly generated from within, allowing the energy as much freedom as possible. More generally, they are imposed from without. We have a particular style of doing this here in America, which I call the Authority Complex.

In the University

It is visible throughout the university and forms one of the great unities of college life. Advisers police permissible study lists. Dorm mothers police permissible hours and clothing and sex. Deans police permissible political activity. Professors police permissible readings and methods of learning. In each case, the justification is, "for your own good"; and the effect is to inhibit autonomous adulthood. One consequence is that people in college look, think, and act alarmingly alike. If the measure of the existence of freedom is a rich diversity of behavior, it would seem that the Authority Complex inhibits freedom as well.

In Our Government

The Authority Complex permeates our culture. That we call Korea and Vietnam "police actions" and have proudly named ourselves "Policemen to the World" is not just a coincidence of phrasing. Nor is it surprising that our main response to the crescendoing black problem is to beef up police forces with men and equipment. I am choosing only the most immediate and dramatic examples, but everywhere the Authority Complex is busy setting limits on other people's energies. Again it is "for their own good." Being exploited and ruled by dictators is better than being Communist; the government will solve the "black problem," give it time and don't listen to the militants. Here again, the Authority Complex enforces a narrow range of behavior. Governments must not change outside the narrow spectrum of what we consider politically permissible, or they will be toppled by the CIA or bombers. Negroes will act like proper niggers, or be shot in the stomach like Huey Newton or jailed like LeRoi Jones. And here again, the other side of the coin is freedom. It is no accident that most of the world sees America as setting itself against a black liberation struggle at home and against struggles for national liberation at scores of places across the globe. Freedom and the Kindly Kop seem somehow incompatible.

Mixed with Punishment and with Children

Some people will draw back at this point: not, I hope, because I display my political sympathies, but because I may seem overhasty in confusing the notions of Authority and Cop. Please come back, we are all in this together. We inhabit a culture that at all its levels has the matter of authority frightfully mixed up with punishment and reward; and that everywhere covers this structural mess with a pastel paint job of good intentions. Benevolently the dean reprimands, the dorm mother locks in, and the professor, inescapably the living arm of the machine of grades and degrees, casts shadows of stronger punishments indeed with every gesture. And, of course, the ghettos and Vietnam, with their different flames, are living Hells, in the sense of being places where sin is punished while Heaven is promised.

We seem unable to construct social or educational authority not embedded in a punitive framework. Our motto might well be, "Eat your carrots like a good boy, or Papa spank." For the Authority Complex extends to the deepest and most intimate levels. As children trying to create identities—which is to say, learning to set limits on the expression of our energies—we generally find parental authority expressed in a style that coerces rather than evokes appropriate behavior from us. With parenthood as with government, this coercion is mostly slow and undramatic. The structure and dispensation of punishments and rewards to children is almost entirely unconscious and unseen, carried out in the subtle language of gesture and inflection. Spankings are the rare Vietnams of the cultural imperialism that dominates the world of the nuclear family.

The true motives of the family, like those of our foreign policy, are not simply benevolent. In each the Authority Complex operates in the interests of Power, to preserve and transmit an established order.

Confronting Freedom and in Bed

One index to the Authority Complex's pervasiveness is the thirty-year controversy over Dr. Spock's *Baby and Child Care*. The book's important feature is that it suggests, however partially, a way to help a child learn to develop self-directed behavior, and thus firmly breaks with the basic American model of child-rearing. (This break is extended much more radically in A. S. Neill's book *Summerhill*.)

Lately critics have been laying all sorts of unwanted social babies on Spock's doorstep, claiming that his book and its odd notions are responsible for hippies, lawlessness, sit-ins, pacifism, and civil disorders. And I think this is true, at least in a partial sense. For the 20 million copies of Spock that were consumed in the raising of those still under thirty have surely helped to shape our somewhat different notion of freedom.

Freedom is the tonic in the chord of change our young generations sound. Our visible motion and change—in educational reform, in political action, in the domain of private behavior—is all toward increased freedom. What is astounding is the consistency of the response this motion draws. At Berkeley during the FSM, when we thought we were fighting for political rights and to affirm a new community, the campus administration kept saying: It's a problem of Authority. The radical Right declares that rock music breaks down our obedience to Authority. Narcotics officers, the President, grammar school teachers, and bewildered parents of twelve-year-old teenyboppers are chanting in a growing frantic chorus: *The kids ain't got any respect.* And they are right. For in America, Authority, given its common style, becomes increasingly incapable of commanding respect from the young for any reason save the fear on which it is ultimately based.

The age at which this conflict surfaces grows steadily younger. Its arenas become more varied and more intimate. The problems of freedom and learning characteristically associated with the Authority Complex dominate the parent-child relationship in our culture, despite recent modest shifts of social behavior. And the Authority Complex thrusts its stick into the bed as well as into the cradle. Its peculiar pattern of fixed roles embedded in a punitive framework, garlanded by confusions of good will and destructive self-interest, seems to characterize our marriages as well, which, like private minor universities, are heavy with unmet human needs and mute pain.

Like, Everywhere

A human culture is a single and consistent entity. The personal and the social, the individual and the public—each bears all the others' imprints; they fit together. So: Papa Cop, meet Teacher Cop. World Cop, meet Lover Cop. You are the same image and process in different clothing. The

Authority Complex is only one of our culture's key metaphors, but it is strong and deeply entrenched. And as far as learning and social change go, it is surely the most important.

IV. IMPERIALISM AS A GUIDE TO HOW THE AUTHORITY COMPLEX INHIBITS HEALTHY LEARNING

We can understand the workings of the Authority Complex at home and in school by considering its operation on the largest social scale. Here it appears as an imperialism exercised over underdeveloped countries with rich natural resources. Clearly, the skills needed for self-directed learning in these countries are severely crippled. *They do not define their own problems:* they are told, for example, that their need is to earn a degree in anticommunism. *They do not choose and develop their own resources:* we kept Cuba a monocrop sugar economy for decades, while her peasants waited like unread books to be used for her good. *They do not formulate their own procedures:* our foreign aid comes accompanied by lesson plans and teaching assistants generated in American universities. And certainly *they do not evaluate their own results:* the CIA and the Seventh Fleet are merely the crudest of our grading systems.

Characteristics of the Authority Complex

Several features characterize our stance as Teacher-to-the-World. Our authority is imposed, not because of its genuine relevance and usefulness to the needs of those we exploit, but because we choose to impose it as an extension of what we see as *our* role and *our* needs. It is coercive, backed up by punitive force. It displays itself in hierarchical, top-down structures of power, which are imitated throughout its domain: we are top dog, and that we wind up supporting dictators or juntas in many of the countries we exploit is no coincidence. Always it controls change to preserve the status-quo of power relationships. Always it is accompanied by a cultural imperialism, which is to say that our impact extends to all levels of the exploited society. Slowly the pressure, not so much of our presence as of the way we exert it, begins to affect social structure and entertainments, educational systems and marriage, to press them into our image. (Japan is a fair example.)

It Stunts the Autonomous Learning Skills

There are two important things to say about the way our style of authority in the international arena inhibits social change. The first is that it stunts the development of autonomous learning skills by pre-empting them itself rather than leaving them to the learner. The second is best expressed by a classical characterization of imperialism. A nation imposes an order on another nation for the sake of its own interests. These interests are not limited to *expressing* its own ordering principles (in the case of capitalist imperialism, according to *Fortune* magazine, these are the need for expansion and the thirst for profit and other forms of power); they also, and more importantly, include the *preservation* of its ordering principles. To be blunt about it: America feels that if she does not shape the world after her own image, it will not only shape itself, and thus constrict her expression, but her own nature will have to change in response. The survival of an order is at stake.

It Imposes Order for Its Own Sake

To impose order for the sake of preserving that very order is the deepest motive of the Authority Complex, and the one most actively hostile to the natural development of order in the system imposed upon. The Authority Complex always somehow comes on defensive, as if it had something to lose. Every high school teacher I know complains that he or she spends a major portion of energy simply maintaining the role of teacher as authority figure, rather than helping the students meet their needs. (This expenditure shows up less obviously in upper-middle-class schools, because kids there are trained to respond to displays of expertise rather than to shouts as authority symbols.) The parallel in the case of black and white poor people is clear. Though the OEO programs were designed to include "maximum feasible participation of the poor," in fact almost all have been completely controlled by local governments, with no representation of those affected. Why? Because to share control would have resulted in new power bases developing among the poor; and the local power structures would have changed as a result. The most poignant example, however, is probably that of the pot laws. Millions of kids all over the country know that there's nothing wrong with pot. So the key argument remaining to Responsible Citizens who have read enough to realize this is, that kids should not smoke it anyway, because to smoke it breeds disrespect for the Law. Dig that: obey the order simply for the sake of preserving it!

It Paralyzes the Meta-Skills of Learning

Colonial imperialism offers one last insight into the mechanics of how the Authority Complex snarls healthy learning. The imposition of an external order for the sake of maintaining that order is actively hostile to the development of new orders or identities, not simply because the learning skills are pre-empted, but because the meta-skills of change become violently distorted.

Recall them. They include being able to find out what you need or want to become or learn, and being sensitive to your natural and personal process of learning or change. But when a country's goals are formed largely by the vision of another country, and when its own development and consciousness are artificially distorted to ensure service to this vision, healthy thought about "where next?" and "how?" becomes impossible. The strongest response to these questions tends to be, "not *there!*" and "not *that* way!" Most of the energy that would be devoted to them is absorbed in a paralyzed and paralyzing stand-off. It is a sad fact that exploitation does not generate an efficient opposition.

Let me leave you to fill in the parallel with the student taking his objective-choice final exam in the Zoology 1 requirement, while I go on to the third meta-skill of learning: being able to interact with others to help learn what your learning is and what you want to learn. Though I speak of this process as a conversation, the key conversation of learning, it is not limited to words, on either the social or personal levels.

It Arbitrarily Limits the Conversation

It is not generally realized that Socrates, who knew a lot about learning, was an anti-imperialist. But he was, for he laid down one strong precept: *Follow the conversation where it leads.* Even his own pupil Plato betrayed him, by those dialogues that were not only beautiful and well-intentioned but also rigged. This says something about how hard you have to work to keep a healthy learning scene going.

Follow the conversation about process and goals where

it leads. Here at last we come to the critical problem with the Authority Complex: Its presence in a learning environment hopelessly scrambles the conversation on which the health of the learning so intimately and totally depends. In the terms of colonial imperialism, to impose an external order (for the sake of preserving it) means that the social conversation going on in the subject nation is fatally and arbitrarily limited. It proceeds in a *closed universe of possibility,* whose boundaries are dictated not by the conversation's internal logics but by the requirement that the structure and power relationships of the present Authority be preserved. Thus it is everywhere blocked by artificial and arbitrary limits and cannot proceed freely.

V. A MODEL OF A HEALTHY LEARNING GROUP[2]

The name of the new game we are trying to learn to play is "freedom." We are in desperate need of new ways and new institutions to guide our behavior: individually and socially, we need desperately to learn.

Yet our culture's central failure is its inability to help its people and itself learn how to learn. This failure is rooted so deeply and broadly in the culture's identity that to remedy it will involve no less than passing on to another culture. Rather than learn to change our culture, we must change our culture to learn. It is a bootstrap operation; I do not know if it is possible. All I know is that some people are trying to learn how to begin, and trying to define a science of beginning.

[2] Much of this model is taken from a paper by Cynthia Nixon, drawing on the thought of the organizers of the San Francisco State Experimental College, circa late 1966.

So begin with the notion of the self-directed learner, who is able to change his behavior to meet his needs and thus has learned how to learn. What he does is *create knowledge:* he creates knowledge appropriate to his context.

Authority-Centered Learning Again

Our current model of education views knowledge as something that has an existence apart from its learner or knower. I think this is not knowledge, but data, and I mean this of matters as diverse as Democracy and the Tychonoff Product Theorem of mathematics. Each must in some essential sense be re-created from raw materials before it becomes useful knowledge in the knower.

But given our current notion of knowledge, our model of education is knowledge-centered, in the sense that it assigns roles to its participants on the basis of their relation to this knowledge. The expert makes it, the teacher owns and transmits it, the pupil absorbs it. In any given learning group, these roles are assigned relative permanence. Given his expertise, his bankroll of knowledge of a certain subject, the teacher becomes the authority figure of a class, and *all* authority becomes permanently vested in him. We call this "role-defined authority"; and it does bad things to autonomous learning, partly because it almost always turns out to evoke the Authority Complex.

This is true even when the "teacher" is not embedded in a system of tests and grades and similar punishments. We know only one way of relating to authority in this culture, and our expectations tend to create a punitive framework, whether or not authority has a whip in its hand. (This is one of the main stumbling blocks in creating groups with more flexible patterns of authority.) Considering teachers and students generally, it seems to me that the least part of the punishment/reward framework running through their relationship, in class and out, is expressed formally, as in graded tests. Most occurs in a generally wordless dialogue of approval, reproof, glance, and gesture, in which both parties participate equally. I was simply amazed, in the experimental program in which I taught, at seeing what happened to kids I normally would have considered to be cardboard C students. When they couldn't find someone to play that game with them and help them reassure themselves that they were C students, they gave up the role and became significantly more independent and creative.

A Field Theory of Learning

Suppose we start, instead, with the behavioral view of knowledge as that which a learner creates, and learning as the evolution of appropriate responses in a context. Then it seems more useful to configure the roles of expert-teacher-pupil back into a single *field situation* and try to understand what does and should go on in the field in which the learner is embedded. To begin with, the field clearly must be viewed from his perspective. And from this perspective, for someone simply to hang knowledge up in the air, as by a lecture, and expect the learner to incorporate it into his personal patterns of thought and behavior seems unrealistic and inefficient. Is this to define teaching? For the learner, the "teacher," or rather the "leader," instead becomes whoever or whatever acts on his environment, the field situation, so as to draw him into new and appropriate behavior.

Two things are important about the idea of a learning field. All the elements of the field are seen as being active—each contributes to producing a change-inducing (or retarding) climate or field. And each is necessarily changed by any change in the field, including those it initiates. This seems both a more accurate and a more worthy model than the current one in which change is largely thought of as the result of action-at-a-distance, originating from a static central source, which does not change in the process (the teacher, the administration, the departmental structure).

This model is more useful for making change than the current one, which regards students as neutral, irrelevant, or even hostile elements as far as producing a learning field goes. In the present system by far the largest single teaching resource in the daytime university—the students themselves —goes almost completely unutilized. And when students *are* used, it is with the explicit title of "apprentice teacher," as if they had somehow to become a different species to be able to share their knowledge.

It is worthwhile to view the dynamics of institutional change in terms of field theory. Here again, in the university, students are traditionally viewed as neutral, irrelevant, or hostile to the process of change: like colonials in an imperialist empire, or niggers in the fields and ghettos. As in these places, in the university too this view is becoming increasingly difficult to maintain as revolt and repression proceed.

But students are, in fact, active agents of change. There are precious few schools where significant change is underway, and at most of these the students have initiated it. In the institutional landscape and the classroom, we are having to think anew about agents of change.

A New Style of Leadership/Authority

Field theory helps us conceive a fundamental shift in the pattern of authority or in the style of leadership, if we think of authority as being vested at each moment in whoever is the active agent of change in a group's learning field.

In a group context, learning displays itself in the ability to *go on:* to use an awareness of the group and individual styles of learning and of the emerging nature of a problem, to produce an appropriate behavior—which in turn changes the group's learning field. The learner, in *going on* consciously, shapes the direction of the group's development. Alternately put, the learner—rather than the teacher—is the group's leader. Thus the central problem in the design of learning groups becomes that of good leadership.

The Problems with a Familiar Style

This requires a different notion of *leadership* from the one that forms the basis of contemporary *teaching.* Authority-centered learning models generate static and comprehensive rather than flexible and partial styles of leadership. A teacher's expertise in a knowledge area expands into a permanent and overall authority/leadership role for the whole learning context.

Acceptance of leadership by role, rather than by appropriateness or quality, is bad training in itself. It stunts development of the skill of deciding how to use possible leadership resources and limits the options open in any working situation. Second, role-leadership is coupled with Yin paralysis, the permanent passive-and-receptive quality in the follower or pupil role, which directly conflicts with the active and aggressive attitude that is a crucial component of self-directed behavior change. Finally, such static handling of leadership seems to be coupled with serious problems of student motivation. The model "solves" this by bringing in a punishment/reward system to motivate learning, which bears no intrinsic relation to this punitive framework.

Qualities of a New Style

Conversation is a flow of energies. In authority-centered learning, much of the authority's energy is devoted to establishing and preserving control; and most of the learner's energy is absorbed in dealing with or against the Authority Complex. In a free learning group, energy goes instead to developing a different style of authority. Freeing-authority is shared, democratic and flexible, rather than fixed in hierarchical roles. Its self-interest is always clear; its power is by example rather than by coercion; and it empowers rather than weakens those exposed to it. Its function is to help individuals and the group to discover and generate identities that satisfy their needs. It frees conversation to continually generate its own limits, from within.

Usually the function of guiding a group's development, however badly, is called "teaching." But "teaching" and "learning" are alternate and interdependent descriptions of a single human process. And so learning, in our sense of leading, involves not only the creation of knowledge in the learner, but also the conjugate part of this process: the communication of thought and behavior to others in a way that enables it to be useful to them.

Since in this model the creation and exposition of knowledge are inseparably intertwined, within the group education takes the form of a discourse. The group's process is a conversation, which moves wherever appropriate (remember what the Authority Complex does to that?). And if the conversation is at all successful, there is no need to bring in artificial exercises designed to test whether the learners have "mastered" certain information. For it is impossible for the learner to *go on* from the material if he does not have it at his disposal. The *going on*—following the conversation where it leads—is itself the test. It is being constantly conducted in the striving for a conversation that will involve each participant and develop his ability to lead the group. For this reason, the group's conversation will be constantly concerned not only with information about the problem being approached, but also with information about the patterns of learning and interaction and difficulty present in the group. And the most evident difference between this and the standard model is the new balance. We talk hardly at all about such matters in a normal class. But don't think we don't feel we need to. The single most persistent phenomenon you find in experiments in higher education—within or without university walls—is their turning inward upon themselves to become conversations about the nature of the learning process and group interaction. *This emphasis is impossible in authority-centered learning, for to deal well with difficulties in process involves challenging the structure and control of the Authority Complex.*

Since the goal of each member is to be able to take on the group's leadership when appropriate, he wants to develop the ability not only to learn and present information, ordering principles and basic assumptions, but also to facilitate the learning process for others by clarifying problems, unblocking difficulties, and so on. Clearly, this demands attention to a wider spectrum of skills than those usually involved in the roles of teacher and student. It requires a sense of the individual learning patterns of the group's members and a deep sensitivity to group dynamics, which is to say, to all the concerns that arise when you think how intimately we impinge upon each other in a group where people are changing. In fact, the spectrum of skills involved in this model is broad enough to suggest that good learning makes possible creative and appropriate action both within one's work and simultaneously upon the quality of one's life.

In such a learning group, the ability to assume leadership is expanded by watching others lead, or, alternately, learning is catalyzed by watching others learn. This suggests that the best resource people are advanced students who are capable of re-creating learning experiences they have only recently experienced; or even people skilled in this *style* of facilitating learning but not expert in the specific material being studied. It also suggests that the best way to help others learn may be by displaying the raw chunks of one's developing understanding, with all their sloppy edges dangling and all the ego-danger this involves. (People who have spent a long time actively playing Authority Complex roles generally find this quite difficult to do.) This model also assumes that the group is sensitive enough to its processes to discover what's hanging it up, and open enough to change dysfunctional behavior. The reward for this is a healthy conversation about learning, which can develop naturally once the meta-skills are freed by unscrambling the authority problem.

How to Make Them and Why They're Reasonable

A learning group organized in this style begins as a set of students who have some idea of what they want to learn and how they want to learn it. They may decide to recruit more learners to fill out the group and, if needed, people to serve temporarily or permanently as knowledge resources, for example technical experts or group-process specialists. In any case, some core of people prepared by previous learning takes the lead at first, say by beginning to present the ordering principles of a body of knowledge. They direct their leadership and the group's work so as to invite the active participation of the others in affecting the directions of inquiry and study, and in providing additional knowledge, old and new.

Two factors encourage a response to this invitation. First, the fact that the work is self-chosen is a powerful internal motivation; so is the opportunity to be genuinely instrumental in shaping the curriculum. This model takes seriously the notion that people will choose to learn what they are enabled to *choose* to learn. Second, each participant begins with a beachhead of leadership, which he can then expand, to provide the necessary fracturing of the initial core authority. For he is the authority at least on his own position in the learning field: on the state of his learning, on the group's ability to satisfy his needs, and on his ability to elicit appropriate behavior changes for others. And this authority is significant in a group centrally concerned with mutual participation in a field of mutual interaction, where it then provides a common denominator of leadership.

A Piece of Theory That Spins Around Love

This brings us to the last essential element of this model, and I state it strongly. *What ya need is love.* You just can't learn with people you don't care enough about to feel for in some essential way, like for them being who they are. This is a kind of caring that is not dramatic but that is indispensable. We are not very good at it, and it needs to be worked hard at to create the atmosphere of trust on which the successful functioning of a learning group largely depends.

For it is critical that each member be perceived and perceive himself as learning and responsive, rather than as the player of a stereotyped role which rigidly limits the conversation of his growth, prisoning him in a closed universe of possibility. His exposure to good examples of behavior-change, learning, on the part of others in the group may lead him to feel that the rules governing his behavior and the group's behavior have been expanded. That is to say, he may indeed have had his mind blown by an example, and his self-limiting set of expectations shaken. But there must still be an atmosphere of trust in the group for him then to be able to make a statement, a guess, a touch, or an attempt in the open space that that shaken fence of expectation may have left him. The act of learning is always doubled by some genuine risk of genuine failure, even in mathematics, just as it is always a therapeutic attempt, in the sense of trying to satisfy a need. The act of learning is also always an act of freedom, in the sense of an attempt to move freely in an unstructured space, creating one's own structure and behavior. And you cannot move freely when you're hung up in satisfying other people's expectations, or when you feel you have something to lose. What is needed is a modicum of trust based on a willingness to let people be who they are, in order that they may be able to take genuine risks in a search for learning. There ain't much of that in the standard classroom. Maybe we can do better.

IV.

Open Space

LEARNING AS DEATH AND BIRTH

BEGIN WITH a simple cyclic model to describe the act of learning or of social change.

Human energies, bound and flowing, form a stable system. Some are involved in maintaining the structure; some are expressed though it, with various degrees of health; and some are repressed or latent, connected with unmet needs. The structure breaks. An open space without coherent structure results: a Chaos. It contains not only the energies expressed or repressed by the structure, but those formerly bound in maintaining the structure's coherence, and the scattered fragments of the structure itself. In this live open space, tools, skills, and knowledge under some form of control—freeing or authoritarian—act upon and with the energies and fragments. Out of Chaos, a new coherence emerges, a new structure. Energies flow and hang until change again becomes necessary, and the process repeats.

From this perspective, significant learning or change in human systems is always explicitly revolutionary: it involves the death of one order and the creation of another. The rhetoric of this description is social and dramatic, at odds with our cultural mythologies about learning. In the real physical world, of course, change has proven to be quantized and discontinuous. But our social sciences lag behind our natural ones.

Whether the change be the elimination of racism, the learning of a mathematical theorem, or the recognition of love, what is involved is always the disruption of an organic human system, its death as an integral entity; and a birth. After learning to conjugate a Spanish verb or express a sigh, the new human system does not differ much from the old. But it *is* new, and its birth may become easier and more appropriate when understood as revolutionary.[1]

If learning is revolution, the goal of our new education is not a degree or a state, but a *process:* a healthy process of change and its attendant skills, in response to our needs and desires. Our learning to create this process seems to have three components: learning to break free from old and crippling frameworks of control; learning to think about the process of change; and learning to handle and build in the freedom we create and grow in.

Given this cyclic model, the key questions of learning

[1] See the diagram on page 139, which portrays the cycle and also indicates the area of this chapter's concern. This view may seem weird. But since leaving school and the official systems of knowledge—so curiously limited in their ability to teach people how to learn—I've been re-examining familiar things, and this is how they look to me.

theory become these: How is open space created, recognized, and maintained? What happens within it, and what is it good for? What skills and what forms of authority and control are necessary to survive and to build with health in Chaos? How are they developed? How can we construct human systems that will die gracefully when their time comes, or at least leave their people empowered to build in response to real needs?

Some first answers to these questions appear when we examine my generation's experience with *free learning in open space*.[2] For we are involved in a many-leveled system of alternative education which transforms us as we invent it; and by considering its examples we can accumulate a more detailed model of our working knowledge of the process of change.

THE FSM AND THE OPEN CIRCLE MODEL

The Cop-Car Episode

On October 2, 1964, a police car drove onto the main plaza of the Berkeley campus of the University of California to arrest a young man at a civil rights table. A thousand students entrapped it with its hostage, and the Free Speech Movement began in high gear. A microphone was placed on top of the car. Sock-footed, Mario Savio stepped up to speak. He was followed by a hundred others. From that unprecedented podium, they spoke for thirty hours, creating the first true public dialogue I had heard in America.

The open space was not only that created by the neutrali-

---

[2] You might look at the "Digression of Definition" on page 111 before reading further, for I use these terms often before trying even so loosely to make them precise.

zation of campus and legal authority. It was an internal open space of live energy gathered without expectations to limit its expression. No one had ever captured a cop-car before, nor spoken from its top within such an immediate, deep and ongoing crisis: no one knew what form of speech was appropriate. Hence a diverse multitude of viewpoints—on history, politics, poetry, morality, law, tactics, and our feelings—appeared from a richly various population. None dominated or subordinated the others—unlike a normal political rally —which is to say that no central Authority was re-created. This permitted a deep commonality of feeling, perception, and intent to emerge.

It is hard now to remember the fragmented alienation that was the endemic state of pre-FSM Berkeley. In the open space around that car was born a long-latent group consciousness, which since has broken and reformed many times, growing slowly stronger and broader, into Community. At that moment it was sufficiently intense and coherent that, for the first recent time within white America, a group of her young were willing to face beating and arrest by 600 cops to defend what was theirs. In the pure, energy-filled Chaos of that conversation a shared understanding was born also. The politics, analysis, and strategy of the FSM were realized full-blown in those early hours; and the next three months of this first major campus movement were devoted to working them out in practice.

The Movement's Structure and Process

This working-out was accomplished in a different sort of open space. The FSM had a visible political structure: campus groups sent representatives to a large executive assembly responsible for policy-making, which elected a small steering committee to make immediate tactical decisions.

But neither body had any significant *control* over the movement's members and their voluntary actions. Their main functions were in fact to handle information: to coordinate its flow within the movement and across the interfaces between the FSM and other campus power-groups, and to represent the FSM formally to the outside world. Power of course resides in the control of information, but at worst such power is only indirectly punitive. In this case it was used to enable the FSM's members, by making information-flow within the movement as free and comprehensive as possible (thus decentralizing power).

A distinctive style of organizing social energies resulted, one familiar to crisis politics. As a need became visible, a group of volunteers organized spontaneously to learn to fill it. Quickly some thirty autonomous groups involving over a thousand people appeared to fill a spectrum of functions ranging from legal support to entertainment, from research to publicity. In general the two central committees were powerless to define, order, or direct their work; they could only facilitate it when possible, and by spreading its information help spread its example and style.

Later accounts tried to explain the FSM's power and success by picturing it as efficient and highly organized, run by a core of highly skilled technicians, like some functional American bureaucracy. In fact, it was nothing of the sort: groups would form and be working for days before the steering committee even learned of them. Skills were mostly developed *in situ,* in a process of free learning, from fragments of past skills and training usually meant for other purposes. I had never before seen my peers able to come together on a mass scale and generate new work in response to their needs. Here many of America's elite and frustrated youth felt for the first time that they created coherent, satisfying, and productive work that used their human capacities. The space they moved in was both open and rich, in senses they had not encountered before.

The Universal Sit-In

The FSM climaxed in the first mass disruptive campus sit-in. A thousand students marched into the administration building "to bring the machine to a grinding halt." They expected arrest and police violence as well as suspension or expulsion from school.

In the freed space of that building, during the fifteen hours before the cops came, the West's first free university conducted its first classes atop civil-defense disaster drums stored in the basement. Movies were shown on the walls. A Chanukah service was held, followed by traditional folk dancing. Singers and instrumentalists performed in the stairwells. They were barred from the study hall to which the top floor had been converted, and avoided the improvised infirmary and kitchen. Pot was smoked in the corners, and several co-eds had their first full sexual experiences on the roof, where walkie-talkies were broadcasting news to the outside. The steering committee made political decisions in the women's john and organized in the corridors.

To an open space—here physical rather than political or conversational, and of course always psychological—the students brought their entire selves and concerns, true to the deep and multileveled nature of the conflict. The result was typical of what flowers in open space. Masquerading as a sit-in, an entire society-in-miniature was created in the liberated territory of Sproul Hall, using all the resources available.

Confrontation Politics and Personal Growth

One aspect of the FSM illuminates the question of liberation and growth and the connection between their social and personal levels. In the six months following the sit-in, literally everyone I knew who had been deeply involved with the movement accomplished some major and long-delayed change in their personal lives. Examples were various: they left school, town, or their mates; some decided to finish their Ph.D.'s, take up painting, stop smoking, or get married. For all, the changes were intimate and deeply therapeutic.

Thus interior psychological space was opened by participation in a highly successful mass movement. Two factors seem clearly involved. First and simply: *a sense of public, collective empowerment carries over into the private domain*. Social behavior that shatters expectations of what is possible creates psychic space, in the form of a larger, partially opened universe of personal possibility. (Conversely, individual learning of all sorts is inhibited in a stifled society.)

The second factor has to do with why people were in fact *able* to move in their open spaces, and is more complex. In the FSM, the anger of America's white young was directed for the first time against their parent, liberal institutions. All observers agree that a long-gathered and deep anger and frustration—with the institution's processes and effects on the students' lives, and with their own inabilities to function —provided much of the energy that built and ran through the movement.

These gathered emotions were catalyzed into available energy during the charged hours around the cop-car, while students discussed the administration's inept atrocities and waited for the cops to recapture the car. For most, it was their first serious demonstration. Each had to deal directly with his own live anger and fear—the immediate tip of a massive iceberg—and manage some temporary resolution. Most chose to stay, to resist dispersement nonviolently and continue the struggle afterward, and to face and endure the uncertain consequences of their choice.

The movement's later development can be viewed as the acting-out of anger in a social theater: the articulation and expression of collective repressed emotion. The main target was the administration, which continued to provoke conflict during this time. In widely varied symbolic theater, the students dethroned the coercive parental authority described above as the Authority Complex. Harsh emotions became tools to break, rather than reinforce, control. In the open space thus created, and in response to their *other* feelings and needs, there flowered a rich and various community and culture, and a multitude of individual changes.

Observers of campus conflict are familiar with the enormous amounts of energy liberated in the participants, with the striking efficiency of its translation into productive social and personal work, and with the heavy charges of anger and fear that must constantly be dealt with on many levels. It seems that to engage directly with these emotions is deeply therapeutic and freeing in a nonspecific way.

I believe that this connection between personal growth and the experience of being able to express anger holds true on the largest social scale, though modified by other factors, and is critical in explaining the connection between the recent political movements among the blacks and the white young and the broad movements of cultural change that are spreading in their wake.

The Open Circle Process

Let me turn to a model of a learning environment that exhibits more directly the cyclic paradigm of learning sketched above. Its main features were visible in the cop-car episode; I have observed it in many other contexts and have created some of these deliberately. As a mass learning form, it can be used as a tool with a high probability of successful operation under the right conditions. These include the presence, among a group of people, of a sufficient critical mass of emotional energy—long stored up, or attached to some recent event—and the need to create a public con-

sciousness, not at all monolithic, which individual consciousness can relate to and be defined against.

Several hundred people are seated in a circle—the geometry is psychologically significant. They include a small core
group that organizes the form's energies by catalyzing and
maintaining open space. The process begins with the break-
ing-open of space, through exhortation or ceremony, or a
piece of angry or joyful theater, like the ritual murder of
interrupting a planned speaker. The event must combine
naked emotion with heavy and appropriate cognitive content; the dissonance between these is crucial to releasing
energy. The aim is to provide a freeing example, to break
open the expectations of what can happen in the circle, to
provide an authority that does not limit or enforce appropriate behavior but gives permission to express what is there.

The core group keeps the process open by preventing the
redevelopment of the Authority Complex in any of its forms
—such as a faculty member speaking at length or in continual response to questions from students; prolonged two-
person debate; cooperative effort by a small sub-group of
sophisticates to keep the conversation focused on a narrow
ideological track; and so on.

The core group deals with the steady resurgence of the
Authority Complex by isolating the individuals responsible
(if any) and effectively removing them from the conversation; by making new behavior to break the expectations that
re-form even without provocation; and by speaking directly
to the larger group about the health of its process. The core
organizers must deal also with the Authority Complex latent
in their own presence, especially while the impact of the
opening event lingers. (For example, the larger group must
not feel that it is *necessary* to put on a show or stand naked
in order to speak in the circle.) The core group defines
space with its energy, then draws back to leave the space
open. When core members speak with the authority of organizers and tenders of the discussion, they speak only of its
process. This authority must not be used to lend false weight

to their personal speech as members of the whole. If this distinction is impossible to maintain, as is often the case in large groups, they are silent personally.

On one occasion two of us began such a process among students at an educational reform community meeting. All our past expectations and conditioning urged us to hang on to control after we first spoke. My companion kept calling on people and asking them to focus their discussion; I sat on the floor crosslegged, rocking violently, acting out with my body my frustration at *knowing* what everyone should, of course, agree upon. Finally I controlled *him:* sent him to shush musicians at the back so people could hear, and do other control-things to facilitate the meeting. Our drives to control were thus neutralized in the conversation, which went on for hours with high tension and freedom.

The pattern of a successful open-circle process is generally this: For, say, half an hour after the opening, speakers cope with their reactions to that event. These are always quite mixed and include much hostility (which usually accompanies the breaking of expectations). Then people's less transient concerns take over. The conversation becomes various, not uniform. It is not debate, being poor in counter-argument, or continuous logical development of a topic— the style of authority implicit within such forms of conversation is not flexible enough. Rather, the key mode of an open process is *testament.* Freed not so much from direct constraint as from the subtler tyranny of limited example and expectation, people improvise to fill space with whatever they have to express and feel is appropriate. They speak as the public fragments of a divided consciousness. When enough fragments have been presented so that the consciousness becomes clear enough for individual and group needs,[3]

[3] This form isn't hostile to goal-oriented discussion: by it groups may make tactical or political decisions. In the cases I've witnessed, a critical factor of such decisions has been information about the internal states of the persons and the group making them—information difficult to come by within a less flexible form.

the process is satisfied and typically breaks up without a climax or a formal closing ritual. When the process is working well, most of those who speak are not accustomed to performing in the public of their peers, and the emotional quavering in their voices as they present their real concerns is the surest index that open space has in fact been created.

As with all open processes, the quickest way to close this one is by creating a climate of fear. Most open circles fail when their speakers turn from testifying to arguing against what others have said—reasserting by their stance of Critic the presence of the Authority Complex they have internalized.

EXAMPLES OF SOCIAL AND CULTURAL GROWTH IN OPEN SPACE

Some understanding of how growth occurs in open space comes from examining five major social and cultural institutions now being developed by the white young.

Underground Radio

The prototype "underground" radio station was San Francisco's KMPX, which early in 1967 began broadcasting an after-midnight hard-rock-and-rap program once a week to the enormous latent audience of hip young in the area. KMPX was then an obscure, struggling FM station, its airspace weakly held by a polyglot of ethnic/religious programs. Given the response to the new programming, the station was *open* to displacing the old segment by segment. Within a year, KMPX radiated New Culture twenty-four hours a day to an audience exceeded only by one local AM station, and changed the listening habits of a growing community.

Since KMPX was the first of its kind, there were few past expectations to guide and limit the conversation of its growth. Programming began by freely exploring the rich and changing music we called rock, and then expanded to include Bach, Ravi Shankar, jazz, *music concrete,* and old radio serials like "The Lone Ranger." Drop-in interviews with musicians and others of interest to the audience began happening unannounced. Sunday afternoons developed into a forum on matters of community importance, like abortion and the Great Pot Test Case and Vietnam. During a local newspaper strike, KMPX broadcast favorite columnists and a daily news summary compiled by *Ramparts;* a sister station went on to develop a new and wildly inventive form of dramatized news presentation. KMPX began to generate dances and demonstrations almost by itself. Its announcers were casual about mistakes and frank language. They announced the arrival of pot shipments, reported lost dogs, and warned listeners about batches of poisoned LSD for sale.

In an open space, a many-faced institution was growing in response to the unmet needs of an emerging community, generating new ideas and examples of what a radio station might become. The speed and flexibility of its growth were directly due to the high degree and quality of feedback between KMPX and its audience. The announcers and engineers belonged to the community and responded to its constant phone calls, often putting them on the air. The station was even physically open to its listeners, who crowded in bearing food and their desires.[4]

The open space could not be maintained. The station's success made it the focus of powerful commercial and social influence from the larger society. Within a year, control of

[4] When steering committee members faced decisions during the FSM, they sometimes went on campus, stopped the first twenty people wearing buttons, and asked them what they thought should be done.

the broadcasts passed from the programmers to the station's managers and owners, and to undiscriminated advertisers. None belonged to the community; all represented outside social and economic interests. In a classic sequence, the Authority Complex re-entered and pruned KMPX's brief various garden back to acceptable limits. The station's staff struck to regain control, were unsuccessful, and left. KMPX's programming went downhill to a safe plastic hip style. The original staff was powerless to better this when hired to revamp a station owned by a major media-chain, for its style of control proved inimical to freedom.

By 1970 there were three hundred "underground" stations. Few had enjoyed even KMPX's brief flowering, and almost none had developed significantly beyond that model. The lesson is general: only collective control by the community involved in and affected by an institution can keep its space open.[5]

Rock Music

"When the mode of the music changes," said Plato, "the walls of the City shake."

The art medium now called "rock music" deserves study as an open social form. Though rock is blues-based, its evolution has been so rapid and decentralized that—in contrast to tradition-rooted forms like jazz and classical music —an Authority Complex operates relatively weakly within it, and its limits are radically open. The form's technology is one factor in this—since records and tapes are cheap, plentiful, and ephemeral, their influence is as unconstraining as their production is rapid. Also, rock is generated from a re-

[5] The best present model of this for radio is offered by the listener-supported Pacifica Stations in Berkeley, Los Angeles, New York, and Houston (though some other stations are more advanced in their internal organization as collectives).

markably decentralized base of small, changing groups with wide-ranging cultural inputs, who are rather responsive to local community audiences. The freeing style of authority inherent in this generative form works to keep the medium open and preserve its vitality.

In this open domain, the young are inventing music anew, with a freed sense of what is appropriate to the task. The measure of a form's freedom is the diversity of behavior it contains and develops from what is available. Rock now embraces and integrates musical styles and elements drawn from every American subculture, and from most major musical cultures known to the rest of the world and to history. Its instruments range from violins to computers, from tin pans to theremins. Its content—as the Birch Society has long recognized—is a many-leveled message about freedom and the destruction of the old style of authority, which is mirrored in the structure and process of the medium that bears it.

But counter-forces work to close the medium. By 1969, they were already beginning to damp its live diversity. Though the music was created from a decentralized musician base, it was produced and distributed through the centralizing apparatus of the music industry, which operates in hierarchical power-modes within an economic reward/ punishment scheme, for the sake of preserving and extending its order. And though music is of all expressions the one in which the intrinsic authority of example should carry most clearly, within the Form of rock the force of an over-riding Authority Complex has biased evolution and has restricted and standardized the language.

Here we can study in some detail authoritarian closure as it occurs in a communications medium. As a mediating valve in the cycle of energy between musician and listener, the industry regulated the information it carried. The principle of regulation was neither free dissemination of all (musical) viewpoints, as in an open-circle process, nor the focused dissemination of a community consciously putting a medium

to its own building use. Instead, the industry chose music to push on the basis of its potential marketability in profit competition (and cultural "safeness"), and promoted musicians on the basis of their integrability into industrial production. A minute elite of decision-makers reinforced these choices with sales propaganda which tapped all the conditioning of their audience to re-create the hierarchies of Star and Superstar and convince people that what they got was what they needed.

Through this valve the rich output of people's first explorations of the open space of a new Form was restricted. Hardly was the Haight unveiled in '67 before the record companies were at work, defining and marketing a pabulumized San Francisco Sound. The Top Forty DJ's, their monopoly of most city audiences still unbroken, played it to death as an In thing. In thousands of garages across Amerika, kids hungry to make it as a group grabbed at the Sound, seeking something sure to get it on at the high-school dance, something the local promoters would find likely, or just one cut to send to RCA. Through a multitude of such cycles, rock music has grown stale. As of 1971, this Form was back under familiar control.

Rock Dances

Rock music has an open and eclectic aesthetic which characterizes the other art forms—painting, clothing, poetry, graffiti—at the growing edge of the young culture, and which is foreign to the parent culture. Call it the Santa Claus Aesthetic: one never knows what the medium wearing it may bring. This aesthetic is a phenomenon of first growth within freeing forms, fed by open access to treasuries of raw material. Yet it may not be ephemeral. For the Santa Claus Aesthetic is surely also a function of the emerging nature of those who invent and delight in its gifts; and perhaps, in this age when we resurrect and ransack the cultures of the world and the past and human consciousness transforms itself by miraculous technologies, it may presage a stable cultural style new to human history.

Such dreams came naturally in the heady atmosphere of the first rock dances, held in the now-legendary Fillmore Auditorium and elsewhere in San Francisco. "Rock dances" is a thin misnomer for these first successful experiments in mass total-environmental theater. The battery of media used has become familiar: films, liquid light projections, strobo-scopic and "black" lights; incense and foods and feelables; live music and tapes. Their total and many-leveled impact overwhelms psychic barriers. *To attend simultaneously through several senses to intense semi-related messages creates an internal dissonance that expands and opens inner space.* Technicians of the mixed-media form were im-mediately familiar with the behavioral consequences of what they called "sensory overload."

The great halls held open space: physical, psychological, cultural, historical. Live energies of longing and contact re-fracted through a myriad of cross-cultural interfaces to open space further, as Hell's Angels, hippies, media-men, activists, socialites, teeny-boppers, blacks, and sorority girls came to-gether in fantastical costume. In that space people sang, danced, rapped, took pictures, played instruments, voyeured, seduced, served Kool-Aid, painted faces and floors, spun in rings, stood drowned in light, freaked on acid, wept in corners, played balloon-ball, took notes and chanted, spun wildly through the crowd crowned with ivy or in the raw. There were no necessary roles, no established norms of clothing, conduct, or motion. Beyond their irreducible interior imprisonments—often dramatically lessened—the participants were free to define themselves and "do their own thing," even though that phrase was not yet current. The halls became a rich, compact arena for the free, improvisational theater which the young are developing now in the streets, classrooms, and supermarkets.[6]

In America and the West, the white young had always learned dances created by others, sometimes varying them slightly in learning. In this process—caricatured by the white feet and black feet, 1-2, 1-2, of our childhood comic books and adolescent social nightmares—the structure and operation of the Authority Complex are elegantly displayed. But in the open space of the Fillmore Auditorium, many were freed to learn a new style of learning how to dance. In a whirl of motions—polka and cha-cha-cha, ballet spins and gymnastic stretching exercises, mambo and bunny hop, twist and camel, waltz and intercourse, kaleidoscope modern dance—from a treasury of fragments and their own natural gestures they learned to synthesize dances whose names were only their own, relegating imitation to its proper place in the process of free learning.

The closed universes of personal possibility were broken open by the force of mutual example. In a climate that tolerated any collection of motions, guided by their own sense of coherence, individuals created and expressed their own dances. They were limited primarily by their physical capacities; by their abilities to grasp and combine disparate elements into coherent expression and to tolerate the cogni-

---

[6] See Abbie Hoffman's *Revolution for the Hell of It* (Dial, 1969), for a lucid exposition of the dramaturgy and social function of this style of theater.

tive and other dissonances centrally involved in this process; by their senses of trust and fear, and by what they had in their selves to express. The particular importance of dealing with fear in this process of learning will be clear to most who remember learning to dance (even in a crippled way), or who strive for emotional openness.

Mixed media are not enough: the open space was not maintained, within the halls or for persons. The halls settled into successful commercial operation, in the familiar centralized forms of the profit economy. In ways direct and subtle, and in the style of the Authority Complex, this re-enforced old limits on behavior and expectations. This process was even acted out physically, while the capacity overcrowds of greed were compressed into a uniform mass on floors that had no space for dancing, and life-theater turned into passive concert.

The process of closure took about a year. The mass media played a considerable part, by shifting the nature of the audience and its expectations. But I do not think they hastened closure, despite the way we cursed them for cheapening this too. For, though closure processes are various, their common period seems to be some nine to eighteen months[7] in any new form or institution that does not contain a subcomponent that functions explicitly to keep the form open. The process of closure begins when dominant power relationships, in social or psychic space, start to be seriously challenged.

The Fillmore moved to Fillmore West, which might better be called Fillmore Lost. But its prototypical classroom for personal and freely developed dance and theater continues to be re-created at be-ins and happenings—especially at those felt to be of historical and cultural importance. This

---

[7] See the discussion of periodicities of learning in Chapter VII. I am speaking here of forms that are unified through physical or electronic contact; closure may take longer in others.

Event consciousness is instrumental in creating open space. It is one version of the Hawthorn Effect,[8] a general term for the way people's behavior changes when it takes on the important aspect of being an object of deliberate study. (The Effect is radically different when study is evaluation within a punitive framework.)

Two other factors involved in the successful creation of this learning form deserve mention. Typically, as in crisis politics, there are many objects, groups, actions, and individuals that provoke and invite participation and active response. From one perspective this means that the drive and instinct of play are strongly excited; from another, that as a functional form such a process of energies is rich in feedback loops. Also, these events are often *free,* both in the simple economic sense, which is psychologically important, and in the deeper sense of an ethical mood prevailing—one that licenses giving out and sharing without requiring return and is often catalyzed by the example of the musicians.

Free Youth Ghettos

History has known other youth ghettos, less extensive and deliberate than those being created throughout America. Never have they contained "youth" largely in their twenties, nor served as the principal cradle for what Kenneth Keniston[9] speculates to be a second, para-adolescent developmental stage unique to post-industrial society and thus to human culture. Robert Lifton has given us the term "protean man" for the selves that may be the full products of this stage: selves capable of wide and continual transformation

[8] So called from its pioneer description in a study of the motivation of industrial workers.

[9] In *Young Radicals* (Harcourt, Brace and World, 1968) and later papers.

and application, bearing with them their conjugate society, which also may be called protean. What environments of learning and change will produce them, and how? This is perhaps the key analytical and political question of our age; surely radical social reconstruction depends upon it. One way to begin to poke for answers is to try to identify and understand the real learning processes that have so far been at work among the young who generate these speculations.

America's free youth ghettos still largely coincide with her college campuses, where they first developed in an incomplete form. Now, in a fuller form, they are growing in every major city. Their prototype appeared in San Francisco's Haight-Ashbury district.

Over a few years, perhaps 10,000 of America's most freed youth occupied the open urban space of a declining neighborhood, seeking with varying deliberateness a place to build a local society that would extend and embrace their individual changes. A tenuous ghetto grew denser. The Haight came to collective consciousness of itself as a distinctive place roughly at the end of 1965, aided by a successful neighborhood political battle to avert the carnage of a freeway. This consciousness was marked and defined by the development of a spectrum of small formal and informal groups—political, social, cultural, economic—whose functions were to clarify the nature of the society emerging there, to guide and express its growth, and to begin to develop institutions appropriate to its needs and nature.[10]

The Haight flowered in peaceful space for roughly a year. Then media discovered it and created the Hippy, and it was swamped by an instant media deluge whose only precedent was the destruction of San Francisco's North Beach colony a decade earlier. The hospitality, trust, and resources of a young society were overwhelmed and its further growth

[10] See Chapter IX.

agonized and distorted. While Scott MacKenzie sang, "If you come to San Francisco, wear a flower in your hair," the speedy economies of tourism and Mafia amphetamine pumped strange elements into the open arterials that nourished the Haight. When the hungry young arrived in force, they found a social sewer.

But there was another, ephemeral Haight never captured by the media, whose development, nature, and destruction have been described only in fragments already outdated. That story is equally about the growth of freedom in America's young, as their lives sketch a new society that feeds cruel hopes of its possible survival, and is too complex to go into here. Still, the original Haight presents some important parallels to the "rock dance" model of a learning environment.

First, the individual consciousness of its members was opened not by multimedia *sensory* bombardment, but by an analogous process in more general media. The catalogue of input is hopelessly long. Television brought the first indelible images of black liberation. The Bomb spoke in their nightmares, while they listened to a new music on transistor radios, read paperback science-fiction, dreamed of touching the moon. They were exposed to all the explosive potential liberations of a sudden qualitative change in man's social and industrial technologies, and to the deaths that these equally threatened. Raised among the gathering contradictions of a liberal corporate capitalist state unable to cope with its problems or maintain its authorities, the inner barriers of their perceptions were corroded by casual lay psychoanalysis and psychedelic drugs. The media were new and penetrating and bore intense, discordant, incoherent energies and images of life and death. The young came to the dance hall called Haight with their minds blown.

Second, the social norms of the Haight were those of its dancers at the Fillmore writ more broadly. They defined a context whose participants were somewhat freed to explore the dance of their selves as they had that of their bodies. There was no effective collective concept of deviant behavior. The boundaries of permissible and possible behavior became drastically enlarged under the multiple thrust of radical examples.

The media phrase "do your own thing" is a weakened version of the Haight's acid motto, "freak freely"; and members of the broader community now becoming self-conscious in America most commonly refer to themselves as "freaks." To freak freely is to let out fully and live in the energies and natures that have been repressed by our society through a process most usefully described as "niggerization": a process in the style of the Authority Complex, which inhibits the development of individual and cultural identity. The concrete experience of life among people who gladly think of themselves as freaks, as niggers learning the beauty of their black and other selves, is a carnival dream. For in a climate with almost no operative concept of deviance, bewildering in its variety of cultural input and individual example, personal change becomes richly possible.

Third, of course, collective values and aesthetics were also revealed and developed in the space opened by the drastic diminution of that internalized Authority Complex that governs public and private behavior. The emotions of varied and explosive personal liberations overlapped and reinforced one another. They encouraged exposure, sharing, tolerance, mutual involvement and support. Norms and expectations of behavior developed, whose authority was freeing rather than constraining. (Their tangible symbol was the Haight's most typical social ritual, the offering of a joint of grass to the friend or stranger entering through the open door.)

Within the space they opened much that was ugly occurred—though more that was beautiful—in terms of specific aesthetics that people shared. Indeed, the *public* presence of ugliness and failure seems to be one essential feature of the operation of an open form.[11] For such a form to continue successfully, its beauties must overbalance its uglinesses in a way that nourishes a commitment to an overarching aesthetic of freedom within which individual aesthetics can be pursued; and it must develop ways to deal with its failures. Making failure a visible element of process is a necessary beginning—in this and other ways, the parallels to personal therapy should be clear.

The imprint of a collective aesthetic of freedom is apparent in both the intent and the design of the institutions that began to evolve in the Haight to service basic human needs. Successful experiments in creating and distributing on a mass scale free culture, free food, free housing and clothing, and free medical services began and progressed to some degree of institutional sophistication and stability, embodying an open and participatory organizational style. Correlated attitudes about sex were evident. So, most strongly, was an ethic and psychology of personal property new to America—an open one, which seems appropriate to the full society of post-scarcity economy whose uncontrolled premonitions now fill the houses of the middle class and excite our imaginations.[12]

To some extent, all these values and phenomena seem to characterize every revolutionary context or process displayed in our Western history, despite the constraining influences of particular ideology.

Fourth, the birth of revolution is glorious and noted for personal transformation: in it prostitutes turn pure. The Haight, like the FSM, was a rich and mobile environment of

---

[11] In this sense, the present openness of Amerika's ugliness qualifies it as an open form.

[12] Goodman, Theobald, and others have speculated about the economic processes and institutions of post-scarcity society, but the subject of its personal and social psychology has hardly been touched.

free expression, of mutual interaction and need. For a time its energies were not focused to do immediate battle; and its internal social climate was even more nourishing, and incredibly tolerant and patient. Such a context is intimately therapeutic.

The Haight was a concentrated laboratory for the process at work in America's young, which may be seen as the therapeutic reconstruction of individual personality in a simultaneously developing social matrix.[13] The clearest examples—which I believe to be extreme versions of the typical individual process—involved the recovery, re-integration, and therapeutic growth, in communes, of personalities whom LSD experiences had pulled over the edge of what we inadequately describe as psychotic breaks. In a process inextricably involved with the evolution of its context, I saw such persons rebuild and build newly their selves with relative degrees of rapidity, humaneness, and completeness, for which nothing in my previous experience—neither example nor rumor—had prepared me.

I imagine the "success" ratio, however you measure it, was not very high. Surely it dropped as the young community grew paranoid, strained, and swamped, before its therapeutic lore was well developed. Still, I saw enough. I do not believe that the clumsy, fragmenting operations of our specialists and specialized institutions match the present

[13] The interplay between engagement in personal and in collective reconstruction has necessary rhythms (and definite periodicities, which begin with those described on pp. 241–8). Many a movement activist has burnt out for a time or forever by working too long in a phase of intense outer activity and not honoring the rhythm of her need for space to recuperate and integrate her changes. (Such misjudgments of need are common in the absence of careful collective lore about tending ourselves through change.) Symmetrically, rest turns ripe and yields motion; but its ripeness is often wasted stale by groups who fail to grasp that public engagement renews private refreshment. (Only through heightened political consciousness can a group manage a regenerative balance of inner and outer engagement.)

effectiveness of such total-context therapy, let alone its potential.

I will return to the question of what skills and factors are involved in such reconstruction, but several are familiar already. Examples of successful change in process provide ratification and encouragement. Without a strong concept of deviant behavior expressed in a punitive social framework, fear is dramatically reduced. Trust is an all-important variable, as is the supportiveness of the context. The tolerance of the Haight was not simply neutral, but often active: at its best it led people to encounter and engage with all that was strange, including the brokenness of their brothers and sisters.

Certainly the Haight held a highly selected (though diverse) population. Their psychological profiles resembled those of the FSM arrestees, who as a large group tested out with unprecedentedly high scores in a cluster of variables centrally involved with free learning ability: autonomy, impulse-expression, fantasy-freedom, and others that contribute to the psychological aggressiveness and openness characteristic of good learners.

Are more general populations capable of undergoing such processes of learning as those described here? Can they deal even this minimally well with the experiences and tools of open forms? Much evidence suggests that they can. The opening of space is a recursive activity now progressing in a favorable climate of historical potential. Minds blown by the FSM came to the Haight; and the instant televised images of both blew further minds across America, opening the universe of the possible. It is now clear that these two events represented the leading edge of a massive motion among the young, and that the technologies of change, which prepared their participants, have been operating throughout America with effects that are only now beginning to become apparent and are still accelerating.

The Berkeley Switchboard

A compact example of the reconstitution of authority in open space appeared in the interior organizing process of the Berkeley Switchboard, a standard hip community service agency coordinating housing and transportation, providing medical and legal aid and so on, for one of the Haight's sister communities. Sponsored by the Free Church—an experimental ministry itself sponsored with few expectations by a collection of liberal groups and churches—the Berkeley Switchboard's organizers were given free space in the form of a house and being left to invent their own thing.

Their constraints were operational goals: to achieve a stable internal society, which left its members free to create and coordinate their work. The style of this micro-society necessarily had to be that of the democratic commune or extended family which the larger community is evolving as its distinctive experimental life-module, often with a specialized work-orientation. In this example, the work was central, constantly evolving and therapeutic (the changing learning to help the changing change), which may be why some aspects of openness characteristic of this form show up most extremely here. The Switchboard had to organize itself around a constant flow of visitors and new members and major turnovers in its work functions and force—and around persons who were freaks learning to work while freaking freely, who like as not would file cards while stoned on acid.

Sleeping bags, filing cabinets and freaks invaded an open space, graced by the attitudes of the Haight. At first there were simply no rules. In a voluntary behavioral Chaos, people lived and worked as they pleased and invented elementary forms of cooperation. Services struggled into being. Garbage piled in the kitchen and collected rats. Drunken bikers beat itinerant hippies with chains in the living room.

After it became sufficiently clear that such phenomena seriously hampered the Switchboard's work, rules were instituted, bearing the authority of their self-conscious and public creation, and backed by ostracism and physical force. Such creations were difficult and instructive for a community deliberately oriented toward tolerance and nonviolence.

Compassionate hospitality led them to open the place as a crash pad; a glut of transients closed space, and they had to learn to restrict the numbers without closing their doors. The Switchboard's people dealt constantly with this problem of developing appropriate limits on the free expression of their natural energies and impulses: limits that would not cause these to wither, but would permit them to flourish in a total social ecology.

The community's distrust of the Authority Complex and its reluctance to legislate helped create an environment in which rules and social norms were devised only when collectively felt to be absolutely necessary for survival and function. Such rules came about in response to specific and mutually recognized problems. They were tailored to suit the society's immediate nature and needs and—in this high-feedback and participatory environment—were constantly open to challenge and revision. Their governing aesthetic was that of minimal constraint consistent with operational goals.

Here the process is elegantly displayed; but this style of reconstituting authority is visible in each of the learning environments described above. To build successfully in such open spaces requires in individuals not only the ability to tolerate and experience intense expressions of emotion, but also the ability to generate and deal with high and rapidly changing flows of social and personal energy. They must also be able to maintain themselves and function within the ambiguity and anxiety, the tensions and fears of partial social and psychological chaos. *In large degree, the appro-*

priateness of what they build will be proportional to their ability to sustain these dissonances and endure these stresses.

A critical question, then, is how are these abilities developed and improved? The most general answer is as important as it is simple: *by practice,* by a progressive sequence of relatively successful exercises. (The importance of such monotonic chains of experience in developing new behavior, within whatever framework of reward and failure, is well known throughout learning theory, even on the rat-running level of simple conditioning.)

From this perspective, most of the learning events described above are seen to be models of typical environments that depend on and nourish these abilities. Their historical progression occurred around some actual continuity of individuals—though its implications and echoes are now nationwide—and furnishes a partial and parallel recapitulation of the process of the development of these abilities within individuals. All of these learning forms—from confrontation politics to therapeutic community—are reproducible technologies and are re-usable in varying degrees and adaptations. They are coming into wide use.

FORMAL EDUCATIONAL FORMS

Before continuing on the question of what tools develop the psychological skills necessary to change, I want to deal with some institutional environments of free learning that exhibit what is built in open space.

The Tussman Program

The Experimental Collegiate Program of the University of California at Berkeley—informally called the Tussman Pro-

gram, after its organizer—began in Fall 1965 in the open
space of a former fraternity house. The two-year program
included 150 freshmen, and a faculty of five professors and
five advanced graduate students drawn from many disciplines. The formal curriculum each term consisted of intensive nondisciplinary study of a *small* core of readings
drawn from a major epoch of cultural change, with three
scheduled lecture/seminar hours and one paper each week.
This, and the expected extensive informal interactions, accounted for four-fifths of the students' class load. The Program's plans were at best sketchy; it hoped to develop them
in the process of evolving into a self-governing community.

In several senses, then, the Program was an open space.
Its first years furnished a compact, luminous example of the
crippled growth of free learning in the live but partial presence of the Authority Complex, and of the territorial competition between the two.

Real needs are revealed in open space. Entering a program explicitly promised to be theirs to help construct, the
students tried to make it responsive to what they saw as their
immediate needs, both personal and social. These may be
symbolized by—but were by no means limited to—their
needs to deal with psychedelic drugs and the War, felt most
intensely in the climate of Berkeley. In each case, the tasks
were to choose some action or relation to the problem, to
encounter and deal with its personal consequences, and to
interact with others variously involved in this process. But
drugs and the War played at most a peripheral part in the
lives of the senior faculty. The professors were not interested
in revising their conception of the Program to make these
concerns central and resisted attempts at this.

The difficulties in implementing these needs were reflected
in the Program by internal political struggle. This was
largely concerned with educational governance: with the
questions—which at first seemed genuinely open—of how
and by whom the curriculum and its styles were to be shaped

and implemented, and faculty chosen and retained. By the year's end the answers were clear: the students had no formal say or effective power in these matters. The governing group was not open, and it came to be rigidly restricted to the senior faculty. (Even within their small ranks, the only stable mode of power and decision they could evolve was not communal or consensual but autocratic, operating in the classic style of the Authority Complex.)

Despite this, within the space of the Program, authority was heavily divided and conflicting in interest and style. This tension was maintained largely through the teaching assistants, who accounted for most of the direct student/faculty contact. In them overlapped the authority of their nominal roles, to which the students responded from deep conditioning, and the opposed and freeing authority of their examples as persons whose condition was close to that of the students, and who were struggling *visibly* with the same sorts of problems.

Whether personal or social, space in which conflicting forces and styles of governance struggle is electric with social and psychological dissonance.[14] Such fractured authority is typical of incoherent open space (coherent open systems are a different and Utopian matter, though these notes are meant as a guide toward their construction). Such space is fertile for growth, *provided that most of the available energy is not bound rigidly into the conflict* but can be disposed in a flexible and appropriate balance between the requirements of growth and the development of an internal and external framework of authority that will permit it.

In the Program's case, the students' "academic" and other learning was on the whole adequate and often considerable, as measured by both the system's standards and their own; and they shared an intense and painful laboratory in the struggle of freedom and authority. But too much energy was

[14] See pp. 355–65 for an example.

in fact bound into the unsuccessful conflict and its immediate demands, and their knowledge, skills, and will were undeveloped. The students were unable to reconstruct an effective, collective authority of a different form from that of the Authority Complex.

Before its power their concerns retreated into scattered private work, and the Program's human space became frozen in a permanent and standard division. One territory was public, common, and institutional; in it the Authority Complex held unchallenged sway, which was achieved and symbolized by firing the teaching assistants at the first year's end and eliminating them from the design of the Program and its successors. In the other territory, among a scattered community with no effective group structure, the students tried to deal privately with those needs for change and learning which the Program no longer held the possibility of satisfying.

This ultimate territorial partition was reflected early on by a tendency among the students to divide into two fairly sharply defined groups, determined not so much by what they needed to learn as by the styles of learning for which they had been prepared. The Program's internal process forced and clarified this division. One group did not choose to try, and generally were badly able, to function outside of an authority-centered learning framework.[15] Though the others were not successful in establishing a collective alternate framework, as individuals they were distinctly more sure in their self-directed learning skills and better able to deal with the anxieties, dissonances, conflicts, and emotions of the free learning process within the Program's society. In these and other skills, the students' unperturbed self-evaluations were generally accurate—a general truth that points to the importance of building change-systems that depend on

[15] That much of their real learning was in fact somewhat self-directed is moot, because they were not conscious of it as such.

the conscious self-selection of their participants and allow them maximal self-direction.

The contrast between authority-directed and self-generated behavior appears in every partially open space. In group interaction, as the politics of situation unfold, people sort out into subgroups that reflect these tendencies. Yet both tendencies inhabit each person in some unique balance —as if this man were 30/70, and that one 60/40. This private balance is not fixed, nor are the characters of the social roles one plays entirely determined by it. Both change in response to the need of the social drama for players to fit its roles, so that he who would be a rebel in Sparta might be a tyrant in Athens, as many members of the Program found.

On the social or the personal level, this division escalates into polarized conflict whenever the context is not rich enough to satisfy both sets of needs, for a learning environment that refuses support is as tyrannical as one with no doors to freedom, and makes people as panicky. The polarization along psychological capacities and orientation split the Program's staff—not entirely along lines of age, a hopeful sign. Most of the professors—the Program's head, in particular—were unable to endure the chaos and emotions necessary either to build within the Program a structure of governance and learning that the students felt dealt with their major needs, or even to engage with much intimacy or effectiveness with individual persons around matters the student felt not to be peripheral.

True, the professors' experience was deeply different from that of the students and had not developed in most of them the necessary skills. But beyond this, they were simply, deeply, and humanly terrified: of Chaos, of contact, of the anxieties of freedom and building newly, of the unknown depths and content all significant learning must involve— the eternal terror in response to which Hobbes articulated the political theory of the Authoritarian State.

In this case, no social mechanisms developed to deal therapeutically with the terror, which instead the Program's process intensified. Both sorts of students came to feel themselves adrift and unsupported. The professors reacted classically, by closing whatever was open. Some acted this out by reinventing and restricting office hours and minimizing contact with students; by firing the teaching assistants, whose presence forced real contact with another reality; and even by literally fainting several times. Mostly they came increasingly to define their self-interest negatively, as the prevention of the destruction of their personal and social authorities. The remedy was to reassert total control wherever possible and to avoid the space outside this domain. To this they applied their energies successfully. Authority in the Program was tightened along unreconstructedly Hobbesian lines, in practice and in conscious theory. Despite its exterior features of newness, the Program collapsed toward a standard learning form, fragmenting and familiar in its process and consequences.

It is worth mentioning that the key professors involved in the Program's failure were noted and active political liberals: its head was a well-known exponent of civil liberties and responsibilities, one was a prominent member of a progressive school board, and another a constitutional lawyer in behalf of radical causes. The process of their attempts and failures to deal with the problems involved in creating a major new learning environment is typical, in outline and in detail, of a wide variety of related attempts by their peers.[16] Clearly any style of educating has its own conjugate politics. The political knowledge and sensibilities of the American mainstream—including in particular the Liberal current generally reflected in our present formal systems of educa-

---

[16] Since 1965, many campuses have deployed such semi-autonomous mini-colleges as part of a broad offensive of containment aimed at the freer energies of today's students. See "The Context of Campus Violence," in *The Wedding Within the War*.

tion—are simply not adequate to the problem of constructing on any human level systems of free learning, or, equivalently, systems capable of continual and appropriate change.

The Teach-In

Properly, an analytic catalogue of my generation's new learning forms should deal with the Teach-In, the first example of which was the Vietnam Teach-In at the University of Michigan in 1965. As a way of creating and structuring space for learning energies, teach-ins can be understood as intermediate between the models of the Tussman Program and the free university.

The Free University

What happens when the needs, orientations, and energies that were absorbed and distorted by struggle within the Tussman Program find a more genuinely open space? What first forms evolve naturally? Their ideal modular unit has been described above as a free learning group. Such units typically exist within a larger institutional form, visible in the hundreds of free universities and student-generated experimental colleges that have sprouted on campuses and around free youth ghettos.

Almost all campus-based free universities come to involve some 6 to 10 per cent of the students—indicating a class of persons psychologically predisposed to experiment with the content and process of learning. Yet the constancy of this proportion, from working-class state schools to private elite universities, implies equally that such personal readiness to experiment comes about in response to objective social conditions and the potential for collective experiment—again, as if a chance to play a new social role drew forth the players. Given this fraction's involvements in politics, drugs, etc. (as reflected in Free U curricula), the figure of 6 to 10 per cent provides a rough estimate of the fraction of (white) college youth willing to venture the edge of social change on an ongoing basis.

The first successful Free U was begun by San Francisco State College students in 1965. Three older students grew tired of grousing about the school and went down to Registration to hang out and gather volunteer groups of freshmen to talk about their education together. After a semester, some members created an interdisciplinary course for their general credits, with cooperative professors; in several years this evolved into a General Ed study group to design and implement major changes in San Francisco State's undergraduate requirements. Other members set about organizing more classes for whatever people wanted to learn. The next semester began with seventeen student-generated experimental classes, which soon banded together to form the Experimental College. Two years later the carnival multiplication of learning groups involved 2,000 students, and the E.C. was discovered by the media and echoed in East Lansing.

The original organizers of the E.C. developed and analyzed a distinctive style of catalyzing change. Generally in our culture the unit of change is conceived as a homogeneous mass population, like an economic or Economics class, to whom a rhetorical appeal is made, in the name of History, Learning, or whatever, urging appropriate change. (When possible, the rhetoric is backed by force.) This model describes equally the teacher lecturing, the style of the American Left of the thirties, and the social and economic legislation of the Johnson Administration.

In the contrasting model of the E.C., change is catalyzed by creating a climate of small, autonomous groups engaged in satisfying activities that generate the energy for them to go on. Change is stimulated more by building and exhibiting actual working examples than by trying directly to influence the whole of a large population. The presence of such new examples is, technically speaking, a *mindblower;* that is, it breaks expectations as to what forms of personal and institutional behavior and reward are possible. In this expanded universe of possibility, those with available energy and skills can go about constructing their own examples: not in imitation, but after and out of their own sense of needs. Drawing attention to new examples is no problem, for the spectacle of people engaging in genuinely satisfying activity is rare enough that the vibes this generates are picked up by those who are ready to move.[17]

On an intimate scale, this model describes the catalytic mechanism of leadership in small free learning groups (compare pages 65–6). It also describes the multiplication of functional groups within the FSM and the Haight. On a broader social scale, it accounts for the almost instant reproduction across America of the examples of the FSM, KMPX, the Haight, rock dances and be-ins, communes, Switchboards, and free universities. On these two scales, the role of media in spreading examples is essential and deserves careful study in view of the way the mass media market false expectations along with real news.[18]

Organizing processes of this sort—i.e., that propagate real examples by media and direct contact among people ready to move—catalyze growth that is sudden, simultane-

[17] The problem more often is how to moderate exposure, to avoid a glut of the ill-prepared coming to close the space and resources of experiment.

[18] In particular, the fidelity or corruption of an example's transmitted image seems to depend on how strongly an editorial Authority Complex operates within the medium, and thus ultimately on whether the structure of power within the medium is centralized or decentralized. (Network television and the underground press furnish two contrasting examples. See also "A Highly Abstract Digression" in Chapter VII.) The information conveyed by such images is somewhat independent of their corruption, however, for it is also a strong function of common culture and common needs among its recipients.

ous, and deeply decentralized in that its forms and standards fall under no central control, not even an aesthetic one. (Consider the case of rock music.) The institutional form compatible with this free organizing process has a structure with decentralized editorial control and centralized administrative facilitation.[19] (Contrast the music industry.)

The clearest example of this form is the free university, a cooperative association of voluntary learning groups investigating a broad curriculum in a variety of old and new styles. Typically, the groups are completely autonomous within the institution they form, which is governed by a decision-making group open to all who wish to participate. Such a form can operate with gratifying success, as in the case of the E.C., which not only flourished in its classes but was able to execute an open-ended series of major organizational restructurings over several years, each time strengthening group growth and opening new space.

This capacity was the product of deliberate design. The E.C.'s organizers set out to develop an institutional mode that would prove flexible to change, able to modify its nature to suit its discovered needs. The ongoing conversation responsible for this development also elaborated the model of a free learning group described above, of which it was itself a remarkably successful example. A collection of autonomous experimenters engaged in evolving fluid cooperation, and beyond them the Experimental College itself, functioned as a laboratory that tested its theories on, and applied its understandings to, its own shape and workings. Thus, like a model conversation, the core group became not only a focus for research and propagation but also its own product and end.

This operation of the E.C.'s core group within the larger form is a clear example of a *reflexive institution,* con-

---

[19] Such processes and forms are also dealt with in Chapter VIII.

taining within itself explicit mechanisms for consciously examining the state and process of its growth and for changing itself in response to this learning. The institutions of our culture are all petrifications of the Authority Complex; their reflexive mechanisms work ineffectively when they even exist. But in order even to survive in this age of accelerating and chronic change, which dramatically exposes Man's condition as the active and involuntary creator of the changes of his being, all human institutions will in some sense have to contain functioning mechanisms for their own *continual* change.[20] This holds true on the small-group level and also within the interior, personal space of each changing man and woman. On all three levels, these mechanisms are analogous. They center on *the consciousness of process* and its deliberate manipulation. In the case of the small group, the reflexive mechanism is visible not structurally but in its operation—as a set of roles and rituals for bringing group energy to focus on problems with process.

In the case of the E.C., several institutional processes overlapped to make the reflexive mechanism highly visible. The E.C. was a natural host for groups learning together about educational change; and these groups in turn generally contained the people who were instrumental in shaping the E.C.'s form and growth, who formed its ongoing organizing core and who studied it within itself. Often they even received class credits within the formal parent institution for their study and organizing work. Thus the reflexive mechanism of change existed as a model sub-unit of the E.C.: unique only in its function, typical in its interior form and process and its nourishment by the larger structure.

[20] Analysis of their construction and function seems most appropriate from the cybernetic perspective on the processing of information, which offers simple and instructive models and theory. See Gordon Pask, *Cybernetics* (Fernhill, 1961), and his later papers on *heter*archical control systems, which provide a model of authority and control distinct from that of the Authority Complex.

It is crucial to note that this reflexive core group was neither a study group nor an element of a check-and-balance system. It was *empowered,* in part because its membership overlapped with that of other change-seeking subgroups, to open all of the system's energies into self-directed change. And it was open to active participation by anyone. (The contrast with the standard mechanism of change in American colleges is immediate and deadly.)

Beyond this, the general conversation about structural and educational change in the larger institution—San Francisco State College itself—came to be visible, centered, and organized *as such* in the Experimental College. The conversation was strong, well organized, and implemented with political skill which had been developing for six years within a climate moderately favorable to institutional change. Consequences included the design of a new student center and the complete revamping of the school's general education requirement, both accomplished totally within the E.C.; and a general loosening and revitalization of San Francisco State's curriculum and of the process for instituting and crediting study within it.

The Experimental College was in part deliberately conceived as an experiment to develop a multi-phasic agency of institutional change within the larger institution, capable of whatever thought and action were appropriate. On this broader scale, we see again the successful operation of a reflexive form.

The main skills involved in the E.C.'s reflexive success were those of political consciousness. They were developed by learning the structure of power—on all institutional levels—and how to manipulate it.

Considerable open space was generated by a style of moving which aimed at avoiding a polarization of the environment's energies into opposed and paralyzed forces, frozen in conflict and expectations, and tried instead to make visible *common areas of self-interest* on which parties could begin to move cooperatively. In interaction with faculty and administrators, students upset expectations by not adapting the confrontationist postures currently expected of activists and by initiating and making visible bodies of serious work. The E.C. itself, not being clearly either within or without the larger college, had an ambiguous institutional identity which confused expectation and response, opening further space.

These open territories began closing as soon as new growth reached a point where irreconcilable conflicts of interest were clearly revealed, as seems to be the general rule. In this case, open conflict began when the E.C. and the larger college contended for scarce physical space for their expansions; and when the E.C.'s styles and content began to make ponderable demands for space and credit within the larger institution, and thus for significant change in its forms and processes. Later, black and white student political movements—in whose generation and nurture the E.C. had been critically involved—were directed against the college itself, demanding massive change, and by early 1969 San Francisco State became the battleground of the country's longest continuous student strike. The space of ambiguous identities closed quickly and permanently; further building at San Francisco State occurred only in space pried open by the leverage of painfully cultivated skills and power. These were inadequate to preserve the E.C. After Governor Reagan appointed Hayakawa as Occupying Authority, control tightened, student funds and official sanctions were withheld from the E.C., and it finally died.

The Experimental College had a typical free university curriculum. Its subjects of study were mostly change-oriented: the perspectives and skills of social change; the skills of small-group interaction and the learning process; tools and workshops in various species of personal encounter and therapy. (Most of the remaining courses dealt with the products and production of a new culture.) The curriculum's methods were innovative and generally therapeutic, and were often explicitly designed to this end.

In liberated territory, guerrillas build hospitals and schools to care for the needs of their people, and factories for the machinery of the wars of hunger and freedom. The metaphor holds in rich detail. Understood broadly, it describes the creation of space in territory and among people dominated by the imperialism of the Authority Complex; it understands what is built in that space, and why; it prescribes strategies for simultaneous struggle and growth on all human levels, for extending the space and building.

THE PSYCHEDELIC EXPERIENCE

From social forms to the human interior is no long journey. The sweet smell of grass will take you there from corridors and rooms wherever the young are learning. For the "psyche-expanding" drugs—marijuana (grass), lysergic diethylamide acid (LSD or acid), and related chemical agents—along with confrontation politics and a new music have provided the most intense learning experiences shared by large numbers of the young.

By 1969, perhaps one and a half million had dropped acid, and ten times that number used grass regularly. I class these drugs together because their immediate effects are similar in essence, though grossly different in scale, and their cumulative effects are comparable on both counts. Like Ac'cent (MSG), the psychedelics are a colorless, tasteless spice that heightens the flavor of whatever is cooking in the personal and social stewpot. They bring out and accelerate whatever change is going on, good and bad, in all its contradictions, and the deliberate will can use them to fix and extend what changes it will.

The surface parallels between the psychedelic experience

and participation in free learning groups, especially those oriented toward encounter and therapy, are immediate. Both result in a "high" or "stoned" condition, characterized by heightened inter- and intra-personal openness, and by a sensation of containing and being embedded in higher flows of psychic energy. The more often one has these experiences, within broad limits, the more permanently stoned one can become—with the aid of other disciplines to preserve their breakthroughs—and the more able to use contact with any source of live psychic energy to generate and sustain the high condition. (In drug culture, this phenomenon is called "contact high.") At first one just sits there stoned: dazzled and reveling in the perceptions, the sensations, and the energy flows, encountering the emotions these arouse. Then one begins to learn how to deal with the flow: it becomes a tool whose various colorations and powers are open to exploration. Successful experiences develop a greater sense of control within and upon these energies, wherever control is possible and appropriate.

But the parallels run deeper. For group learning, like all human change, is a cyclic process of breaking established patterns to create open space in which new ones are formed, and the psychedelic experience gives basic insight into some of its key features. The mind construes the reality of experience, and patterns are its image. To break open cognitive or social patterns is to break open simultaneously the minds that project their coherence. Thus the adverb usually used to describe the psychedelic experience—*mindblowing*—will serve well to name the first process of the cyclic paradigm. Aldous Huxley spoke of the experience as opening the doors of perception. Into the house of the mind comes knowledge that transcends its immediate system.[21] This phenomenon of

21 The echo of Marcuse is deliberate and precise. See his *One-Dimensional Man* (Beacon, 1964) for insight into the mechanisms by which our culture inhibits the development of social and cognitive knowledge transcendent to its system. That Marcuse has become an intellectual idol

transcendence is responsible for the intimate and age-old association of psychedelic drugs with mystical insight and religious culture. For the purpose of our analysis, however, the knowledge is of needs, existences, resources, and potentialities not previously realized. (The skills and meta-skills of free learning are grounded in consciousness of these things—see page 47.) Such new knowledge does not simply extend the system it appears within. Within, and ultimately without, the mind creates a new order.

A Digression of Definition

The *space* of a human system is not a vacuum but a collection of *elements,* organized by functional relationships or *interconnections* into a *form.* The space and form are *closed* insofar as new elements and interconnections are predetermined, and *open* insofar as they are not. *Free learning* is the organizing of form in open space: it generates new varieties of form, relationship, and element. Organizing in closed space is something else again: here form changes its scope but not its nature. Space fully organized by the style of the Authority Complex is only one possible variety of fully closed space (others may be less pernicious). Space governed partly by the Authority Complex and partly by another mode is *incoherent,* and open to the extent that the two organize there in live conflict.

Such abstract concepts provide a frame for any level of social reality. Some examples:

(1) Your consciousness is a tissue generated from experience: elements of perception are connected and these connections built into higher order. In our culture most of these connections are causal: *if this, then that:* $((A \rightarrow B)$ and

---

of the young—the impossibility of whose transcendent appearance he so brilliantly described—is a choice irony.

$(B \rightarrow C)) \rightarrow (A \rightarrow C)$, following the logic of hierarchy. To a great extent you choose not to admit into your space elements and connections that do not fit your categories. Still, you know what incoherence feels like.

(2) Consider a group of people, *A,B,C* . . . They are elements of the group's space, as are their extensions—their cars, houses, productive technologies. *A* and *B* are in love, etc.; *A* and *C* argue politics, etc. These are connections, $<AB>$ and $<AC>$. But $<AB>$ and $<AC>$ are also elements, for in the process of the group these relationships may themselves be functionally connected: one factor of $\ll AB><AC\gg$ may be the way $<AC>$ draws off anger from $<AB>$; and so on. Now the group gets a new member, *Z*. Is its enlarged space more open? Probably not, if it's a business firm and *Z* is a secretary (though there's always some chance *Z* will seduce the management into turning production to new priorities). But if the group is a white commune and *Z* is black or a physician who can teach people to heal each other, the space opens.

(3) Recently the whole of human space has opened into radical incoherence by the appearance within it of new elements—qualitatively new means of production, which open the possibility of new relationships of every sort. In this space two principles of organizing contend.[22] All the examples in this chapter may be understood as experiments in shifting the balance between them.

Back to the Track

The psychedelics enrich individual perceptual space with new elements and new connections. Neglected or repressed sensory and emotional experiences and memories reassert

[22] Their characteristic mandalas and features are described in Chapter VII.

themselves, often abruptly, and new varieties become immediately accessible, sometimes by seeing old ones in newly reflected light. What springs into consciousness is partly what already presses to enter; in this, selection is a function of the mind's immediate state and needs. But in significant part, selection seems to be truly open and random. Both the emotional relevance and the unpredictability of what appears in the opened space are the principal triggers of the fear that characterizes this—as any other—learning experience and leads people either to avoid it or to freeze within it, unable to deal with its demands and possibilities.

Beyond this, the psychedelics facilitate the connection of diverse elements and thus the formation of new patterns or metaphors. (For this reason they are becoming the favored chemical tools of painters, writers, musicians, and visionaries.) Psychedelics enlarge the universe of possible similarities or commonalities among elements, by expansion, rephrasing, or relaxation of its limits—or, equivalently, of the functional rules that govern the recognition of what we may broadly term "similarity" or "connectability." In mathematical terms, the family of possible mappings-with-functional-structure (morphisms) among elements becomes enlarged, not so much by the addition of elements as by the passage to a higher level of abstraction that admits broader or wholly new concepts of morphism.[23] (In the cybernetic description of process, the corresponding passage is to a higher order of control—one that makes possible heterarchical rather than hierarchical control systems.)

In terms of poetry, the domain of possible metaphor expands. As García Lorca described it, the new metaphor—and the live energy of its creation, the tension that resides in the fresh, real joining of disparate elements and opens briefly

[23] Beyond this, the concepts, constructions, and processes of mathematics all bear important analytic models for aspects of the learning process, though they have been little studied in this light.

On Learning and Social Change

a new way of seeing or consciousness—is the core act and substance of poetry. The principle holds as well for the human poetries of learning and creating new social forms. When dissimilar metals are mated and heated, electric energy flows from their interface. And when man and woman, black and white, or two bodies of knowledge are scraped clean and put into new contact, raw energies are generated to turn toward new form.[24]

Within groups freely learning, the enrichments of element and connection parallel in detail those of the psychedelic process, on levels not limited to perception and consciousness. In particular, new connection among groups and among persons, and within each of these, begins with an organizing process—perhaps not evident as such—that makes visible aspects of similarity, in the form of common nature, needs, or interest. Whether it is possible to build on this common territory, and what is built and how, depend from this point onward in the process upon a complex of factors and remaining inner and outer limitations: need and choice, power, skills, taste, and tangible resources.

In groups, new elements and connections are suppressed or prevented by a limiting authority collectively subscribed to and created, as in the classroom game, and generally operating in the style of the Authority Complex. The blowing of the social mind is accomplished by the neutralization of this authority, in three ways: removal, repression, or confrontation. In the case of psychedelics, understanding the appearance of new element and connection scarcely seems possible without better understanding the nature of human consciousness and its changes; and this in turn depends in part on fully understanding their biochemical foundations. The recent researches of biochemistry in general and biopharmacology in particular suggest strongly that the analogy

[24] See the remarks below about cross-cultural learning; and in Chapter V about hybrid learning forms.

of the social process applies within the mind down to the cellular level, and that the psychedelics may function by neutralizing or suppressing inhibition of biochemical or neurological processes that are always present, actively or latently. (The biochemical functioning of such inhibitions within the cellular or systemic ecology is itself parallel to the Authority Complex as a system of control.)

Whether the young are guerrillas or not, it is natural to find hospitals and schools in their principal toys. The psychedelics provide general therapies and learning for which the young feel keen need. Grass and acid are used extensively as deconditioning agencies to prepare for new behavior in a culture that lacks the tools and skills to deal adequately with its pervasive and deep fears, angers, anxieties, and tight linear constraints.

• Fear is the first encounter. There is the outward fear—decreasingly tangible but highly symbolic—of breaking social law.[25] It is reduced by intimate embedding in a smaller, peer society, which not only sanctions psychedelic use by example but exhibits from this use experience and knowledge of evident attractiveness (whether to need or desire). After this come the endless layers of the onion of inner fear. In entering space essentially unknown, progress into the levels of the experience is measured directly by the peeling of these layers. From outside, the tools of this progress are mainly peer support and knowledge about the process and its phases. From inside, the tools are a series of spiritual rituals and disciplines, which teach the renunciation of coercive power and control and bear the reward of increased

[25] Parental and social authority are in this case quite specific and fairly easily avoided, save for 200,000 grass busts annually. Thus the psychedelic experience provides an arena in which fear may be investigated at considerable depth without proportionately dangerous social consequences.

ability to draw strength from one's being and nourishment from the partial harmonies and triumphs of one's changes. But tools alone are inadequate. That act or state of the will which faces fear itself, stripped of all names, is always necessary.

• The rituals of psychedelic use—the joint passing round the circle, a trip with a guide—are functional sacraments.[26] They are rituals of beginning, of entrance into a community of shared learning. Involving joining and some setting of norms, they are the most public of the simple transactions of trust so important in dealing with the emotions of the change process. They reinforce trust indirectly as well. For they are constant symbols of the creation of the counter-authority of peer-oriented learning, which in turn sanctions the relevance of shared knowledge about the process and its phases and trust in this knowledge as a tool against the first enemy of fear. The rituals also invoke the Hawthorn Effect and the sense of one's own presence as being centrally important to the process at hand—a key to fruitful participation in any learning group.

Like any good learning society, the psychedelic society is one of voluntary self-selection, of mutual exposure and support, of open struggle with the process of learning. Without a strong concept of deviance punitively expressed, fear is dramatically reduced: the climate becomes one in which failure is not only openly permitted but is followed by support; and in which people can learn to trust their own motions, rhythms, and common sense.

---

[26] Rituals are live magic, which reinforce a culture's realities. Americans might drink from a common cup, but instead they clink separate ones in a ritual that began when men poured a bit of their drinks back and forth for safety against being poisoned by each other. But for grass smoking we choose a form symbolic of open community and mutual trust. In this circle we define ourselves by an illegal *con-spiracy*, "breathing together" forbidden chemicals to explore beyond the Law we were taught.

• Fear leads to anxiety. The psychedelics act to de-fuse this at low levels, when present or internalized sources of fear are not too strong to be handled. But when control over them is shaky, psychedelic openness often unhinges it: anxiety is magnified by negative feedback into paralysis, or sometimes into breakthrough, revealing the naked fear beneath. (Barbiturates, tranquilizers, and heroin seem to act on anxiety independently of fear and to magnify neither.) Anxiety lives in *If . . .*, and through its lens vision is oriented toward future and possible experience. The heaviest experiential characteristic—immediate or enduring—of psychedelic use is that one lives more intensely within the *presence* of one's experience, inner and outer.[27] Anxiety leads to and comes from the blocking of psychic energies by the mind's internalized authorities. But these, from logic to super-ego, are de-compulsified by grass and acid. In particular, the anxiety that knowledge, action, and experience itself be immediately coherent within a well-known and rigidly ordered framework seems to relax. To this extent psychedelics are a technology of deep relaxation, of *letting go*.

• The effect of psychedelics upon anger and aggression is strongly debated. Some believe it to be direct inhibition. A considerable mythology has grown around this viewpoint, expressed most strongly in the edicts of some political groups —in particular, those that most clearly display their own Authority Complexes, like the YSA—that their members not smoke grass because it corrodes political consciousness and action. In fact, the first significant community organ-

---

[27] The wide use of psychedelics is thus intimately connected with the aesthetic of spontaneity into which the young are growing. In *The Uncommitted* (Dell, 1970), Kenneth Keniston describes how the mechanisms of accelerating social change condition us to the psychological stance of "living in the present." He does not speculate about the changed styles and needs of learning that this stance may require and permit.

izers among middle-class white youth were the neighborhood dope-dealers. But the mythology is beginning to fade
only as experience makes clear that hippies will fight when
attacked and will move in newer political forms.

The notion that psychedelics de-fuse anger is at odds with
their general effect on emotions—to facilitate consciousness
and release, especially of those usually repressed. In fact,
studies of grass-smokers in the Haight revealed that, while
most experienced unusual levity or sexual impulse while
under the influence, nearly all experienced unusual anger.
Of course, this has something to do with their being perse-
cuted as social criminals for their drug uses and other habits.
But surely the connection of psychedelic experience with
openness to anger is organic. A national survey of college
students after Cambodia[28] showed that 9 per cent of non-
smokers believed that major social change necessitated violent revolution; 13 per cent of light smokers; and 29 per cent
of heavy smokers. In this we see correlated with psychedelic
use both the receptive consciousness necessary to forming
any new political attitude, and the aggressive consciousness
necessary to forming this one.

My own view is that psychedelics act not on the roots of
anger and aggression but rather on their often considerable
magnification and redirection by anxiety. Grass and acid
heads may appear passive in part because their aggressive/
Yang will was always yoked by anxiety to destructive uses,
and now, having been uncoupled by the aid of these drugs,
drifts confused and untrained in what to do, or is absorbed
internally in Holding Together within partial Chaos.

• The higher one's state, the less choice there is about incoherence and dissonance: they force their way in through
open doors. The choice is to endure them, or to close: either
by rejecting them or by contriving higher orders that embrace them. The appropriateness and strength of these higher
orders depends partly on other knowledge and skills, and

[28] *Playboy* magazine.

partly again on the ability to sustain the openness of Chaos while building within it—and thus on being able to reduce to manageable proportions the fear and anxiety always present when facing the abyss.

In psychedelic experience, the appearance of new elements and new connections leads directly to dissonance, of perception and consciousness and, over time, to tolerance of this. As psychedelics also facilitate making new connections —which, in any organizing process, is the basis for developing new coherence—their use provides the strongest general training I know for the skills of dealing with the Chaos of learning. (They aren't likely to come into favor in the educational Establishment, however, because an alteration in the broader priorities of learning is usually connected with their use.)

Psychedelics affect the perceptual level, but not directly: rather, they act upon the perception of perception, i.e., metaperceptually. They do not make you feel (see, etc.) new things. They lead you to *feel* (*see,* etc.) what you have been feeling but not feeling, from the skin level inward to the collective unconscious. In general, this action induces a doubled consciousness: consciousness itself plus meta-consciousness. You become not only newly aware, but aware of your awareness. This meta-consciousness may be generated by repeated access to an alternate state of consciousness that fluxes and wanes. It may also be due to the specific nature of that consciousness. For "psychedelic" consciousness is one of continual qualitative changes—in fact, "the changes" are the most general characteristic of a psychedelic trip; and those familiar with the experience comprehend this phrase instantly. Thus this meta-consciousness centers in an intense consciousness of the changes and the process of their experience.

To speak precisely of matters meta-mathematical or cybernetic is awkward without symbols. I'll call this meta-consciousness *process-consciousness* hereafter. It can be induced or strengthened by many agencies, but I suspect all their ways are parallel to the one described. This reflexive consciousness seems to be the component of inner space which is analogous to the reflexive mechanism of a reflexive institution. It is equally the personal analogue of the process-consciousness of a free learning group. Its development on any of these three levels leads toward its development on the others, though this may be inhibited by many factors, and such action is worked out slowly over time. If this development is blocked on any level, process-consciousness will tend toward parallel diminishment on the others; for consciousness tends toward integrality.

Process-consciousness bears with it a conjugate aesthetic, an aesthetic of continuous, qualitative change. We have met it above as the Santa Claus aesthetic; it might better be called "protean." Its eclectic sensibility goes with open universes and is typical of the indigenous arts of the young.[29] It deals in abrupt changes within a many-stranded consciousness, in sharp contrast to the aesthetics of that linear consciousness Marshall McLuhan[30] describes as the product of our culture's particular visual and other media, and which may be equally well seen as the product of the hierarchical control systems of the Authority Complex. This protean aesthetic admits mystery, incoherence, and sudden change as central values.

The psychedelics de-compulsify and diversify the linear mind. They are typical of tools that help you to *be* where you are; and thus to linger and wander along paths that start right *there*—as all the beginnings of free learning do—and that future/anxiety-oriented sight overlooks. As much as

[29] James Joyce, who was a morphine-head, was an early literary precursor. More recent and popular are Joseph Heller (*Catch-22*) and Ken Kesey (*One Flew Over the Cuckoo's Nest*), whose books, in literary representation of Marcuse's analysis, described American society as a gigantic, self-closing Language System—albeit one that could be transcended by a simple desperate act of will when its closure and exhaustion became inescapable.

[30] In *Understanding Media* (McGraw-Hill, 1964).

process-consciousness, the protean aesthetic they induce is itself a tool to this end and for the building of non-hierarchical, flexible systems of authority.

Even in casual use, the psychedelics induce consciousness that is revolutionary in its very texture; it is a consciousness adapted to changes and thus to Transformation itself. I consider them at length because they are indeed magical drugs, and their experience yields many models to illuminate the mechanisms of Change.

Yet the broad consequences of their use are not intrinsic but depend upon context and the consciousness applying them. Used in full and searching purpose, psychedelics are powerful agents for the complex self-transformations that must accompany the transformation of our society. But in Amerika today much of their use is unfocused, confused, and self-destructive.[31] The society of psychedelic use operated as a healthy open space for a few years in the Bay Area in the mid-sixties. Under great external and internal pressures it began closing in 1967. The quality of shared purpose and knowledge about psychedelic learning became diluted. As acceptance spread, the fear barrier diminished, and people began turning on more for exterior social reasons, or for escape, than in search moved by inner need. Thus the technology spread unaccompanied by its software, so to speak, and its uses became degraded.

Other factors in the closing of this space include the action of Hip Capitalists, who supplanted the early psychedelic missionaries to peddle good, ersatz, and poisoned drugs indiscriminately to "their community"—not as sacraments of knowledge accompanied by use-lore but as naked commodities in profit-greed. Equally important has been the

[31] Though the level at which action is purposeful may be deep indeed. How are we to judge those who use psychedelics to disable themselves for the "normal" uses of society, in an age when survival calls for our giving up the greeds of the Ego and dismantling the inner machineries of Control?

over-pressure of government and law, which have suppressed knowledge and, in league with Hip Capitalism, guided the white ghetto youth community through destructive habits into growing mass addiction to speed and smack. In this, government policies and actions have run parallel to those directed against black communities since the late sixties, to prevent ghetto rebellion. The Black Panthers term this "drug genocide" with good reason; but here the focus is cultural rather than racial.

This whole subject deserves separate discussion.[32] But one thing must be said here. The psychedelics do open a revolutionary consciousness—on the first level, by opening one to inner and outer reality. But social reality is pretty confused and painful these days; sensitivity is anguish as well as ecstasy. *Whoever does not move to fulfill new consciousness, by changing social reality, must move to deny it*—by repressing it directly, or by manipulating it to adapt oneself to the dominant power relationships. Those who cannot gain strength through moving to change objective conditions deepen their impotence by numbing themselves to the pain, via speed, smack, and nonchemical means. Thus grass indeed leads toward the numbness of heroin, as in the old cautionary tales, unless we make something else real.

SOFT LEARNING FORMS

Most of the learning experiences described so far are "hard," in the sense that their primary objectives are specific external goals, like political change or building a functional social form. But there is a class of "soft" learning forms whose

[32] For more remarks see my articles in *Drugs: For and Against* (Hart, 1971) and in *Organ* (#IX, July 1971).

main motive is—or should be, for they are often misused—
the general development of learning skills that occurs during
their process.

Within our specialized and fragmenting culture, soft
forms occur formally mostly as stigmatized remedies for
psychic crippling, in the various forms of classical and modern psychotherapy and analysis. Since 1965 they have
started to proliferate in quick and multiplying variety,
largely among the white young, who are coming to accept as
natural the need for constant deliberate learning of the skills
of learning, but also among orthodox professionals (again
mostly young) in the fields of social work and change, who
are belatedly discovering the need for such tools.

In addition to the conventional forms of therapy and
analysis, soft learning forms include group therapy, the
Synanon Game, encounter groups, sensitivity training, psy-
cho- and socio-drama, Synectics,[33] a variety of nonverbal
games, and to some extent meditation and other spiritual
disciplines (which deserve separate study). The rapid spread
of these examples is described by the process-model of the
free universities. So is the ingenious and unpredictable
multiplication of their varieties—a characteristic of free
growth using richly diverse inputs in open space.

The processes of each soft form are easily isolated and
observed, the more so since most totally lack a more-than-
private social orientation and an explicit functional em-

---

[33] Synectics deserves special attention, and not just because it's the
only soft form sponsored primarily by industry. A deep though very
verbal game, Synectics develops and serves as the main tool for a semi-
permanent team, who integrate diverse backgrounds into a structure of
flexible roles and constant attention to process. Synectics trains for
personal and, especially, team skills in the basic act of industrial or
artistic creation. It trains people to create new metaphors, which can be
made tangible and applied. The method of Synectics is elegant and
powerful; and its processes of team training and team working are lucid
paradigms of free learning. See William J. J. Gordon, *Synectics* (Harper
and Row, 1961).

bedding as elements of an adequately comprehensive process of freeing change. This makes them both less effective and less interesting as objects of study. All deal with the slow or sudden dismantlement of internal authority systems; some attempt their replacement with something new. These especially illustrate clearly the vital importance of the trust generated and the security given by participation in a peer community of experiment or mutual-learning-and-aid, as well as the necessity of creating climates in which failure is not only permitted but followed by support, and in which people can learn to trust their instinctive motions, rhythms, and common sense. They undoubtedly hold innumerable fascinating insights for a comprehensive theory of change.[34]

Taken together, however, they seem to illuminate no new major feature of the process of free learning. Conversely, the phases, problems, and skills of this process are all more or less completely revealed in the operation of each soft form and can be equally well described by the corresponding perspective and concepts. The terms of psychoanalysis offer a particularly convenient base for this description (e.g., the solving of a major technological problem can perhaps best be analyzed as deep therapy for a social and cognitive tension) and exhibit in more detail some aspects of the subprocess of rebuilding identity.

There are deep implications in the spread of these soft technologies. Freud came to America, not with his first translation in 1911, but when his concepts escaped the elite clinic and academy and, transformed and anonymous, entered folk-thought as common tools. Such slow processes are bringing to cultural life the magnificent knot of meta-

[34] The newest soft forms spreading in 1971 were the *permission groups* of radical women's therapy and *co-counseling,* a nonhierarchical group therapy centering on personal emotional release. Both operate with heavy norms against negative expression and for positive—setting a context useful for a while but surely half-blind in the long run.

phors—sociology, anthropologies, existentialism, psychologies—that the West has generated in this century through which to view man's actively *changing* condition.

Now for the first time the nature of human interaction itself—especially the workings of man as an animal learning with difficulty—has become the proper and natural study of the young. Our time lurches across a great divide. Our cultural concerns shift from economic scarcity and things to psychological scarcity and persons, in concert with our industry as it shifts from goal and replication to information and process. *The most important consequence of the spread of the soft technologies is not the temporary languages they create but the consciousness they induce.* It is a reflexive consciousness, a consciousness of human process, compatible with the cybernetic consciousness of our hard technologies; and it is essential to change.

The induction of process-consciousness, like some other sub-processes of free learning, is a recursive process: one that extends its results in progressive stages by applying the previous ones. The clearest model for this is the "bootstrapping" operation of computer cybernetics: generating a program to generate a program to generate an adequate program for a problem. Bootstrapping has powerful analogues in personal, group, and institution development. In this case, with the process-consciousness generated by the soft technologies, pioneer workers in education among the young are becoming able to improvise new soft forms or learning games designed to produce specific skills whose variety has no apparent limits yet. This deliberate art is so new that little has been written about it. Yet I believe it to be the leading edge of creation of a new science of learning, which can radically empower group consciousness.

Soft learning forms are also spreading among private industry, which finds in them a tool with no immediate dangerous political consequence for developing certain skills of employees to increase efficiency and profit. Hard learning forms might develop these skills. But to be successful in this, such forms, I believe, must have as their objectives changes, constructs, or experiences that lead directly out of the systems of centralized and coercive power, fixed and hierarchical roles, which uniformly characterize the administrative, productive, social, and psychological processes of our economic institutions. Conflicts of interest appear immediately, and personal and social conflict follows. In private industry, as elsewhere within the domains of the Authority Complex, such confrontation can be tolerated only within narrow limits, as a safety value to prevent, rather than aid, change. Thus "hard" free learning experience—which always involves some form of social organizing—is quickly halted or repressed. (Here, as elsewhere, hard free learning forms flower only when they can defend a base of open space.)

Soft learning forms, on the other hand, seem to hold no terrors for industry. Their moderate use seems possible within any confined space without soon expanding its larger limits. Their broadly world-reconstructing influences seem to be damped and absorbed by the larger operations of the Authority Complex. Thus soft forms are coming to be deployed by our established institutions of government, education, and industry not only to develop limited skills in ways that do not threaten basic power relationships, but as instruments of containment, to adjust, direct, and inhibit energy that might flow freely. A standard reaction of college administrators faced with student "unrest" is to provide encounter groups to absorb it.

Overall, soft learning forms—and the broad spectrum of new therapies, gestalt/Reichian/bioenergetic/body-remedial, that cluster with encounter groups under the Esalen umbrella—are being employed in liberal consciousness rather than radical. That is, in a framework that teaches that there are no *root conflicts of interest* and nature unresolvable by compromise, but only *problems of communication* between people or of the self with its deep reaches. This line is a hip version of the standard Amerikan mystification that change is ultimately only a private affair; and under it soft forms, like misused drugs, function mainly to help people learn how to adapt to their niches in the established structures of power.

Surely we need better contact with our selves and each other; we are ill for its lack. Yet most of the breakthroughs people achieve in soft forms now cannot be sustained in the everyday social climate. These forms are crippled in their power as learning agencies because they are not designed to help people create the structural social change necessarily conjugate to personal change. To the extent that soft-form learning is not organically related to transforming gross social relations, it is bogus learning, gaudy dress to hold interest in the same old roles of a destructive social game— a bourgeois indulgence in experience, dangerous because it pretends by itself to portend ultimate remedies for what is a very real and general crisis.[35]

Yet the technology of soft forms is young, and the question is still open as to whether their cumulative effects can at least release energy and serve as useful preparation for the hard open struggle to change larger forms. The speculative framework of this book points this way. For soft-form skills to be translated toward the satisfaction of broader needs, the needs must be recognized and the skills understood as appropriate. The question depends on whether an Authority Complex can function indefinitely to prevent the development of a consciousness of needs and resources. Throughout our present systems, it seems not to be able to.

I think the immediate utility and eventual consequence of soft forms depend on their being deployed as elements in a framework and process of self-directed change oriented toward comprehensive human goals. We are greatly in need

---

[35] Notice that the "human potential" movement is all phrased in terms of the potential for private or intimate growth, and not in terms of the human potential for *collective* commitment, nurture, concern, and justice.

of vision about their integration with other technologies of change, for the partial liberations of subjective condition that soft technologies work are the key to an enormous release of human energy, in which the action to liberate objective conditions can and must be grounded. It is time to liberate these tools from the Liberals, and redefine them, redesign them for revolutionary use.

This process is beginning slowly in some communes with high levels of consciousness. Yet young groups working on political change have almost universally avoided soft forms rather than try to discover their uses as tools to their ends. I think this choice is a dangerous mistake, which has much to do with the way the political face of the youth movement is growing backward into familiar, limited, and harsh political forms and languages, having been unwilling —more than unable—to work seriously and well on its inner processes and persons. This current failure and the quite limited success of soft forms within industry both point toward key and symmetric principles. *Politics with bad learning and learning with bad politics are equally limited and futile. Healthy change requires deliberate attention to both its product and its process; work on either is crippled without conjugate work on the other. Neither personal identity nor social identity can be successfully recreated alone: they are conjugate and must be dealt with simultaneously in their full depth.*

WOMEN'S, GAY, AND MEN'S LIBERATION

The consciousness-raising groups of these movements deserve a separate chapter as learning forms. I would not venture to speak for the two more established movements; and my experience with men's groups is too young to discuss.

SOME SUPPLEMENTARY PARADIGMS
OF LEARNING

Before pulling together this excursion in change, I want to examine briefly some related paradigms.

The Flute

Music itself furnishes the purest models, both of men learning to cooperate among different qualities, and of men generating structured series of change.

I cross the register-break in a dying slide *pp* from b to e' near the beginning of a Debussy piece. I undercut, lips too fluff-lax in anxious relaxation. Ears mark the distance from some Platonic standard, tuned more to the difference in timbre (weak, husky with exotic overtones) than in pitch (a bit flat). Lips tighten a trifle at the corners, pull the airstream flatter, harder; hands roll the trembling tube inward a little, should more. Sound steadies and bells in the room, and I attack the next note.

One thing, perhaps the most important, about playing the flute: I seek that relaxation which permits the basic problem-solving cycle—evaluate/formulate/assess/decide/implement/evaluate—to proceed properly. Each instant of a note's life is a microcosm of choice; grass and attention slow the process enough to observe. What are the traps? If I am anxious for or about the next note, I do not listen to the one I am in. *Be where I am.* If I am anxious to hang on to the goodness of where I am, for fear any change may make the note more sour, my body translates this into frozen fingers and lips that cannot move. *Don't be afraid to let go, learn to have nothing to lose.* To move in holy indifference is not to be passive: I choose the changes I press on that sound. But only after actively *be*ing where I am and free to move, with neither fear nor possessiveness (which also is fear).

I enter a note overtense, try to relax, let go too much control; my lips are seized with a sudden trembling. Later in the phrase I am loose enough to leap a ninth with no change in timbre. Holding that looseness, again and more broadly my lips begin to quiver erratically; unable to control themselves gently, haunted by the muscle-memory of tight control, a legacy of cramping now released to rage through the tissue walls. That is always the problem in learning: how not to freak and pull back while beginning to create anew a new control in that chaotic space liberated from an old order or grasp. How, dogged by the ghosts of my own state, to ride with the uncontrollable vibrations of energy, hoping they do not tear apart my tone or self while new order is created from within.

The Act of Poetry

The Poet, be his medium words or society, sits before a candle burning, dripping, playing with its pool of wax in a cold room. He pokes his finger toward the hot core of the body of wax, pulls back. In its wake the world is seen for an instant, clear and specific in its distortion, as on a drop of quicksilver. But in no time the process of filming-over begins, a layer of wax congeals and deepens into opaqueness. He watches the lucent quality of the molten interior persist, diminish, disappear. The tentacle of the pool solidifies. On its surface, as in the minor Romantic poets and the welfare system, he can see only blurred and indifferent reflections of the complex energies that surround him. With his flesh, as much as he dares, he pokes at the rim of the flame, to lead its melt down again to a stable place where he can break the skin already forming.

By this process form builds. Each new integral tentacle of

its substance flows over the others—where soundly, melting into them—and is configured by its own momenta and their shapes. As it rises, form comes to complete the circle around the flame, whose energy is not wasted, and the Poet comes to stare transfixed: first into the depth of the basin of clarity, eternal around the wick; then into the Fire itself, enmeshed in its severing and rejoining of the elements.

Thus our language and our institutions are skins through which we mediate our connection to the Cauldron, constantly to be broken and reformed as the Fire withdraws beneath them. Every fresh metaphor stales; every school's service is outgrown in a year or millennium and carried on in diminished routine, which no longer engages Invention. When we are not held prisoner by cold wax, Invention's energy turns to drawing forth or breaking open new pattern.

.   .   .

The condition before Form is like unto nothing, but it makes me think of a Center, the Well of Metaphor, a place of pure molten heat, of clear light. I slip or plunge in, go to some depth hands outstretched, the light penetrating them, rendering even the bone translucent, erasing my sight. Then I am cast back, realize my ordinary outlines coming into focus like the shadow of a swimmer surfacing. As I withdraw through the zone where things separate, I become conscious that in my hands, congealing into Form, are clutched fragments of that primal Stuff. Their heat still live, my flesh twists and fuses to their shapes. Some time after I surface these embers grow cold, become merely their matter. I pry my fingers loose and go down again.

The Teachings of Don Juan

In a gem-like study of learning disguised as ethnology, Carlos Castaneda records the oral teachings of the Yaqui Indian Don Juan. Derived from a different cultural base, the main paradigm of his teachings parallels and illuminates our cyclic paradigm. I quote it almost in full because it is too beautiful and condensed to paraphrase, and because it gives the clearest account I know of the spiritual disciplines necessary to the act of learning. It describes the process of a "man of knowledge."

A man of knowledge is one who has followed truthfully the hardships of learning. A man who has, without rushing or without faltering, gone as far as he can in unraveling the secrets of power and knowledge. He must challenge and defeat his four natural enemies.

When a man starts to learn, he is never clear about his objectives. His purpose is faulty; his intent is vague. He hopes for rewards that will never materialize, for he knows nothing of the hardships of learning.

He slowly begins to learn—bit by bit at first, then in big chunks. And his thoughts soon clash. What he learns is never what he pictured, or imagined, and so he begins to be afraid. Learning is never what one expects. Every step of learning is a new task, and the fear the man is experiencing begins to mount mercilessly, unyieldingly. His purpose becomes a battlefield. Fear is the first of his natural enemies. A terrible and treacherous enemy, it remains concealed at every turn of the way . . .

He must not run away. He must defy his fear, and in spite of it he must take the next step in learning, and the next, and the next. He must be fully afraid, and yet he must not stop. And a moment will come when his first enemy retreats . . .

Once a man has vanquished fear, he is free from it because instead he has acquired clarity—a clarity of mind which erases fear. By then a man knows his desires; he knows how to satisfy those desires. He can anticipate the new steps of learning, and a sharp clarity surrounds everything. The man feels that nothing is concealed.

And thus he encounters his second enemy: Clarity. That clarity of mind, which is so hard to obtain, dispels fear, but also blinds.

It forces the man never to doubt himself. It gives him the assurance he can do anything he pleases, for he sees clearly into everything. And he is courageous and stops at nothing because he is clear. But all that is a mistake; it is like something incomplete. If the man yields to this make-believe power, he has succumbed to his second enemy and will fumble with learning. He will rush when he should be patient or be patient when he should rush. A man defeated in this way will fumble with learning until he winds up incapable of learning anything more. He may turn into a buoyant warrior, or a clown. The clarity for which he has paid so dearly will never change to darkness and fear again; but he will no longer learn, or yearn for, anything.

To avoid defeat, he must defy his clarity and use it only to see, and wait patiently and measure carefully before taking new steps; he must think, above all, that his clarity is almost a mistake. And a moment will come when he will understand that his clarity was only a point before his eyes. And thus he will have overcome his second enemy, and arrived at a position where nothing can harm him anymore. This will not be a mistake. It will not be only a point before his eyes. It will be true power.

He will know then that the power he has been pursuing for so long is finally his. He can do with it whatever he pleases. His ally is at his command. His wish is the rule. He sees all that is around him. But he has also come across his third enemy: Power.

Power is the strongest of all enemies. A man who is defeated by power dies without really knowing how to handle it. Power is only a burden upon his fate. Such a man has no command over himself, and cannot tell when or how to use his power. And naturally the easiest thing to do is give in; after all, the man is truly invincible. He commands; he begins by taking calculated risks, and ends in making rules, because he is a master.

He has to defy his power, deliberately. He has to come to realize the power he has seemingly conquered is in reality never his. He must keep himself in line at all times, handling carefully and faithfully all that he has learned. If he can see that clarity and power, without his control over himself, are worse than mistakes, he will reach a point where everything is held in check. He will know then when and how to use his power.

The man will be, by then, at the end of his journey of learning, and almost without warning he will come upon the last of his enemies: Old age. This enemy is the cruelest of all, the one he won't be able to defeat completely, but only fight away.

This is the time when a man has no more fears, no more impatient clarity of mind—a time when all his power is in check, but also the time when he has an unyielding desire to rest. If he gives in totally to his desire to lie down and forget, if he soothes himself in tiredness, he will have lost his last round, and his enemy will cut him down into a feeble old creature. His desire to retreat will overrule all his clarity, his power, and his knowledge.

But if a man sloughs off his tiredness, and lives his fate through, he can then be called a man of knowledge, if only for the brief moment when he succeeds in fighting off his last, invincible enemy. That moment of clarity, power, and knowledge is enough.[36]

To this account—which, though drawn from the searching-out, with the aid of psychedelic experience, of "paths that have heart," seems perfectly general—I can add only two things. When clarity is not used only to see, it functions to create expectations; it reveals limits—or possibilities, which are also limits—that seem self-evident and self-justifying. And when power is used without fully self-conscious control (process-consciousness), it creates coercive and inappropriate rules; however benevolent its intent, it operates in the style of the Authority Complex.

The way out is to release that control, to make power not a possession of the ego. To realize that power is a mutual conspiracy, among men and between them and the universe; to find a path with heart, a path that traces the consequences and responsibilities of this realization. Such a path is an ethic, an aesthetic, a metaphysic: name it as you will, it is alive.

[36] Carlos Castaneda, *The Teachings of Don Juan: A Yaqui Way of Knowing* (Ballantine, 1969). Castaneda's second book on his apprenticeship to this Indian sorcerer—*A Separate Reality* (Touchstone, 1972)—is even more elegant and astounding, in itself and as an essay on learning.

That path whose beginning I know is called the Tao. It leads through an elegant and comprehensive understanding of change, though by that point one does not write it down. Before then, it gives much insight into the process, the phases, the forces and motions of free learning—especially into the conjugate rhythms of change and into the nature and construction of authority that furthers rather than exhausts. Increasingly, I am coming to be able to understand the skills and phenomena of change through the metaphor of the Tao. But that is a different story—it is only after one has passed beyond a thing that it can be written down—and likely in a different style.

I should note here that the social image of the renunciation of control has been phrased most clearly among us by David Harris. It lies at the heart of the total life-metaphor with which he helped found the Resistance, a self-catalyzing organizing process that became the purest strong political movement among the young during the late sixties. Resistance focuses on the draft and through it on the coercive power of the "community" over the individual. To rebuild a total framework, begin by reversing our society's terms of power, and of "community" which does not honor the responsibilities of commonness. *Build community that defines itself not by whom it excludes, but by its capacity to be open and include. Create power that empowers those in its domain and does not define their powerlessness.*[37] *Invent love whose laws are these natural functions.*

We must believe that this is possible. Our growing experience taunts us with hope. Though Harris and five thousand others went to jail—having vanquished fear, though perhaps resting overmuch in clarity—the years they chose to accept were few and their preparation strong; they

[37] Harris speaks clearly of the difference between the *idol,* the man whose example enfeebles because it is mysterious and inimitable, and the *hero,* whose example empowers because it springs understandably from a common life-circumstance. Contrast the American and Cuban adulations of Che; consider leadership in learning groups.

may come out the best men of my generation. Beyond jail, Amerika moves in reaction to kill; to accept the next live escalation of her control will be a death we may not grow soon enough to avoid. But that does not taint Harris' phrasing of the key tasks of the community of free learning.

A Personal Note

My mind started opening to the concept of *open space* sometime in the later years of work with "my" analyst, Arthur Gladman. I remember realizing it concretely one day in my hobbit-hole on Ridge Road, surrounded by rich encroachments of objects, a junkyard treasury of life-trips. As from somewhere outside I saw how little room there was to move, watched the constrained dance I threaded through the small avenues left among books, bed, mobiles, jungle, ticket-stubs, the vulture in the bathtub. Suddenly I understood how I reproduced physically the cluttered confines of my psychic space. There also I diminished my freedom of motion by grasping too hard the accumulations of experience which I kept to define myself by, and leaving, in the passageways of daily routine, little room for anything to happen.

This was back in '63 or so. Had I been more in touch with my body, I likely could have read out through it the feeling of suffocation I was experiencing in my inner and outer roles—like so many in pre-FSM Berkeley, energy pulsing in a closed system. As it was, I opened up as much space in my room as I could, pushed things to the wall, and proceeded to blow some holes in my mind. I think it was even before I got into grass and acid that Gladman led me to understand directly the existence of what I now recognize as the primal fear of Chaos itself. I remember how hard it was for me to grasp that my fears were not all assignable each to dread of specific injury or pain, but welled also from a deeper stratum, in reaction to the void of dissolution and the un-forenameable beyond. (In the light of our interplay I caught sight also for the first time of my capacity for deadly anger, spontaneous as a cat's claw springing from its sheath.)

So the roots of this metaphor pass through the private practices of psychology. Given the consciousness of the time, our therapeutic dialogue lacked much social perspective and a political edge. Yet I gained vision by it; and in the space it helped open many Events happened, through which I moved with others to remedy its lacks.

Six years later I was asked for an essay for a book on Summerhill. I spent some weeks setting down what I then understood about the process and psychology of free learning, i.e., this chapter. All the major new learning media of my generation seemed to embody similar patterns and phenomena, fleshing out a more detailed metaphor of open space and pointing toward a cyclic model of the process of Change itself.

As I tried to spell it out, I felt flashes of despair—and not only because I was recording such dry skeletal sketches of the rich domains of experience I was traversing, seeking an inner Form. But also, I was writing of matters already two to five years old, trying to describe an initial phase of the evolution of free systems, while around me the dialectic of our movements and my own life had quickly progressed to new phases of consciousness and need. By the time this book appears three more years will have flown; even more are we dealing with orders of question beyond the fragmentary vision of this metaphor, and the events it interlaces have disappeared into History. (By this schedule, how long will the thought forming now take to surface?)

Yet the cycle is continually renewing, and whatever knowledge gathered of it becomes useful again, as all who move for liberation go through their versions of these changes.

A RECAPITULATION

How can one comprehend the learning of a generation within pages? I have sought a narrow focus: to slice across our main change-experiences in a way that reveals some of the structure of the process of free learning and its characteristic phenomena and skills. The ways people free space and build in its openness can be abstracted and detached from the real history of a particular culture. But they can be understood only *through* such a history; for their understanding is their use, which is real. So I deal with the learning of my experience, the understanding that we now exhibit, in all the imperfection and life of a beginning;[38] and try to indicate some of the flavors and directions of our change—in part because change must be understood within a context of particulars, but also because our particular transformation points toward Change itself.

The redundancy of my account is not due simply to windy choice of detail, but also to the deep unity that underlies all of our major changes. *Within each most of the main features of all may be discovered*—in effect, I have tried to slice diagonally through a series of parallel studies. It is time to collapse this overlapping account of the changing flesh of a generation back down to its abstract skeleton—the cyclic model of learning outlined at the beginning of this chapter—and see what has been gathered along the way. I will use a summary of diagrams, supplemented by some miscellaneous

[38] Due to this, the detail of my analysis is limited to the earlier stages of the change cycle. So much remains to be dealt with, especially the particulars of how old and new skills are brought together to bear on the building of new form. The full-scale practice of psychoanalysis is rich with models that describe the maturation of change. Yet I am suspicious of them, for they describe the reconstruction of personal identity within larger social relationships that remain essentially unchanged.

notes. These diagrams index most of the topics considered above and set them in perspective with some others, as important but neglected.

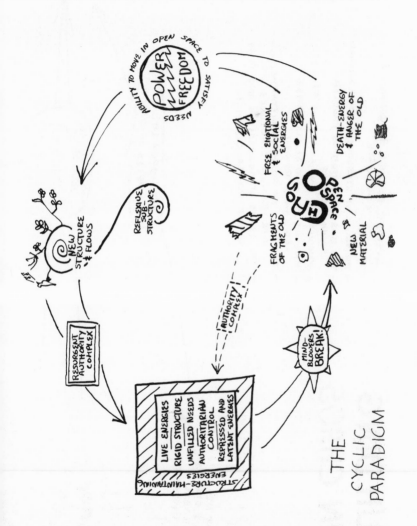

THE CYCLIC PARADIGM

BUILDING
IN CHAOS

SPECIFIC FORMS & ENVIRONMENTS
CULTIVATE:

- THE SKILLS OF REPRODUCING THE KNOWN
- THE BASIC AUTONOMOUS PROBLEM-
  SOLVING SKILLS
- KNOWLEDGE AND SKILLS OF PROCESS
- KNOWLEDGE AND SKILLS TO SEE
  AND SHAPE POWER
- THE SKILL OF FORMING METAPHORS,
  INTEGRATION, COHERENCE
- THE SKILLS OF AGGRESSION AND PLAY,
  WHICH POWER CREATION

ACT UPON THE
RESOURCES OF CHAOS

TOOLS, SKILLS
KNOWLEDGE,
POWER
CONTROL

NEW
FORM

OLD AND NEW
FRAGMENTS & ENERGIES,
AVAILABLE
IN RICH DIVERSITY

CHAOS

INTENSE FREE EMOTIONAL
ENERGIES

INCOHERENCE & DISSONANCE.
COGNITIVE, PERSONAL, SOCIAL

THE KILLING ANGER OF A
SYSTEMS DEATH

FEAR, ANXIETY

DEALS WITH THE PROCESS
OF CHAOS TO KEEP MOVING
ON IN OPEN SPACE

SECURITY
CREATE TRUST BY:

- VOLUNTARY SELF-SELECTION
- ENTRANCE & OTHER RITUALS
- MUTUAL SUPPORT IN COMMUNITY
  OF CHANGE WITH AN ETHIC
  OF SHARING
- EXAMPLES OF SIBLING CHANGE IN
  VISIBLE STRUGGLE & SUCCESSFUL
- LEGITIMATIZED & ACCESSIBLE
  PEER KNOWLEDGE OF PROCESS
- SENSE OF COLLECTIVE EMPOWER-
  MENT & OWN STRENGTH
- BROAD TOLERANCE OF FAILURE
- LEARNING TO DRAW NOURISHMENT
  FROM THE PROCESS OF CHANGE;
  CELEBRATION

RELAXATION
BUILD TOLERANCE BY
EXPERIENCE IN:

- ACTING OUT ANGER, AND GEN-
  ERALLY FREAKING FREELY
- PSYCHEDELICS, AND OTHER TECH-
  NOLOGIES OF THE UNKNOWN
- SPIRITUAL DISCIPLINES: THE
  TECHNOLOGIES OF LETTING GO
- AESTHETICS OF CHANGE OPEN
  TO INCOHERENCE
- CROSS-CULTURAL EXPERIENCE
- SOFT LEARNING FORMS:

  * ENCOUNTER
  * THERAPY, ANALYSIS
  * THEATER-BASED FORMS
  * OTHER LEARNING GAMES

● BUILDING IN OPEN SPACE

OLD AND NEW FRAGMENTS
WITH THEIR OWN INTER-
NAL STRUCTURES AND
PROCESSES

OPEN
SPACE

NEW ELEMENT AND
CONNECTION;
FREED ENERGIES

USE RESOURCES TO
BUILD THE SUBSTANCE
OF CHANGE ⟶

ABILITY TO SATISFY NEEDS
FREEDOM
ABILITY TO MOVE IN OPEN SPACE

RECONSTITUTE AUTHORITY
INTO PROCESS-ORIENTED,
SELF-DIRECTED AND
FREEING CONTROL ⟶

PROCESS-CONSCIOUSNESS

META-CONSCIOUSNESS INDUCED BY

— A PROTEAN AESTHETIC
— THE INDUSTRIAL, MEDIA, AND
   DRUG TECHNOLOGIES OF
   THIS AGE OF CHANGE

— EXPERIENCE OF TRANSFORMATI

— NEW KNOWLEDGE
— SOFT LEARNING-FORMS

(IT LEADS INTO THE METAPHYSIC
  OF CHANGE CALLED THE TAO.

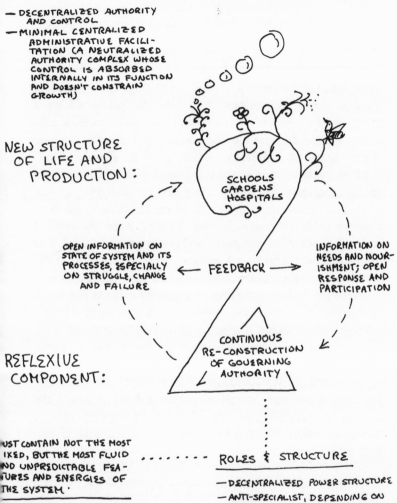

— DECENTRALIZED AUTHORITY
   AND CONTROL
— MINIMAL CENTRALIZED
   ADMINISTRATIVE FACILI-
   TATION (A NEUTRALIZED
   AUTHORITY COMPLEX WHOSE
   CONTROL IS ABSORBED
   INTERNALLY IN ITS FUNCTION
   AND DOESN'T CONSTRAIN
   GROWTH)

NEW STRUCTURE
   OF LIFE AND
   PRODUCTION:

SCHOOLS
GARDENS
HOSPITALS

OPEN INFORMATION ON
STATE OF SYSTEM AND ITS
PROCESSES, ESPECIALLY
ON STRUGGLE, CHANGE
AND FAILURE

← FEEDBACK →

INFORMATION ON
NEEDS AND NOUR-
ISHMENT; OPEN
RESPONSE AND
PARTICIPATION

REFLEXIVE
   COMPONENT:

CONTINUOUS
RE-CONSTRUCTION
OF GOVERNING
AUTHORITY

UST CONTAIN NOT THE MOST
IXED, BUT THE MOST FLUID
ND UNPREDICTABLE FEA-
URES AND ENERGIES OF
HE SYSTEM.

THERAPIES
   — FOR THE DRIVE TO CONTROL
   — FOR FEAR AND ANXIETY

MECHANISMS
   — TO DESTROY CLARITY
   — TO GENERATE DISSONANCE

EMPOWERMENT
   — TO OPEN ENERGIES THAT
      CANNOT BE CONTAINED

. . . . ROLES & STRUCTURE

— DECENTRALIZED POWER STRUCTURE

— ANTI-SPECIALIST, DEPENDING ON
   CONTINUOUS AND FLEXIBLE REDIS-
   TRIBUTION OF ROLES AND SKILLS

— EPHEMERAL AND DISPOSABLE
   CONSTRUCTS AND COMMITMENTS,
   TIED TO THE EDGE OF CHANGE

— SPACE, KNOWLEDGE AND ENERGY
   FOR LEARNING THE SKILLS OF
   LEARNING, OPEN TO ALL

OPEN SPACE

Open space is discovered as such, or through the opening of what is closed. Sometimes it is tangible, generated by a group newly together, a new artistic or social form, a new energy source. Its base may be purely physical, as in the case of the vacant lot in Berkeley where grew the People's Park.

More usually, open space is a matter of consciousness, of seeing differently and newly. Any new technology, physical or social, opens areas or levels of consciousness. So does personal or social contradiction, revealed when the conflict between a system's operations and needs grows critical. The rituals of new identity—of entrance into community, of expression of gathered emotion—invoke new consciousness.

Exposure to new examples of behavior extends the limits of expectation if these are implicit, or breaks them if overt. (When such exposure is direct and mutual between persons, its operation may be understood in the terms of cross-cultural encounter;[39] when it occurs through media, it opens more simply.) Exposure to examples of change or empowerment on any social or personal level expands the universe of possibility of any other level nonspecifically (a resonance effect induced by social and psychological embedding).

[39] Every act of human learning is inherently "cross-cultural" in that it involves crossing a limiting interface of personal and cultural identity into unknowable space, and then reconstructing these newly. Not surprisingly, what is commonly recognized as cross-cultural experience provides training and models for change, especially in regard to therapies for the fear of the unknowable. Indeed, the best general model I know for the functional skills and meta-skills of autonomous learning (and their contrasting counterparts fostered in our present systems) is provided by a study on preparing people to teach within other cultures, written for the Peace Corps from the perspective of trainers in the new behavioral sciences. See Roger Harrison and R. L. Hopkins, "The Design of Cross-Cultural Training: An Alternative to the University Model," *Journal of Applied Behavioral Science, 3,* 1967, 431–460.

Like new element, its conjugate—new connection—creates new consciousness, as though sight passed through the new medium of a flaw within a lens: total consciousness now embraces partially coherent and conflicting visions and opens into incoherence. Such is the action of new metaphor, cognitive or social, before its vitality is exhausted by its integration into a coherent frame. (The example of dissonant mixed-media stimulation is perfectly general, as is that of space governed by fractured authority.) Process-consciousness is a permanent and indefinitely mutable reservoir of incoherent consciousness, leading to new form; and the space that shifting from content-level to meta-level opens is accessible by accident or design. A limited variety of process-consciousness is involved in the Hawthorn Effect, a strong example being the realization of personal or community self-construction in history, which leads toward full process-consciousness.

To open new consciousness is to blow the mind, to break the conjugate patterns of cognition and behavior. Space is freed from the control of the internalized, operant logics—the Authorities—of the mind, the spirit, the society. In the minimum degree, this is expressed in the brief de-linearization of our construction of reality; in the maximal degree, by that state which might as well be called holy indifference, or simple—that transcendent order which embraces the partial harmonies of all that is real and incomplete and within which the Tao of transformation operates in full harmony.

To free space, the Authorities of closure must be removed, counteracted by inhibition, repression, or confrontation, or broken through struggle. In general, conflict is overt at some level of personal and social space, though its ways and forms may be obscure. Behavior that truly reduces the control and threatens the existence of the Authority Complex is not likely to go unnoticed or uncountered.

All ways of conflict are truly dangerous: they threaten failure or, worse, exhaustion of free energy and paralysis.

And they threaten success. For the urge for birth and the fear of death are conjugate impulses, and the struggles for and against new life necessarily mirror and shape each other's tools and consciousness. That closed cycle is familiar, it leads our freed energies back into old forms. Though conflict is necessary now, it can open out of the Authority Complex—which knows no real yielding and is thus incomplete in the Tao—only by opening into a form within which the tools of the death of a system, though live and powerful, can be subordinated to the uses of birth: a transcendent form that embraces the old order within a higher one.

CHAOS

Herakleitos of Ephesos wrote that Strife is common to all; that Strife is Justice; that by Strife all things come into life and conjugate death in a universe of continual transformation. The meaning of his terms is as removed from us in time and culture as Lao-tzu's realization of the Tao. Yet the Chaos of Strife is the elemental condition all our motions disclose and all our systems of knowledge and society are constructed to deny. The action of knowledge at man's interface with his conjugate Universe—the construction, destruction, and reconstruction of natural science—displays the general paradigm perfectly.

About science, as about all systems of applied thought, our cultural mythology is powerful, explicitly anti-revolutionary, and dead wrong. In his elegant little study, *The Structure of Scientific Revolution*,[40] T. H. Kuhn describes how the system of world-construction we call science grows

[40] University of Chicago Press, 1962.

closed, is broken open into partial chaos, and then re-formed throughout, at first freely, in cycles of transcendent revolution. The processes he describes parallel those considered here and extend them in important directions.

If I seem unduly concerned with Chaos, that's because my culture denies this and other Mysteries. Yet the live face of Chaos is one with the existential crisis of freedom and choice, which defines the edge of learning. For this reason the Chaos of encounter and confrontation opens political and psychological space, and crisis politics is rich in learning. In denying Chaos our culture had to provide a substitute. It has chosen tools of coercion to inspire crises that galvanize our development in stiff and inappropriate ways. Our consumer economy increasingly descends from the technology generated for the Warfare State; and every student's later productive life depends heavily on his ability to learn desperately tonight for tomorrow's test. Yet there must be a better way; for death is the message of every closed system.

The structure of Chaos as we experience it is richly incoherent. It holds fragmentary forms and live energies, elements connected in harmony and strife, each pressing to be seen newly in the vividness of being unbound, each a universe of coherence defining by its incompleteness a conjugate universe of higher orders of incoherence. To embrace incoherence is to face the unknowable: it evokes primal Fear.

Fear of the known is specific and is dealt with cleanly (well or not). I take fear of the unknown to be the central psychological/spiritual problem of learning. Its conjugate expression is the use of power to control and ultimately to prevent change, which is correctly anticipated as the death of a total organic system. The question of *when* fear of the unknowable justifies the paralyses of anxiety and power is not my study here. Mind you, I don't object to a little structure in Chaos—enough to hold off the total Panic that closes breath, little enough around the open space of the lungs to breathe freely while we learn to live with our changes.[41]

Various contents of Chaos have been sketched or hinted above—there is no typical example—along with skills involved in building within it and learning forms that foster these. For more detail, confront your life.

ANGER

One aspect of Chaos deserves special mention. If the birth of new forms is the death of old systems, then anger is intrinsic to the process, for no system dies willingly. All the changing forms of Amerika—technological, social, cognitive—now threaten us intimately with the Chaos of our freedom. And as the death of systems gathers, so does anger; repressed and swollen, its unexpected energies now flood into any free space, whether opened in anger or not, to entangle and paralyze growth.

The process of building new form is a bootstrapping one, in which, in order to work against fear, it is necessary to live maximally in and through the open potential of what is being created. This is hard to do in our culture. The nourishment of the will is a function of love: of love for the creation of our being, its substance and process. But our systems of learning, production, and life run by punishment and shame: they *niggerize* us, teach us to dislike ourselves and to distrust and repress our capacities. We should be angry. We are, but fear forbids us to express it directly: our anger sours to the hate of the flesh that becomes the effect of our cities and the strength of our churches. And the conjugate voice of love is stilled equally, souring to greed. People so trained find it difficult to believe in each other enough to

---

[41] And Chaos does have structure. Karen has just walked in with a slip from a fortune cookie, which reads: "Even if we study to old age, we shall not finish learning." And mine, broken open, reads: "If you neglect study when you are young, what of your old age?"

learn from or act with, let alone to create healthy mechanics of change and brave the uncertain hand of history. So the first problem in building a revolutionary movement or learning group is getting people to take themselves seriously, to believe in their beauty and dignity and potential collective power, and to celebrate fully all their achievement. (The cry *"Black Is Beautiful!"* now spreading across America opens the space of our future.)

Amerika is now just waking to formal public recognition that the violence of anger acted out uncontrollably is its grossest national product. As the pace of transformation accelerates, our need for its potentials becomes live, and the frustration of our energy becomes acute. We translate our anger at our death by strangulation within our rigid systems into a general hatred and murder.

Within my lifetime the mainstream of the literature and art of Western Man has turned to a rich expression of powerless agony—in which light I choose my preference for a music of equal celebration and tragedy—as a dying culture races to work out its most ambitious and blind creation: the death of its species and an entire planetary ecology. These are but two of the cultural barometers that register the burden of our anger and point starkly to the fact that—with almost unbroken generality—we do not know how to build social or personal forms and processes that deal adequately with the anger gathering within them or govern its expression. Instead, we generate our continual helpless violence.[42]

We must learn to make our anger open, choose to take

[42] For many years the peace of the Amerikan classroom has been the silence of frustration and the boredom of death. Since 1964 an enormous charge of righteously hateful anger has begun to be acted out against the established educational system. It does not simply vanish in the alternate educational system we are developing. In general, throughout the free universities, when people come together to replace authority-centered learning with a self-regulated group, they must deal with stored and unexpected anger, not only at first but at each group nexus of decision and change.

off the mask frozen in a smile before we are forced to, before there is nothing left to expose but the indirect dagger of our murder. But our culture denies the expressions of anger, dying with polite legislation. We act it out clearly only in wars which grow more removed from control and sports which slowly escape participation, attended by passive audiences. Beyond this, our culture is rich in rituals of inhibition and destruction, while those of creation and expression have lost their vitality.

We are newly rediscovering the positive rituals. They must deal with accumulated necessity, and many lead through anger and violence—but openly, with self-interest proudly clear. Frantz Fanon argues that deliberate violence is necessary to the formation of new identity by a colonized people; all the literatures of revolution support him. If, as I believe, Amerika makes niggers of all her children by the reigning processes of the Authority Complex, which act through her every form and tool, then the play of this violence must be translated in the theater of every action that creates a new identity.[43] For the burden of anger is equal among all her populations, no matter how otherwise favored, and, undealt with, sabotages all their creations equally.

The child's first cry from out of the blackness, free and total, is of anger and fear. Entering through their inescapable purity as an isolate entity into the Chaos of World, the child begins the act of learning, and the will of life transforms these emotions to the aggression that powers growth.[44] However it goes, I know that today anger must be dealt with

[43] Confrontation makes explicit real conflicts of interest and serves an essential function in the creation of new identity. See "Dear Michael: Two Letters on Confrontation" (*Change Magazine,* January 1969).

[44] Anger springs continuously from frustration in the learning process. It can turn for or against the self, to aid learning or to block it. In the individual it becomes introjected, its power directed against the self in a piggishness of negative judgment, paralyzing the will against trying. In groups, such introjection is both personal and interpersonal, equally sabotaging group will. But on either level, when anger-energy is fully

equally with fear in the act of learning; and that the proper governance of anger, unlike that of fear, requires more machinery than the nourished will.

That machinery is built by bootstrapping up from almost nothing. A small functional group cultivates a consciousness attentive to the health of its process: one that recognizes the presence of anger and the need for work to deal with it, and begins by establishing norms of openness to permit its expression. Beyond this, the skills and forms for anger's useful government must be developed deliberately. To give one example: in an educational reform work group oriented toward theater, the larger work process becomes stifled by accumulated anger among persons and frustration of goals. They unblock by recognizing this and shifting to a therapeutic subprocess: breaking into couples who act several energetic cycles of anger/aggression/reconciliation in nonverbal mirror games. The immediate energies of frustration dissipate through body expression. Talking together, they focus on personal conflicts and arrange to deal with them later in another sort of session. Then they resume work.

THE SKILLS OF FREE BUILDING

This essay has a narrow and culture-bound focus because I am young and of the white dominant class, and the skills of interest are the ones we do not have or cannot use properly. Our institutions condition us efficiently in some skills— especially in those necessary to create and function within limits. Our problem is to learn to use these as tools rather than tyrannies of our will: to break them free from the Authorities they are embedded in and bear. That process is one of deconditioning; one model is the psychedelic ex-

---

accepted, grasped, and outered, it reappears as the playful and fierce aggression integral to the problem-tackling will—the Yang motor of *going-on.*

perience. In general deconditioning restores harmony in the competition between skills—for example, between the abilities to defer and to accept gratification, where our training has left us with a harsh imbalance.

Deconditioning and competition do not extinguish the skills in which the Authority Complex has drilled us so fearfully. They remain our tools and are not so much corroded as depended upon less. Acid-freaks can write a straight letter to their Probation Officer in linear typographic logic. This is no joke: as most heads know who have had to respond to an emergency while stoned, the lower reaches (at least) of the psychedelic experience provide a clear model of a free-learning technology which within its process permits its users to reassert essentially full control over their gathered skills when they choose to.

Our culture trains well for the skills that can be trained, given that it is an impoverishing environment for those that must be learned—which include not only the functional skills of autonomous learning but an associated battery of psychological and spiritual skills. These define personal strength and group society and are functional skills on the meta-level, i.e., they are involved in the control of the functional skills. Their best cultivation seems to come in learning forms that deliberately provide for continual rotation among all members of all roles and functions, and thus for mutual training in all the skills of process and content.

We must believe our songs, the cries of our need. The message ringing through all levels of the new art and politics dawning in Amerika is about control, about the fearful greeds of power: it calls, *Let go! Let go!* It calls for the move to a higher order of control that can satisfy more needs than those we have managed. That move is a move of consciousness. Its essence is spiritual, but for the purpose of building healthy functional social groups, and in the terms of linear analysis—which at this point in our history is itself deeply suspect as a tool—I find it is best described as a process-consciousness whose construction and operation is clearest in small learning groups. The model of process-consciousness drawn from them applies also to social institutions and, more awkwardly, within the individual consciousness. It depends in particular upon the skills of the psyche, in ways that have been sketched above.

It also depends upon the deliberate construction of its operation, for reasons most clearly seen on the gross cultural level. Today the process of change is happening so rapidly that we are forced to relate not only to individual changes but to change itself as a phenomenon, and to develop a corresponding and appropriate consciousness. This process is carrying us back toward the fruits of ancient cultures, the visible metaphysics that deal with change—the Tao in particular.

But we must go beyond. *No culture in human history has ever before been called upon to develop institutions and processes whose function is to render healthy the process of change itself.* That this function must be conscious is implicit in its nature, which is to render visible; we are not likely to mistake its appearance. The kingdoms of Old China governed by the corruptions of Lao-tzu's Way did not flourish within the Tao despite their pretensions, which have been taken at face value by later commentators and used to prove the Tao an avenue of powerless quietism into defeat: they were static and inadequate societies. Nor does our own civilization display much evidence of reflexive self-changing capacity. It is clear that our present modes of politics are completely inadequate. Sometimes we generate vital information about process, but in general the information is without action-consequence and thus incomplete.

For a clear example, consider our universities. Within their departments of psychology, experiment has proven for decades that our whole system of testing and grading assesses not knowledge or learning skills, but the success of social conditioning. Yet that system of punitive evaluation continues as the dominant motivational framework for learning. What will it take, short of total revolution, for us to be able to apply our knowledge to our goals?

A culture is an organic entity. The quality of its needs is uniform, within individuals and within institutions. The necessary skills and process must be approached in a total context, within the total society and with the total being— which of course means in ways that run directly counter to the teachings and practice of our fragmenting age.

The problems with our learning are so deeply coupled with the societies of our learning-environments that we must speak in terms of the creation of a radically new order. The social image of process-consciousness must, I think, be a full form of participatory democracy; the functioning of such a consciousness requires that every segment be represented and empowered directly in the governance that affects it. The mechanisms of democratic governance vary from level to level. They are largely unknown, though we have invented some successful and reproducible small-group forms in which they can be painfully studied. There, as on the larger social level, they seem always to require radical decentralization of functional structure and of power—an imperative now clearly faced by our cities, our governments, our educational and productive systems, etc. That decentralization has its interior analogue in the process of learning to let all of one's voices without words have their say.[45] Both seem to require an adequate social and personal taste for incoherence.

Process-consciousness, whose social face is freedom, reflects a total cultural framework: a metaphysics, an aes-

[45] One current aspect of this process is the investigation of decision-making tools from other or earlier cultures—the *I Ching*, astrology, the Tarot, etc. Unlike the corresponding tools of our culture, which gather information about external phenomena, these (however one explains their working) provide information about the *internal* states of the decision-making system. Such tools are essential to process-consciousness.

thetic, an ethics, a politics. Perhaps this is not possible in a full form. The existential crisis of free choice may be impossible to endure on a full-time basis. But history still seems to offer the possibility of a maturity defined not by fixed social and personal identity but by personality whose major commitment is to flexible roles and to change. The construction of a conversation with *no* limits, always instantly open to new elements, connections, and directions, is clearly a convenient fiction: limits must continually be generated for building to proceed. But from *within,* not *without,* and ever again broken in a rhythm of eternal revolution. We have no choice about that cycle; we can learn only to tend the health of its process, which at present means more to make than to prevent revolution.

One danger in dealing with process should be mentioned. The consciousness and control of process can easily become a tyranny rather than a tool. This is seen most clearly in small groups inexperienced in its use, who, by inept work, snarl process worse than they could by straightforward ignorance. Incomplete process-consciousness replaces the Authority Complex as a system of control and conflict that absorbs energy unto paralysis. Process-consciousness must govern the health of its own operation. The answer is a balance in its use, an ability to let go a created consciousness. Surely this is difficult: our creations always call to us to rest in them as sufficient, work to freeze the energies of their creation into proud duration. This process may be read as the pure, primordial operation of the Authority Complex, or, as some modern Protestant theologians are coming to do, as the workings of Original Sin. But it seems possible to go on from there.

V.

The Ecology of Violence in the University (Notes on the Tao of Education)

1. BY NOW WE ARE FAMILIAR with the University as an institution involved in violence. We know that its primary function is to deform the young to roles in the economic process of technological imperialism, and to fit them to be the impotent citizenry of a nation generous with death. Within it CIA agents are trained and defoliants created; its sociologists rationalize the destruction of the black family structure; its administrators act as slum landlords, plant narks among the students and call in the pigs to break heads. Each

campus has its distinctive litany, blood on the ivory tower.

2. In moving away and on from the institution that was supposed to teach me what to do with my mind, I've had to try to understand the violence of the University. Watching as its catalogue of social atrocities grows and learning the ways life within it left me violent and violated, I have come to see it not as a factory whose product has an accidentally ugly surface, but as an entire and coherent *system* of violence. It is a total institution, all of whose parts—structural, architectural, procedural—function together to create an ecology of violence.

3. Needed: a simple, unified perspective on higher education—and most of lower, for that matter—as a destructive system. Most current radical analysis focuses on power, its distribution and uses. But there are violences less dramatic yet more fundamental than those of power-politics. I want to make a lens, melt of metaphysics and some images, through which to view the University as a total institution and understand some of its deeper violence.

4. In the last sixty years, from Freud to Women's Liberation, we've begun to realize that our culture's troubles are most deeply involved in that mysterious complex called sex, so it makes sense to start here. Most beginnings deal with the repression and distortion of sexual energies. Through this lens we see a different perspective: the repression and distortion of sexual *modalities*.

CONSTRUCTION OF THE LENS

5. Primary metaphysic, yes, that's where we have to start. Our culture has a harsh way of handling "opposites." Good and Evil are dedicated to each other's annihilation. Win struggles against Lose, Right against Wrong. "Opposites" fight, the One versus the Other—to death if they can, naturally. Hobbes argued that One's Other was evil; Western society chose to believe him; almost everywhere men grow, work, or live in groups they are governed by this assumption. Metaphysic strikes deep.

6. Take sex, see how the value structure that goes with this metaphysic works out in terms of sexual role. The official cultural version is that man and woman are "opposites." Man strong, *therefore* woman weak. Man aggressive, woman passive, *Q.E.D.* Such oppositions are acted out in social ritual, by opening doors or being asked for a date. Beyond this division, each "opposite" denies its Other. Strong men don't cry. Muscles or logic on women are deformities. Most men numb themselves to the fact that their breasts are sexual organs as fully as women's. Women pluck and shave hair away from their bodies. Men with softness in their style rate low in the pecking order. Aggressive women are still unnatural. Socially a man is defined by his ability to "earn a living," i.e., to exploit his environment for survival; and a woman by her relation to children and a man, in which light she cannot help but exploit them for her identity. We wind up with women incapable equally of anger and of the ability to act in the world; and men who cannot care sufficiently for those or that which their work touches and transforms.

7. That metaphysic whose pursuit some call the Tao deals not with "opposites" but with the poles of a twoness-in-one, for which ☯ is the ancient symbol. Darkness and light are not static states but conjugate processes, each defining the other. Night and day live wrapped in each other's arms. Heat and cold, motion and rest depend Each on the Other. In the Tao, poles create Each/Other by their difference. What exists between them is not the denying antagonism of "opposites" but the tension of interdependence. And the goal of being is not a state of victory, but a process of becoming, built from the harmony of complementary qualities, an integral motion begun beyond the poles and expressing itself through their interplay.

8. In terms of sexuality, we are each of us, man or woman, possessed of both poles in the Tao: somewhat able to act in the world, and to receive it; capable of creation and nurture, giving and taking, leading and following, all concave and convex actions and responses. The cunt can equally be an aggressive organ, and the cock as receptive as any transcendental hole. To become one's person in these terms is to accept all of one's complementary parts into some unique harmony. A man learns that his strength comes not from stern tension but from the rhythms of tension and relaxation. A woman learns that her love is deeper and freer if she lets out her anger. Sometimes, body-locked, we hardly know which is the other, who comes, who receives.

9. The old names for the poles are Yin and Yang; it is true that all may be seen in their terms. Following ancient practice, I used to call them also Female and Male, believing that, though it made for some confusion until you got used to not thinking of "Woman" and "Man" at the same time, it also made

for more powerful metaphor. Thoughtful sisters finally convinced me that to continue describing as "female" all the qualities that have been left to or forced upon women as a class is to perpetuate a sexist perspective. Yet it seems to me that the sexism of its traditional vocabulary and formulation is not innate in the Tao metaphysic, that it can be used as a tool without sexual prejudice.[1]

Sometimes I think the problem with our culture is that it is Yang-dominated throughout, in its psychology and values. Sometimes I think it's that we're conditioned to perceive and behave in terms of "opposites," to divide all the Yin/Yang polarities along the deadly line of *better* and *worse, good* and *bad,* to carry on that eternal quarrel, frozen in antagonistic roles. I call being split apart this way violence. Sometimes I know we can move toward an integral harmony.

VIEW OF THE UNIVERSITY

10.   One mode of teaching is triumphant in the University. Minds are to be filled with information. Image of a hand closing on a piece of data, fist plunging into watermelon. Image of a cock ejaculating. Sock it to me. But there is another mode of

[1] I return to this delicate question on page 186. In reading what follows, I find it takes a constant exercise of consciousness not to lapse into thinking of the Yang qualities as inherently male. I've made this separation even more difficult by using certain biological metaphors that a more disciplined political mind would edit out. I include them in lazy humility, to indicate how partial the reconstruction of my own consciousness is, and also to remind us that the question of the biological grounding of sexism is still not well understood.

teaching, unpracticed, which proceeds by creating an environment, a resource-full context within which growth may proceed inspired by its own direction. Image of a womb, life inside, unfolding.

11. The public rituals of the academic process—publication, the seminar—are in terms of *performance* and *debate,* ritualized aggressive behavior.

12. Diagnosis of the University: excess of the Yang. In this imbalance the mind is trained as a knife only: we learn to analyze and dissect, to fragment and divide, to distinguish cases with rational logic. But there are other skills of the mind, the ones that bring things together rather than take them apart. Call these synthetic, creative, Yin . . . our language is fuzzy and poor in their names, just as we have no organized or useful ways of teaching them. We pretend that "creativity" is mysterious and try to teach the multiplication tables well. Yet creativity has its laws, even as the tables do.

13. When the mind is trained as a knife, its product, knowledge, comes out hamburger, bits and pieces. Certification into the intellectual elite is accomplished by the thesis, a scrap of meat on the altar of Fragmentary Knowledge.

14. *I will say this only once: nothing is wrong with Division itself.* But imbalance is disease. What we need now is the knowledge that unites these fragments, the Yin action that frees us from Yang paralysis.

15. The Yang mode of teaching depends on the conception of knowledge as a thing of fragments, detachable both from other fragments and from the

person who can use it. Like automobile parts, which can be put together one by one to form a vehicle that can be considered independent of the forge that produced each part and the mind that will guide the whole. Such stuff is information. Information-centered education proceeds by the classroom in which "knowledge" is transmitted independent of personal relationship in the production line of class and assignment: the rigid industrial process whose product is specialists.[2]

The very roles that monopolize our model of education are created by defining people in relation to this Yang conception of information: the expert produces it, the teacher markets it, the student consumes it. (But if knowledge exists *in* persons, then the way you get from *here* to *there* is not by isolating and "transmitting" it. Rather, some completely dissimilar process, like arranging conditions to establish a resonance; and new roles, like that of (s)he who tends the environment of its growth.)

---

[2] Since knowledge is a core industry, the forms, roles, and processes of educational institutions dovetail with the culture's dominant industrial process and follow its model. Thus the knowledge specialist is designed to be produced in a form as standardized as an auto part, an anonymous replacement to fit easily into some large machine. Thus high capital investments in certain areas and means of knowledge-production are allowed to dictate user custom and inhibit change; and the social organizations built about these investments shape the uses of power for their own aggrandizement and perpetuation. And thus the authority-modes of the knowledge system follow the linear, hierarchical control-model.

(The identification of education as the largest industry of the modern corporate capitalist state yields an illumination of powerful metaphors to interpret the reality we live through. For thinking about education in Amerika, one should be well-informed in these metaphors. They are dense in the literature of the New Left—e.g., Carl Davidson's *The Multiversity: Crucible of the New Working Class*, SDS. I'd go into this more here, but I'm focusing on a cluster of metaphors that have been less well written about.)

16. The crumbs from the knife of the mind are organized by the principle of Division. We are taught that Knowledge is split up into Disciplines, which unfold their partial structures of understanding in isolate, parallel branches, insulated from contact by special languages.

17. The social image of this conception of Knowledge is the University's organization into Departments. The divided map of information is reflected in their internal and external structures and relationships of power. The smoke's topography is a map of the furnaces in the industries of power—for information is a product of power, a tool to engineer detergents and departmental status. In this way are organized those who, having shaped their minds to knives, come to see themselves mirrored in their blades as algebraic topologists or whatever—defining themselves by the knowledge they create, less by its name than by its fragmentary forms. (The specialist reflex runs deep. When it comes to knowledge of the interdependence and wholeness of systems, which we are currently calling ecology, the first move is to create a new and separate Program or Department to administer this new Discipline. But how can the Department of X justify housing or training a generalist?)

18. Departments form closed, parallel societies. Typically their functional and social structures are bureaucratic and hierarchical, organized in terms of the principles of distinction: associate and assistant, professional and menial. Minor privilege and reward tell class and caste apart. Overall there is little significant deviation from a common norm in behavior, dress, classroom or publication style, modes and standards of thought . . . the sameness

that marks an unfree system. This linear social structure of higher/lower and rigidly normed behavior seems always to appear where people concentrate upon what divides them and not also upon what brings them together.

19. At the foot of the Departmental power-pyramid is the individual professor, in turn secure and dominant in the private territory of his classroom or his specialized bit of research. (Image of baronies, image of the stag locking horns with young contenders in the spring.) The faculty are split apart and isolated by the mode of their production, whether of knowledge or of trained youth. Who drops in on a neighbor's classroom or shares rat psychology with the Renaissance scholar?

20. The space of each classroom is like the other. Rows of identical concrete cubicles, color them pastel or redo them in aluminum and glass, it's all the same. Within each are seats bolted to the floor in identical distance—all facing front, so that no one's eyes can meet except with the teacher's, the best way to keep a group of people split apart. Nowadays the chairs are no longer bolted in rows. The students themselves rearrange them that way, sit equidistant and facing front to Authority. When there are no chairs, say rugs and cushions, people still act out the original architecture of separation, having embedded it in their reflexes, and tend to stay as equally far from each other as the space allows.

21. The principle of academic architecture is Division: it functions to prevent mutual intimacy. Cafeterias are designed to be crowded, for efficiency's sake: their bare walls reflect chattering noise back into the rituals of food: to be heard at dinner you have to

speak loudly, which sends your body through many of the physiological changes of anger. Dorm rooms, study cubicles, offices are constructed like class-rooms, housing identical units in isolation. Where two share any of these square cells, there is still no coming together, for people cramped together in inadequate space build walls against each other from within.

22.   You can tell from the bathrooms that dorms are de-signed to split men and women apart. Such a living context helps make them see each other primarily in sexual terms, encounter each other as fractions and not as integral persons. In the academic and ad-ministrative buildings, johns are set aside for staff, and eating-places also, keeping the social classes apart at both ends of alimental ritual. (Even in the boys' bathrooms of primary rural education, the communal trough is now being replaced by rows of individual urinals, whose porcelain contours beg you to huddle into them and shield your privates.)

23.   It's no accident that a dorm lounge looks like a dentist's waiting room, or that classrooms are de-signed by the same people who design prisons. A certain class of corporate architectural firms is re-sponsible indifferently for universities, prisons, hos-pitals, army barracks, and public housing. For such institutions, which function *to process people* in accordance with the economic scheme, the princi-ples of design are uniform: standardization and alienation, efficiency. All surfaces are hard, paint is tough and non-chip. Academic spaces are designed to turn over their occupants six times daily or once a semester and leave no trace; hospital rooms, to be steamed out after each occupant. Concrete is pri-mary: the institution *is* its buildings with their lichen

of bureaucracy; it is *not* the people it processes. (Likewise human knowledge is thought of as its husk of information, outlasting the inhabitant, expanding in stories around a central core, like some farsighted building program.)

24. Today students are fitted to the shape of the system of information, with its centralized Authorities. In that distant culture whose cities, economy, industries, and political power are decentralized, where the learning of Change is a living Way, there would be no mountains of fact and concrete called Universities. Knowledge would grow in and around the shape of each person. Education would enable each separately and together to create what knowledge they need when, appropriately, and always *anew;* would not be distinguished from the process of life, institutionally or otherwise.

25. Architecture tells us who we are, what about us matters, shapes our dreams. In rooms where you cannot write your name on the walls, the message is to be passive: the environment refuses interaction and denies your presence. The classroom is designed to alienate. Why not? The function of higher education is social conditioning at least as much as the transmission of knowledge. For its continuance, the economic order needs persons trained in certain forms of social response and incapable of others. School trains students to a certain style of authority inside and between their selves. Social order, architecture, information, all shape this climate, telling people, "Adapt to me."

26. Into the standard classroom descends the standard teacher, inescapably sovereign, to rehearse students in the intellectual and social ideologies of his De-

partment/Discipline. He orchestrates the process
that splits them apart. Here, in this arena dedicated
to thought as opposed to action, their training to
divorce intellect from emotion is carried out to its
highest refinement. (What wonder they find it hard
to feel and deal with the anguish built in to their
later work?) The schedules of class, curriculum,
and degree make them learn to fragment their attention and energy; to divide their selves as well as
their work into parts, to be able to standardize production; and to defer both response and gratification, which involves numbing themselves to the
sensations of their needs and the possibilities of
action.

27. The jock and the scholar stand at opposite ends of
the traditional campus social spectrum, to testify
that higher education further divorces the workings
of body from the workings of mind. Hence the environments of classroom and study-room are designed for passive, motionless bodies; and the processes that go on within them are designed to train
people to experience ideas and emotions without
physical response.

Yet what learns is a whole being; in each of us
knowledge is made manifest physically, from the
level of molecular biology and RNA-chain coding
on up. Increasingly I become convinced that physical therapies, constant rituals of body use, and disciplined work on the interface of body and mind
(e.g., hatha-yoga, bio-energetics) are essential curriculum for the integration of knowledge. I also
think that a revolution in our cultural style of conceptual learning is promised by our current early
experiments with learning forms in which people
create and physically act out theater that embodies

the conceptual problems they are investigating. To deal with the body as integral with the mind in the art of learning will require a basic rethinking and reconstruction of our educational environments and processes.

(The divorcement of mind from body and the hostile elevation of mind above body characterize not only the University but the dominant culture.[3] We may understand this as a *Yang tyranny,* brought about largely through the offices of men who have been trained to deny the reality of inner/subjective experience, the claims of energy rooted in the Yin of flesh-earth, and who enact their private limitation into public policy and values.)

28. The classroom process is combative. Within it the young are conditioned to claw each other in competition for an A, a smile from teacher, a fellowship, certification, future power. The process of power in the classroom is normally the primitive politics of aggressive ego-struggle for scarce resources (like public space and last sentence's rewards). Outside in our political meetings we reveal the uses of the mind to which we've been conditioned. When the velvet gloves of the academic seminar are stripped off and the leisurely clouds of paper interchange blown away, what's left looks like a bunch of guys milling about in the public arena, battering away at each other with huge cocks to see whose is longest and strongest.

29. The classroom process of competition drives people away from each other and back into themselves.

---

[3] See Eldridge Cleaver's magnificent little essay on the sex-linked polarities of white and black culture, "The Primeval Mitosis," in *Soul on Ice* (Dell, 1970), which helped lead me to these notes and extends them in turn.

The basic gut-state of most students in class is fearful. A low-trust, high-risk environment; small wonder most people behave timidly in it. But what else can we expect from learning dominated by a framework of punishment/reward, success/failure, in which every motion is subject to judgment?

30. When all is divided in the culture of heirarchy, of Good over Evil, half gets shoved under: anger, black people, the body, whatever's dark and bad for you. Men fight their softness and women their strength. We learn to weaken our powers by exalting those praised and starving the others. Split into parts, you are freaky in some and ashamed of being freaky (or do you still remember?). For what is wrong and the pain and confusion in your head you have learned to blame your self and your private condition. Weakened, divided, we go through our paces learning and living to be integrated into the system of production and consumption.

31. Another name for this game is Capitalism. This is the system that, according to Marx, divorces you from the control of your production; splits you from the sense and production of your self, in the condition called alienation; and divides you from your brothers and sisters and whoever is Other, in the process of keeping you powerless. (Marx built off Hegel, whose metaphysic was homomorphic to the Tao.) Capitalism is a total system, each of its key institutions reflects its characteristics—nothing special about education, a similar ecology of Division holds almost everywhere. In order to keep functioning in its modes of production, repression, and exploitation, such a system must systematically cripple its people and leave them unable to come

together, with their selves or each other. All its institutions will work to this end.

32. Imperialism is the broader framework of our culture.

All depend on the splitting of the One from the Other. Where interdependence is honored, they are not. We have followed a one-sided way for so many faith-full centuries, have built our forms around it. Now the sky turns black with its signature. What institutions will school us equally in the ways of yielding—the yielding up of power and control, and of the Self to the Other, which are necessary to Coming Together—and teach us that yielding is not defeat? How will we recover the halves of ourselves of which we have been systematically stripped; and learn beyond this the unity of our parts in polar interplay?

CODA ON COMING TOGETHER IN LEARNING

33. It is irresponsible only to take apart. The perspective on the University (and its parent culture) I have tried to sketch here carries an implicit prescription for action: since by design all is Split Apart, begin by Bringing Together. That process

has already begun among us: surely most of the good energy now new in your life has been generated by the coming-together of what was divided. So I want to close with some dry notes about the design of coming-together in small groups.

34.   The small-group context is crucial for all learning, academic or not. It appears in various forms. In the University it is called a "class" and is defined in this way: (a) People joined by random schedule and program rather than common purpose, (b) with minimal mutual commitment, (c) come together for brief isolated meetings, (d) scattered in a longer arbitrary time, (e) to encounter each other in one or few of their many dimensions, mainly mind, (f) in an authority-centered society and (g) fixed roles, (h) dominated by a punishment/reward framework of motivation, (i) to learn of a specialized splinter of knowledge, (j) made and known in advance, (k) and beyond this be trained in certain skills of social conditioning and data processing.

How ghastly.

Begin by inverting that definition. People joined by common interest and mutual design choose to commit themselves to come together extensively and intensively over an open-ended period of time, which will shape its own form and limits. They meet each other on as many of their human levels as they can, in a democratic peer society which generates its own norms and internal motivations, to learn and to create the general and particular life-knowledge now needed.

In doing this, they begin to exhibit a social form new to our culture at least. The form goes by awkward names now, when people care to name it: "intentional learning community," "work-family," whatever. Examples are multiplying. (Communes are often of this sort, with differing degrees of consciousness and craft.) Is it too early to guess that this form just now being explored will replace the "class" as the basic small-group context of learning for the young? And will the next revolution in higher education parallel the last, in which a new living/learning group, the Fraternity, evolved to generate a new curriculum, the Liberal Arts?

35.   How do people learn in groups? In the University, formal learning usually goes on in a sequential process of the form

AAA. . .AN, AAA. . .AN, ... ,

where the typical module A looks like this:

A = (a,b) = (listen to a lecture, study and
                    think alone),

or at best:

A = (a,b,c) = (discuss in seminar, study
                        and think alone, discuss pri-
                        vately and informally);

and N is some ritual of judgment, like a test or a paper.[4] Such a sequence does involve some alternation of modes—private/group, listening/dealing-with—but the focus of each of its segments is on only cognitive interaction and content.

A group can learn together in better ways. One simple richer process we've worked with comes by taking the form above, but making the typical module A look like this:

---

[4] That is, you go to class, come home; go to class, come home; . . . ; go to class, come home; and take a test—week after week after year.

$A = (a,b,c,d) =$ (design a new *experience*, go through it alone or together, deal with it cognitively in group and informally, think and study alone).

In this it is easy to see a model for a competent political or social organizing process, where N is a mobilization of social energy in some form. On a smaller scale, an intentional learning group goes off for a weekend to design a learning game—say, about social process—play it and then deal with it; design, play, and deal with another; . . . , and

$N =$ (evaluate and plan for the next work together).

What matters here is that such a process is designed to integrate experience and cognition in an organic way, each giving rise to the other, within each module A. In the University model, private experience can occasionally be "made relevant" to some module; but there is no deliberate place in the process for experience related to cognitive content, nor provision for allowing each to generate the other.

36. Begin to integrate experience and thought by learning in forms that alternate them deliberately. This principle goes further: the way to begin to integrate divided areas of Knowledge is to put them into intimate contact within some form. For example: we have done extended workshops in sexuality and politics, using the form AA'NAA'NAA'N. . . . Here each module of work A is focused on sexuality; and each A' is focused on political behavior. Both A and A' are of the form

$$(a,b,c) = \text{(design and play a learning game,} \\ \text{think in group and then informally} \\ \text{about it)}$$

and

$$N = \text{(evaluation and planning)}.$$

As the cycle AA′N repeats, the initially "separate" subjects come to be known as interpenetrate. Through such group methods an integral conscious-ness, a knowledge grounded in both domains—per-sonal/public, thought/experience—begins to grow and leads to larger action. I mean, we've tried it, and it does.

37. I first learned about hybrid forms of learning by watching an SDS Agit/Prop Theater rehearse in 1967. It was then the only political group in Berke-ley that stayed together well, or whose members enjoyed coming to meetings. They spent half their time horsing; half of the rest, in discussing ideology and half in struggling to translate it into dramatic images with popular impact. I saw that they had to come collectively and individually to a different, deeper grasp on their political thought in order to be able to translate it into a different medium than was necessary in a straight political rap group. Their theater was reciprocally enriched and grounded. Power is generated on the interface where different media come into intimate contact. Abolish monopoly forms.

38. Now that educators are discovering that affect has something to do with learning, they have let emo-tion back on the campus, to go off and play with itself in the ghetto of Encounter and Sensitivity, still split off. But any significant learning involves

personal change, with all its emotions and consequences. The University model of formal group learning is not concerned with these: the individual is left to deal with them where else in his life he can. But a healthy learning group recognizes its collective responsibility to help each person deal with the integral whole and consequence of each act of learning, not only its public beginning. (In our better groups now there are informal norms and formal processes which function to this end.)

39. Last, about process, and the Yin skill of tending it. Formal academic learning deals with content almost exclusively. Whether by the hour or by the semester, the conversation focuses on its cognitive substance rather than on its process. But conversation is a container, a flexible form within which something grows, an environment—not of walls, but of processes. If these are healthy, growth is healthy; if not, not. An obsession with content and little useful custom or language to deal with process goes along with our culture's Yang mode of teaching, data-bit-oriented. Men in particular are Yang-trained to deny the reality of subjective experience and to objectify outer reality. Their personal blindness is reflected in the content/process imbalance of man-dominated groups. Even before Women's Liberation, work groups of women tended to be significantly more attentive to process, though not enough to escape the general Yang clench of our culture.

Consciousness of the environment, whether material or of process, and tending its health are in the Yin mode. A healthy process of learning involves an alternation between the modes: dealing with content or other goal-directed activity until it becomes necessary to deal with the process of work;

shifting levels and working with process, e.g., by opening up accumulated group anger or changing the work's leadership patterns; shifting back to the content-oriented mode. I have written above about process-tending, and the number of people sharing a vocabulary and a tradition of how-to-do-it is increasing rapidly. It furnishes the strongest example I know of how the Yin mode can be recognized and combined in balance with the Yang, toward an integral process of learning.

40. Beyond what I've said already, I believe the health or harmony of learning, group and individual, can be understood and regulated in the Tao by right balance and interplay between the polar terms: experience/reflection, creation/integration, action/rest, unique/mutual, and all the rest, including the Word/the Imagination.

VI.

Glimpses of the Glue

MAXIMS

Lao-tzu began,

> The Way that can be named
> is not the underlying way.

Yet he went on to write 5,000 characters concerning it, while pausing for a cup of tea with the gatekeeper before disappearing into the unknown territories.

What can be said about the Way that is not banal from its perspective, arcane and irritatingly empty from without it?

There is no foolishness like the foolishness of a man trying to write about the Tao.

INTENT

To write about the way the Way appears in these writings. Foolish, distracted by Spring, without ambition.

ANECDOTES

When I was fifteen and one of a lonely handful of weirdos in our suburban high school, I stayed up late nights with Tony, another, helping him transcribe tapes of Alan Watts' interminable lecture series over KPFA—our introduction to non-Western religions and metaphysics. This was in 1955, just after McCarthy fell, when the Thaw was beginning. What Tom Parkinson calls *Pacific Basin Culture* was cresting in its first coherent surge; and from the hills all around the San Francisco Bay alienated liberal kids like us came drifting into City Lights Bookstore, to poke into the Beat ambiance and pick up on its influences.

So I suppose it was there that I got the Mentor paperback on the Tao.[1] It was a wretched translation, and what's more, I misread it with all the undisciplined and introverted romanticism of my adolescence, mistaking alienation for the indifference of the sages. Over the next few years I came back a few times to its eighty-one brief poems, receiving

[1] Lao-tzu, *The Way of Life;* Tao Te Ching tr. by R. B. Blakney (New American Library, 1955).

them with a mind that I now recognize as empty, but that then seemed vague, lethargic, and baffled. I felt slightly ashamed that I never quite managed to ponder Lao-tzu's epigrams deeply, nor applied to their text the same analytical energy I devoted to thermodynamics. I would never have claimed myself a serious student of the Way; and if on fifty jillion college forms asking my race and religion I wrote *human* and *Taoist,* I meant no more than an arcane *fuck you.*

But the joke was on me. Unbeknownst, the purity of that metaphor had infected me; an intangible virus of the central nervous system was at work reorganizing the patterns of my energy and perception. Slow as water, invisible as steam.

When I was twenty-three I met Karen, and we began a long interplay. At first it was phrased consistently in the gross Western mode, all Yang the man's domain and Yin hers. Of course, the fine texture was richer, but you know what I mean. For the time being, we were too busy finding out how we supported the shape of each other's needs, and building a flexible bond on the strength of this, to question the roles in which an exploitive Yang culture had schooled us, or to realize the extent of our imprisonment in them.

During our second summer, when acid was new and tripping a precious investigation, we tripped together and experienced fusion down endless changes. Seasons later, in the moist lace green of a Sur ravine, we went beyond, into the integral state from which all forms reappear.

These journeys had much to do with unlocking that frozen balance. Karen was already engaged with the elaborate permutations of the *I Ching,* which traveled in the same circles as acid. Thus experiences from the core and the surface interlaced. Seeking terms to read out our transcendent adventures and their shadow on our everyday relationship, those we came to were heavily polar.

Sometime in the third year of exploring our complementarity, we turned over in bed. I don't mean physically, we'd done that early. But now, in this grounding-place of our energies, we began seriously to develop our stunted Aspects—my receptive sexuality, her aggressive—and seek new balance. This went on for years, while each tried to help the other with the freakiness and joy of learning a broader being as man and woman.

Slowly we spread reconfiguration from this center through our lives, learning to lead and to follow one another in season. We took turns at the Yang of economic coping, to free each other at times of major change when the Yin-tentative needed space and protection. After the third time, we learned that breaking up was not the end—though its terror was always live—but a phase in a chosen cycle in which coming together and splitting apart gave rise to each other naturally. In the spaces between, I began learning forgiveness and to indwell in my body; and she her anger and to make things with her hands. All this took place in halting rhythms of progress/retreat/stagnation/break-through which we learned to recognize and accept and tried to move in harmony with; and is going on still.

Our fifth summer I spent in jail reading, besides Keniston, Friedenberg, and Joyce, Legge's edition of *The Texts of Taoism.*[2] In this lull of rest between action and action I read, besides Lao-tzu again, the 255 tales of Chuang-tzu. They slipped through my mind like fish through dark water.

In our seventh year we had a wedding. On the boughs over the piled stone altar hung the great Yin/Yang banner Barbara made. While we celebrated our investigation of the polar Mysteries, the guns were sighting in on the People's Park. Race: *human*. Religion (or whatever): *Taoist*. Why not? We went off to honeymoon at an ed reform conference

[2] The Julian Press, Inc.; New York, 1959. In paperback, Dover Publications; N.Y., 1962.

where we did our first serious work as a team. Later while the baby was perking we carried this on into extended work-shops in sexuality and political behavior, sexuality and learning[3]—some of the richest work I shared in as an organ-izer.

When we got back from the honeymoon, Karen hung the wedding banner on the bedroom wall. Even in the baroque jungle of our cottage it pulses like a sun. Each morning at home for a year now our son Lorca has absorbed the gentle impact of its mandala, symbol pure in a wheel of trigrams. Sometimes when I manage to touch him gently I remember how innocently it entered me.

By such intimate processes the infections of Metaphor spread, like sacred clap.

OBSERVATIONS

1. I feel obliged to account for the spotty Taoist readings of my text. I feel puzzled at this sense of obligation, irritated, mistrust it, fear it will lead me to play the wrong kind of fool. After a prayer, I construct a post-facto biographical rationalization for my yinyang uses, thinking to indicate one depth of the roots of thought. I wonder what fraction of my readers will believe that I did not work to decorate my work with polar references—but that these thrust themselves upon me, welled up with such incomplete power that I finally grew weary of the discipline of expressing them only in oblique language, and let them stand like disconnected out-croppings of a deeper stratum in my landscapes. I reconsider my feeling of obligation, compare myself to a man who left his door unlocked and must account for the presence of an

[3] Through five weeks of travel campus-to-campus practicing them, the thoughts of the previous chapter came together.

inscrutable Oriental who has appeared in the living room and has come, through simple inaction, to dominate the family conversation. I overindulge in metaphor (is such a thing possible?). Imagining the chronological progression of these essays, I think of my consciousness as a sea, one I look down on from slightly above, and recall how through the years in certain weathers I have seen the dolphin backs dark in the water, their schools of quick hieroglyphics rising through seasons closer to surface and broader in play.

2.   My applications of a Taoist framework are incomplete and misleading, reflecting the immaturity of my grasp of Tao concept. How much of this immaturity is slovenly, and how much a natural consequence of the Way's terms having begun to engage me consciously only as I neared mid-life? Whichever, there is a pattern to what I see and what I do not see; and its character is the signature of an early stage in a biography deeper than my own.

The pendulum rises to one height of imbalance, is still for an instant; falls wholeheartedly toward the opposite pole, modulating its impulse in transit; arrives to again invert the cycle of energy, whose balance is this interplay.

I seem obsessed with the moment of first fall, pay scanty attention to the balanced and mobile character of the cycle. I rationalize this indulgence in terms of journalistic responsibility, reading my theory in history as reportage about the first broad breakings-away from Yang culture. But my choice of emphasis is equally the product of an apocalyptic personal psychology, itself shaped by the age.

So I speak of the usefulness of opening space, but not of the usefulness of closing it. I advocate decentralization as a principle without honoring the manner in which centralization gives rise to it as need and potential, and is generated by it anew. On the gross level I emphasize release and slight control, and on the fine I avoid dealing with how these necessitate each other. Overall, my shadow of the Tao is neither balanced nor dynamic—like a frozen snapshot of the pendulum starting its descent.

3.   From here, the way of development is:

4.   If your way is reading about the Way, Lao-tzu is the writer—though for several millennia his slick purity has left his students unable to deal critically with the vision he opens or to grasp "his" version as early, limited in history and culture, and capable of radical enlargement. The matter of translation may matter, despite the earlier anecdote. The version by Witter Bynner is much in vogue now. But of all available translations of the *Tao Te Ching* I prefer the grand old clunker by James Legge, now almost a century old. People see its idiosyncrasies as laughable and its misinterpretations as gross. Yet this is the fate of any translation of this elusive attempt to mark an elusive vapor, even if it be vibrant and poetic where Legge's is pedantic and mawkish in its verse.

The unique virtue of his rendering is that he reads Lao-tzu from a perspective so distant from our own that we can see much of what he adds to and subtracts from the old guy naked. Legge was a translator in the missionary tradition of the English upper class, with the fine narrow arrogance of its education and spirit, well versed in the intricacies of Christian dogma, in whose light he cannot refrain from remarking upon the theological inadequacies of Taoism. Still he is humble enough to admit himself often at a loss in grasping what he transcribes; and at crucial points in the text confesses his interpolations by brackets. All in all his obscurations are open, while those of contemporary translations (and of Lao-tzu himself) are still sly to our eyes.

AN EXAMPLE

Control over the rhythm of opening and closing is essential for group development and even for group survival in this time when each beginning, insofar as it's open and authentic, attracts a swamping deluge of people hungry to connect. A shared group culture develops slowly, in organic rhythms, and the openness on which it depends is easily overloaded. Even when membership is closed and visibility restricted to the publicity of example, the stress of openness generates the protective rhythm of closure, or else dispersion.

The first commune in one midwestern college town began from a core, opened its membership (selectively), closed it upon overfilling space, consolidated a pattern of collective relationship. Their door was open to curious friends of friends, whose trickle swelled to a river come to dig the ambiance of people trying to live differently, or to trade at this countercultural information nexus. This current, though enriching, grew to overstrain the resident community, taking space and energy from its inner needs; the doors closed sharply for a time, and then re-opened under severer regulation.[4]

Symmetrically, the closure processes of groups generate the need for opening processes to balance them. "Strongly interacting groups" are well known from contexts of therapy and political action. They rapidly become difficult to enter or leave (closed); this is reflected in their development of unique microlanguages which exclude outsiders and which insiders find rich and are reluctant to relinquish. Such groups are by nature *centripetal:* they generate and depend

[4] At the two-year choice point, the commune fragmented benignly, subgroups dispersing to seed other communes, in particular the first political commune in town. By then, catalyzed by the primal example, a dozen independent communes were sprouting in the student ghetto. (See Chapter X)

upon energies and patterns of interaction that constantly draw the group more tightly in upon itself. There comes to be not simply a wall but a central magnet that impedes escape. Most strongly interacting groups grow more and more intense at their centers, and eventually collapse through enervation and the accumulation of poisonous social wastes within a closed system.

This tendency afflicts impartially political collectives and marriages. In the deliberate stewardship of groups it can be balanced by the introduction of *centrifugal* components and programs, which open group space by motion across the ingroup/outgroup interface. This centrifugal ventilation can be resolved into conjugate modes:

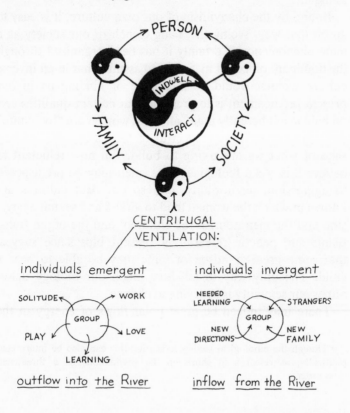

COMMENTARY ON THE PREVIOUS CHAPTER

Concepts reflect the social order that generates them.

In the China of Lao-tzu and the *I Ching,* women were bound in sexist social roles, characterized as inferior, weak, emotional, receptive, etc.; and these qualities in turn were perceived as intrinsically female. As a society's sexism pervades all aspects of life within it, weighting them with sexual value, so the interplay of polar forces throughout nature came to be seen as sexual, and the Yin was taken as The Female.

Bound by the chauvinism of our own culture, it is easy to go on that way, seeing the Yang clench of our society as a male phenomenon. Certainly it has been organized through the dominant offices of men. Yet to assume that in an inverse culture women would be incapable of landing us in our present predicament is to presume that certain qualities are, on balance, inherently male, and that women are "by nature" more empathic, more respectful of the earth, etc. For the sake of what we are trying to build, I'm now reluctant to believe this. As a biological class, men may be predisposed to aggression, territoriality, and so on.[5] But cultures are known in which the women tend to affairs and sexual aggression and the men nourish the children; and the organ transplants and genetic research of present bioscience suggest that some great-grandson of mine may be able to bear a child. The only way to tell how much our biology determines our sexuality is by trying to change.

There may indeed be great polar flows of energy in the

[5] Though the ethological studies indicating this can also be interpreted politically, as research to shore up the foundations of a threatened class order.

universe. The old texts of Acupuncture and Kundalini Yoga describe them in the body, and Soviet bioparapsychologists have begun to map them electronically. Yet even the bio-chemistry of our brains records the influence of our society (as study of schizophrenia demonstrates). As we cannot transcend our culture, it is impossible to prove that one flow is inherently male. Suppose one were able to, suppose the balance of the flows had these *potential* ranges for men and women:

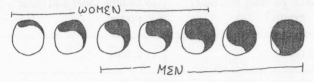

We can conceive a social order that restricted its members' balances to these actual ranges:

Such a society would see the white flow as manifest more typically in men. But how are we to know which case is ours?

So I think we are free to remake the tool of Taoist analysis in the image of the order we would create. To continue using the metaphor of Male and Female is impossible without prejudice—it's pointless to think of qualities like nurture or Inaction as female, if you believe them to be equally appropriate to men.

From this perspective, the principle of Division must be understood in a sex-free way. And we can still use a polar frame to understand the broad motions of men and women in our time, taking the present imbalances to be rooted in history rather than in our genitals:

MEN TO DEVELOP IN THESE	WOMEN TO DEVELOP IN THESE
to cherish, receive	to create, aggress
attend to the inner reaches	attend to the large orderings of society
to let go inner and outer control	to assume inner and outer power
et cetera	et cetera
both to be free and unexploited in these	*both to be free and nonexploitive in these*

It is tempting to say that men need to grow in the Yin qualities and women in the Yang; and I continue to use these classical terms in the next chapter to describe broad categories of qualities that seem to be related.

But again, it is impossible to determine how much of the "naturalness" of these groupings is due to our cultural perspective. Even the urge to classify all qualities into two abstract types may be an expression of our bipolar sexuality, intensified by our obsession with the primary contradictions of sexism and classism. In a time of awakening democratic sentiment, Riemann postulated that through a given point not one but many parallels could be drawn to a given line; his geometry was found to describe the "real" world more richly than Euclid's. Just so, as a non-chauvinist society emerges, it may conceive that to each pole correspond not one but many conjugate poles.

Whatever, reality is too subtle to be described by a simplistic mesh of Yin and Yang. The forces that move are not named by any of their manifestations, even so abstractly. Perhaps it is best to use these terms very lightly, wary of their tyranny over the intricate polar flows whose dynamic they remind us of.

COMMENTARY ON THE FOLLOWING CHAPTER

The Tao yields a technology of conception, a lens to reorganize vision. As such, it is a pragmatic tool for realizing social change, and one purpose of these notes is to soften the mystification with which it has been surrounded.

If Taoist emphasis seems foreign in discussion of the technologies of revolution, this is because of the disrepute brought by its false use as cover for the corruptions of the Chinese emperors, and because we in our categorical culture approach it as a "religion." True, the classical texts are normally read to warn against technological art. But they must be seen in their historical context, rather than as revealed truth. They condensed at a time when the revolution to male dominance was still fresh in their culture, as an organizing node for the repressed Yin. For this reason the Taoist texts—precisely as Lao-tzu warns—do not manifest the balance of their topic, and later commentators have rightly seen them as expounding a predominantly Yin social philosophy (in their dialectic with the culture's dominant Confucianism), a Way which puts inferior emphasis upon the Action in Inaction. There is also the matter of their having formed in a time whose condition and conception of technology were radically different from those which open to us. All in all, like Marx, Lao-tzu needs to be brought up to date.

VII.

Technology and Social Reconstruction

THE SCOPE OF THE QUEST

1. IN THE TAO, order and disorder embrace and move through all. I see ecology, theology, and technology as more identical than distinct, and think our problems stem from our culture's Way of falsely dividing. In the roots of our language, nearest to that place before all divides, *theo-logy* is knowledge of God, i.e., of the action of order (and disorder) through the world. *Eco-logy* is knowledge of the House, in its order (and disorder), i.e., of the workings of whole systems. At this level knowledge is still undifferentiated from practice; and so *techno-logy,* in its

root meaning of "systematic knowledge," is scarcely distinct from the others, and thus might be used, as it was during the Industrial Revolution, to indicate the practical arts, collectively, and their science. All our subjects merge into one, which is nameless.

2.   We are taught to see technology as a pathway of machines, leading up from stone axe through TV. But at its current summit we recognize that a computer is just expensive junk hardware without its software component—its programs, and behind them the systems by which people learn to generate them; and programs and systems of the spirit, parallel to those of the mind but mostly unnoticed. From this vantage we understand that any technology exists largely in the mode of its use. In the hands of animals with a different genetic heritage of aggression, the stone axe would indicate a different technology.

Thus tools draw our attention to the software that operates through them to organize energy. Going on, we see that methodical community organizing and psychotherapy are also technologies of energy-organizing—broad ones, embracing many minor technologies, some employing physical tools. And we arrive back at technology in its root meaning of systematic knowledge in practice.

3.   The full complexity of physical technology is as great as our own—for machines are intimate extensions of the sensing/computing/effecting mechanisms of our life form, and the process of our cognition is compounded from experience through these.

Our son began to invent Geometry when he discovered his fist and tried to bring it to his mouth. For three days he hit himself in the eye with the fist it guided. Finally he grasped that he was not an indivisible point but a complex of sensing parts in spatial relation, and solved the problem by turning his eyes off the fist and concentrating on touch to guide it home.

Months later we got him a set of rings stacked on a pole and topped with a knob. He dumped them off, studied them, put one on his finger a few times to grasp the action, then put it on the pole; put others on, dumped them, put them on again, indifferent to size-order. Then he turned to the knob, which had only a one-sided hole, stuck it on his finger, then on the empty pole, but hadn't enough control to make it fit. Impasse, study. He picked up the pole, which was small enough to *extend* his hand easily, and reversed action by threading it through a large ring; crowed with delight. Then he practiced on a small one. Then he steadied the knob where it lay and managed for an instant to fit the pole in; failed; and wandered off in the daze of just-before-sleep. During these twenty minutes we saw him learning through his body simultaneously a sense of extension and a sense of hypothesis based upon symmetry and example.

From such examples or yoga, we learn that the unit that "thinks" is not the naked brain but includes at least the body entire.[1] Extended as we are, by other flesh and matter, the physical mechanism that generates the patterns of our consciousness includes everyone's entrails and all our artifacts, bar none (and I think much more). Thus our machinery is integral to our every thought—even more deeply than McLuhan argues by citing how printing-press literacy has shaped our cognition. From our tools an astute alien could deduce the politics of old age, the an-

[1] Mainstream educational institutions, save for those of military persuasion, essentially ignore this deep truth (unless you count the laughably fragmented practice of high-school phys. ed.). But most learning games depend upon it.

thropology of love, and our image of Human, as these were actually practiced among us.

4. As we have a technology, industrial chemistry, to tailor molecules, so we have a meta-technology to manufacture our material technologies. These are not chaotic, some operating one way, some another: they form a systematic practice based on an ordered gestalt of principles. The technology of our technology is pernicious, witness the sky turning black; but it is first of all *coherent*. Its organization is everywhere dominated by the unbalanced Yang: Aggression/Centralization/Isolation/Grasping/Domination. Changing this clench is the substance of new politics, whose first directions are plain: moving toward balance in Receptivity/Decentralization/Collectivity/Release. . . .

5. Each level of form's working is made manifest in every other, as along the lines of this mandala, whose dark lines are the focus of this meditation:

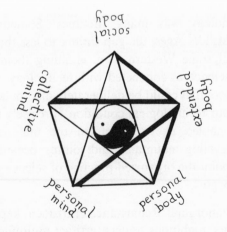

(the focus of this meditation ....)

MAN MEETS HIMSELF AS MACHINE[2]

6.   Our wedding with machinery is lost in time. From the first it altered all about us, in ways that kept changing. But our consciousness of Machine as *entity*, powerful as the nature-god, is recent. True, it often flared up, like freshly discovered fire or Cortez's musketry at the Aztecs, when particular technologies sent change cascading through societies. But such flashes of perception were discontinuous. Only when material invention accelerated to become a steady phenomenon during each man's life, only when each saw many new machines "causing" the transformation of his society before his living eyes, could we identify the Machine as such, and begin to grasp and dread it as an agency of change.

Similarly, when we yoked the stars into astronomy to guide our planting, the gap between the opening of a science and its elaboration into a practical technology was many lifetimes. Sometime after the Middle Ages, the gap shrank to less than the lifetime of some Western men, enabling them to recognize science as connected with technology—as, in fact, a tool that could be deliberately manipulated to change our technological condition (precisely as this in turn enabled us to transform the material continents, leveling mountains and joining oceans). From this point the organized practice of science as we know it begins.

7.   Panorama: Renaissance craftsmen, kept court scholars, ambitious traders, artifact multiplication. By the

[2] Sexist resonance intentional.

seventeenth century our image of the Machine was sufficiently developed for Hobbes to articulate in its terms an image of Man and the Social Body. Governance in Western society, with its authoritarian control of the spirit, is still based on his metaphor, formed in our early flush of triumph at mechanical domination of nature.

8. The impact of machine-connected change continued to increase as the giant baby Man closed his fist around his new rattle and shook it. Soon we were forced to recognize the *progression* of technology as central to our civilization, and men came to speak of the Industrial Revolution. Since Marx's time we've started to explore this recognition and to realize how technological transformation shapes and is shaped by our economic processes and our cognition.

   In my lifetime the recognition has deepened toward understanding ours as the first human culture to be organized around its own continual radical transformation through being geared to high technology. Already the pace stresses us near our limits, forcing us as a species to change our capacities or get off the trolley, forcing us to confront radical transformation as the underlying and naked condition of the universe.[3]

   Thus we meet Transformation through the Machine; and come to invest its joint-and-pulley skeleton with all the emotions we now feel facing the Abyss. As our culture is ill and balks at motion, our feelings are deeply out of balance: we see the Machine mostly in terms of greed and fear.

9. Millennia ago dominance in our culture shifted from female to male; we've just begun to seek balance. Our

---

[3] For this reason the reconstruction of our relationship with our technologies must be based on a metaphysic of Change.

image of power—male, overdeveloped, all Yang in
its action, in accord with our cultural sex roles—
determines our view of the machines that empower us
and conditions their uses. We have made minimal use
of their softer/decentralizing potentials. The beginning concern of political movements with sexuality
opens the first promise of a more harmonious Way
with machinery.

10.   Yang culture embodies terror of all that is holey,
from cunt to death, the dissolution of structure to be
re-formed. Its style is Grasping, in fear of Letting
Go.

Against death, in the ego-greed for unchanging
immortality, the Pharaohs raised the Pyramids by
means of what Mumford calls "megamachines."
Their body: organized ranks of artisans/laborers.
Their power: mostly human muscle. Their organization and operation: the simplest separation of the
skills, the simplest multiplication of the powers, of
one man building a tomb to guard the body from
change. So many units to measure; so many to cut;
so many to lift; so many to place. All under central
control of the head.

In modern capitalist society we armor ourselves
against the present as well as the future; in our
searching for security the Ways of Power have
grown more subtle and complex. But ego-greed still
stirs the pot, moved by fear of diminishment, sharing, release. And in our culture of control, the shape
of our technology (and to some extent the place of
our women) is as it was for the Pharaohs. The pyra-
mid Apollo whose capstone soared to poke she-
moon for investigation was the action of megamachine: so many to calculate, so many to weld,
etc., each with his powers multiplied mechanically,

all working on isolate stones as specialists, coordinated and directed by a centralized intelligence agency.

Our megamechanical organization extends beyond our material industries. All our functional institutions—the army, organized medicine, social welfare—operate as megamachines whose social product is the perpetuation of centralized power. Our educational system is doubly organized around this mechanical image; itself a megamachine, with ensembles of specialists, it functions to train and acculturate people to posts in the social megamachinery. (Hence the system is built upon principles of division, hierarchy, and so on—the comprehensive Yang chord of Chapter V.)

11. To us the Machine is male, and his secret name is Golem.[4] Dividing all, our culture outers what it conceives of as its evil onto the machine, which comes to be seen as an "independent" creation which will rise and turn to destroy us.

Long ago Golem appeared in our nightmares. As our skill with machinery grew, we provided him with hands and a sufficient arsenal, invented in the services of conquest. Now we are busy designing his brain. Out of habit, computers, our highest technological art, are developing mainly within the uses of war and economic exploitation. Now the time for Golem's waking nears, reporters gather at the door with flashbulbs. When he rises from the table, his expression will be dreadful, and his two male fists of

[4] Or Frankenstein's monster, as the *goyim* call him. But Golem is an older figure, dating back to sixteenth-century Prague where the Rabbi Yehuda Löw is said to have endowed a human figure of material stuff with life to be his servant. (Through his not observing the holy Laws, it ran amuck, terrifying the people.)

Violence and Control unbalanced in terrible carica-
ture.

12.   Other images of the Machine as (Hu)Man are possible. We have only their fragments.[5]

LIMITS OF THE IMAGINATION

13.   Many people concerned with bettering human conditions (let alone those of the earth) recoil with
superstitious dread at the prospect of higher technology as a life-furthering Way. Golem haunts us
all in an age whose most spectacular accomplishment is the instant annihilation of cities, in a culture
now recognizing that its most innocent technological
triumph, Rinso White, has poisoned the deepest
waters.

Most of those who are excited about technology
have paralyzed imaginations. They tend to see goals
and consequences on the most rudimentary levels,
in terms of physical satisfaction of physical needs,
as if material means affected man mostly materially.
Thus the thoughtful conceive that the world might
be fed, cities rebuilt, disease prevented, age eased,
learning aided, and so on, by wise use of machines.
But they have little sense of how changed technology might alter our political behavior, the psy-

[5] I can't help wondering what our bowel habits have to do with the
way we view our extension Machine. Shit is each person's earliest
separable extension, one's first experience in material production. Rather
than its being the stuff of art, we are taught that its nature is malignant.
We do not follow our production through its cycle of decay and blossom;
we see it vanished in rushing rituals of water by a loud mysterious
machine. Anonymous the turds depart; anonymous reappear the appliances with which we later armor our shithouses, their bowels as
mysterious as our own. And the rivers run thick with shit.

chology of our cognition, our spiritual sensitivities, and so on.

14. But why shouldn't our minds be in a box about technology? All women and most men—especially intellectuals—are acculturated to take pride in not understanding the technologies they exploit and depend upon. Knowledge of the Machine is conceived of as isolated from other knowledge and irrelevant to most social roles. By our economic processes it is mystified and confined to certain specialized castes of men, and among this technological elite the restrictive training of the mind on unbalanced male principles is most highly developed. Small wonder engineers aren't noted for imagination!

15. Culture-wide, the natural play of imagination about technology has been specialized and repressed. In the arts, it has been confined until recently to a "low" and minor branch of literature. Science fiction investigates the possible futures of our transformation through our technologies, material and other, from fusion energy through somatic psychotherapy to psi and Buddhism, alone and in multiple combination. Once science fiction romances treated ray-guns like six-guns; now they consider ethical systems derived from the needs of life in different ecologies, methane-based or machine-supported. As its body of speculation grows richer and deeper, we begin to recognize it as the signal literature of our self-changing technological society. When we meet Golem, if we survive, we will find that we've heard his poetry already.

Adaptation to change begins in consciousness, and science fiction—the speculative extension of technological man—has been crucial to the present rise of visions with new force among the young. Its impact hasn't really been recognized yet. But many of my generation found it a precious, funky medium for opening our imaginations—not least, about social reconstruction. It taught us to play with our minds about what man might become and how, in all the Ways of his being. Though periodical circulation of its literature never went beyond several hundred thousand copies, a remarkable proportion of the shapers and movers of the counterculture— political and artistic—grew up reading science fiction, learning to deal with lasers, the ethics of heart transplant, and the ecological crisis, long before these became official Realities.

16.   For our repressive systems' maintenance, it is essential that technology and imagination be divided, save in the service of exploitation. Hence in the social geometry of college campuses, we find the artists and the engineers farthest removed from each other, with the engineers nearer the business majors.

Yet people's behavior turns psychotic when they are kept too long from dreaming, a process essential to regulating condition. And a society kept from its technological dreaming, from imagining new machineries of food and politics, cannot regulate its transformation and turns blind deadly.

17.   The case of the engineers furnishes the most brilliant example of the function of our educational system as megamachine. When Sputnik went up in '57, scare flared in Amerika. Under this outered symbol the technological race for military supremacy accelerated: in consultation with the Joint Chiefs, Power cranked the wires and demanded, give me more of dese 'n some of dose. Triumph of megamachinery: within a decade, how many hundred thousand assorted engineers and Ph.D. physicists? Meanwhile Federal support for technological re-

search came to dominate the financial base of university education; man acquired the literal capacity to kill his species; missiles became the dominant industry of the greater Los Angeles Area; computer technology flourished in the high-skill spillover. By 1969 this made-to-order megamachine had multiplied high missilery across land and sea and broke man free from earth to touch her sister.

In the Sierra mountains, on Indian ground, by a warm pool blasted in granite and far from all cities, we watched on a tiny videoscreen the turning of the moon's limb, saw it swell to fill our horizon, felt the slow circling fall. As the first human stepped onto moon surface, Karen was throwing the worn coins of the *I Ching,* an open question. They registered the six Yang lines of the hexagram of primal power —*Ch'ien,* the pure Creative. The screen flashed through visions of starving choking cities. Torn between joy and despair, I thought, those graceless clowns, with their locker-room boys' toys society and poetry of Gee Whiz, they're supposed to represent *me?* I'll be damned! What sad theater that was, its accomplishment so impoverished, with all our dreaming left behind at what should be its flowering celebration.

INTRODUCTION TO DOME-BUILDING: THE TRANSFORMATION OF PERSONAL CONSCIOUSNESS

Lacking a Grand Plan for the reconstruction of society by pious use of ecologically sound technology, my fragmentary projections lead outward from my own life. A specialist in technological dreaming might offer weird and unique visions. I have only images drawn from common knowledge and rooted in personal experience now widely shared.

18.   I write this in the nursery I have just built for the ferns and our son Lorca. Opening out from a hole in a wall of our cottage, it is a modified geodesic structure spanning an irregular space. Entirely skinned in transparent and tinted plastics and sheltered by a small bamboo grove, it defines a magical space, an experience of outside inside. Its snug twin insulating skins scarcely interrupt the continuity of green life, from bamboo to planter over the bed. The two 3/8-caps forming its airy roof are as light as they look, maybe fifty pounds, and already have held in a gale wind. Their patterns of triangle/pentagon/hexagon, tinted in the yellow/green/blue chord of bamboo against open sky, form the two wings of the butterfly of Mathematics. Lights and gems will be its hovering eyes, to complete the image for the child in his crib and for us as we lie on the floor in meditation. Poor and cramped for space even without a kid, we needed it. And joyful energy rises up in me, the payoff from elegance in response to necessity.

Total cost: maybe $150, a week's learning, two weeks' work.

19.   I first turned on to geodesics by reading Bucky Fuller. But what kindled my longing to do was the poetry of Steve Baer's *Dome Cookbook*,[6] which describes the related but distinct technology of *zomes* which he helped develop. Beginning with the work of modern Russian crystallographers and mathe-

[6] Supplanted by a later edition. Lama Foundation, Box 422, Coralles, New Mexico 87048. $3.25.

maticians, Baer extends their results in theory, translates this into architectural design, and describes the process of constructing *zomes* out of recycled sheet metal from the tops of junked cars—and how not to chop your foot off if you salvage them with an axe. Spectral clusters of *zomes* now stand as monuments of collective creation in Lama, high in the sparse mountains of New Mexico, and *Dome Cookbook* circulates in the counterculture, bearing its implicit testament of a man who salvaged the skills of his technological training and put them to the uses of the imagination.

Closer to home, at Pacific School, an experimental high school south of San Francisco Bay, ten domes were built in four months, three by the students alone. In *Domebook 1*[7] the builders tell how— a full practical introduction to theory, different material technologies, design and construction problems, aesthetics, etc., put together in two weeks. It gave me all I needed for the nursery, besides its own delight.

20.   It is the breath of new example, imagination come alive, which inspires us to new behavior. I could sit around reading Bucky Fuller until Domesday. But to see before me, in their own handwriting and funky home photos, ex-mathematicians and freed fifteen-year-olds casually multiplying spherical grace—well, that was something else.

Both domebooks were put together, printed, and distributed by a cluster of technologies that place the producing of a book within easy reach of a semi-skilled, low-capital work group. This format was

[7] Since this writing, it's metamorphosed into *Domebook 2*—Pacific Domes, Box 219, Bolinas, California 94924; $4.20. An astonishing book! I wish a piece of this piece had gotten in it.

first made widely visible through the *Whole Earth Catalogue,* whose explosive popularity indicated the audience and the felt need for educational access to technology. Its motto: "We *are* as gods, and might as well get good at it."

21. Our architecture develops the cube monotonously —though it is only one of the Perfect Forms known to the Pythagoreans and Plato. For them mathematics and theology were configured together. They would not have found strange the notion that living within space generated by other geometrical Forms induces changed consciousness—which is what the current testimony of people who use icosahedron-based geodesics as a technology, not only of housing but of psychological and spiritual centering, boils down to.

22. Like our society, conventional building technology is organized around the concentration of stresses and forces and their treatment by means of brute local strength and gross load-members. Geodesic technology, like a number of other alternates now spreading, differs not only in its mathematical base, but in its essential dependence upon the structural principle of synergy. Its treatment of force is global and flexible, rather than local and rigid. The linear sum of the strengths of its minimal individual components is multiplied many times into the strength and stability of the whole system, which appears only as the dome is brought to completion as a living structure.

Having built normal houses, I can swear that to build by such principles is a radically unfamiliar experience and changes your consciousness. Even your routine awareness and trivial mistakes are of a new nature—of combination, permutation, and edge-effect. And I can't describe how at completion you're aware of a new form quickening under your hands, coming alive in a way unknown from usual building. But all dome-builders speak of this moment with awe and treat their domes as if they were creatures who could be kept in health or wounded.

23. Cognition begins in the body's action. Building a dome is a yoga, a stretch of action-road along which consciousness changes. The road's stations are the repeated failures of expectation and the incremental learning from each. No mystery: the lessons are quite specific. Time and again you design a member or place a prop from a long accumulating gut sense of what strength is necessary for support; or cramp your body to lean gingerly on a hub. Each time, your expectations prove to be gross or unnecessary, your anticipations are revealed as fearful. And what guides you shifts from a grasping for security toward a sense of the delicate power of wholeness.

24. From our experience in the physical world we derive the metaphors that undergird our understanding of all else. We were raised in a Way that taught us that hierarchies of importance, strong and weak members, were implicit in building. What would be the spontaneous politics and social constructions of children who played with struts instead of blocks and who early internalized a Way of building in which all components were equally essential, effort evenly distributed, and the power of each dependent on and multiplied by cooperation? Is the social image of a geodesic dome a society without strongmen?

SOCIAL DIMENSIONS OF DOME TECHNOLOGY

25. Down to Amerika, where the Government reports
that housing costs an average 20 to 25 per cent of
a family's reward for production. A family with kids
needs roughly 1,000 square feet of floor space. Conventional building technology costs begin at $17 to
$20 per square foot, labor included. The current
estimate is that 40 per cent of American families
cannot afford to own the cheapest new capitalist
home. Under our exchange system, such a home
costs roughly two and one-half years of an average
family's productive work. Financing in a profit
economy runs this to four and one-half to five years.
(Taxes and upkeep figure extra.) Cheap prefab
construction can bring these figures down to around
$12 per square foot and three years' work.

Geodesic buildings equally adequate to physical
needs, safe and aesthetic, cost less than $3 per
square-foot-equivalent for foundation, structure,
lofting, and utilities core. This is the cost of
materials. They are minimal, and the routines of
building are few, simple, and precise. Most are
easily hand-automated. So labor is greatly reduced.
And its nature is changed. A variety of specialists
and their skills are needed for a tract home, but
anyone defthanded can build a dome. Thus, even
given our present habits with space, an average
family can own a dome home for three-eighths of a
year of productive exchange for materials, plus
three-eighths of a man-year of its own labor in
building.

26. From any humane perspective of ecology or economics, our conventional building technologies are

enormously wasteful of materials and human work. Low-skill synergic construction technology makes radically more possible the vision of universal adequate housing in America. *Fact:* while our cities choke and rot, one year of the military budget could buy materials and land to house 40 million people well in geodesics—and also to train and pay the men in military servitude to build them within this period.

27. Such technology has political dimensions. It invites user design as well as construction, in each way severing dependence upon specialists and weakening involvement and support of the system built about them, the megamachine of the housing industry. Slashed capitalization requirements weaken user control by the economic system. Aesthetically, technically, financially, the living unit thus tends to self-determination. Geodesics are a clear example of a technology that empowers people to determine the conditions of their lives.

Any technology points such specific directions; who knows how deeply they already run in us? (I just flashed on where I first turned on to the possibilities of transparent plastics as a housing material. It was sometime after World War II. I was maybe seven. Donald Duck Comics came out with its first touch of science fiction, an issue devoted to the future and inspired by the imaginations of General Electric designers. Donald and his nephews wandered in a world of consumer wonder. Caught in a rainstorm, their host unfolded an infinitesimal square of clear plastic into a tent-umbrella. And I thought, *Wow, would I like to make a fort out of something like that* . . .) Assembled on modular principles and thus relatively reusable and portable, and permitting a greatly lessened proportional investment of work in housing, geodesics encourage our drift from being fixed in location to a semi-nomadic life-style more matched to a culture of changes.[8]

28. What do all these abstractions come to in this time of history? I am a young man with a lover and a child and friends now facing the choices that will determine our adult lives, and through them the reconstruction of our society. Low cost/skill synergic housing technology grants us radical mobility. After building the nursery, Karen and I know that we can move anywhere, anytime, and make ourselves a home adequate in space and grace for $2,000 worth of materials and a season's labor; and that a group can move together on such terms and easily build in a way that blends with whatever land receives us. Before this, the straight choice was to be tied to twenty years of payments at a rate that forced you to work at a steady "job," and all that implies. The only option was to build by yourself conventionally, by fragments, while working and renting. Those I know who tried this found the process occupying all of their life's "spare" time for three to five years and faced any further move reluctantly. So these new technologies free our life decisions from some heavy constraints.

29. Of course, it's not quite so simple and rosy. Weepy fingers of bamboo hide our nursery dome from the

[8] In the Tao, it is not Nomad *versus* Urb, but a balancing of motion and rest, each generating the other. Both as a utopic cultural projection and in the most immediate and tangible personal senses, we are seeking a Way of life which cycles harmoniously between travel and indwelling, between city and country, between community and isolation—and, beyond these to which material industry applies, is balanced in the polarities of engagement/retreat, creation/reception, etc.

roving search of the city building inspectors, cruising with the fleet of Berkeley police. For to live in a dome is to live beyond the Law—literally, since they are legal only out in country not subject to the Uniform Building Codes.

As with Simon Rodias' towers in Watts, the codes and inspectors comprehend neither the driving impulse nor the structural principles that flower into geodesic domes. Designed to guard human life, the codes base their expectations on cubic architecture and stud-and-beam construction and arbitrarily outlaw the accomplishments of a more efficient technology—and the social consequences of its wide adoption.

30. It's not simply a matter of being behind the times. The Law is not free to change. Great economic and political interests are vested in keeping the codes as they are. For lumber companies, the codes protect and enforce the profitable waste of the planet's dwindling forests. For the closed racist plumbers' and electricians' unions, with their $10 per hour wage scales, the codes outlaw use of the high-efficiency, light, flexible plastic piping and conduit that now make plumbing and wiring safe, accessible technologies to the handyman. Such relation of Law to the greedy interests of power is general throughout the construction industry, and to the uses of all other major technologies.

31. The growth of large, dense cities is isomorphic to the development of centralized political control: their populations are more manipulable, psychologically and physically. Today urban population density and authoritarian bureaucracy escalate in runaway feedback, heading for the explosive crisis already visible in the progressive breakdown of the

physical and social systems of New York City. In such a meta-stable ecology, one element of the dynamic is the protection of the technology that both makes the cities possible and dictates their forms, by the political and economic power systems that flourish within them. The skirmishing between dome-builders and building codes is a perfect example of how the decentralization of power comes into conflict with its organization into centralized forms. For a decentralized, mobile population, which radical housing technologies make possible, does not lend itself to systems of centralized control. Free up the codes! Power to the People!

EXTENDING THE DOME, IN SUFFICIENCY AND SOCIETY

32. At a commune in the California mountains they are building a methane generator for the thirty light homes among the trees. It will take their food and body wastes and yield them gas for heat, cooking, and light—they don't *like* electric light—plus good compost. The technology is adaptable for a one-family dome. Depending upon the ecology of the location, a more ample *energy-independence* could come by supplementing this with generators powered by water or wind; by solar cells, expensive but elegant; or by another technology of sun-energy, like a steam generator run by a Mylar parabolic reflector. Such sources would feed a sophisticated battery storage system—a moderate investment, until the technology involved gets better. But even now, tied to a small system of reconditioned auto batteries, they could supply current for light, the

low-drain appliances made possible by sophisticated
electronics technology, and occasional heavier
power use, like washing-machine or soldering-iron.
Decent steam-generator technology would make
heavy-power independence ecologically sound in
tended forest land. It is available by dirty tools already, portable and within the reach of group
means.

33. I hope next spring to build a living model of a
family-sized dome which will be a literal green-
house. Inside, the quality of the light will be diffuse,
the shadows edged with translucent green from the
sunlight filtering through steam, condensed between
two-foot-spaced plastic skins, and through the garden whose moist roots bedded in clear perforated
cradles will inscribe the dome in hydroponic lati-
tudes and longitudes. And at the pole, sunset will
gather distilled in the reservoir below the solar still.

Within the skins of a thirty-foot dome will fit
2,000 square feet of garden, under intensive hydroponic cultivation. Polyethylene breathing panels on
the outer skin will exchange new and used air. How
many gallons of water cycle through a tomato's
growth? Here the water, circulated by hand or
power, will be retained within an almost-closed
system, making the dome desert-suitable. The nutrient input will be regulated; it will come from
methane-generator compost plus chemical supple-
ments—supplied by an industry replacing the
present life-destroying fertilizer and insecticide industries. No doubt about it, they can be retooled, if
production and distribution are freed to follow the
people instead of bind them.

Such a large dome-system, perhaps extended by
a ground-level closed system using special films to
trap solar energy for more rapid growth, if artfully

cultivated could support the people living within it, at least if they were vegetarians. To build and run it for a year would add $500 to basic dome cost. After that, running costs would be very low, at most $200 per year. What living in this relation of completion with the rituals of their food might do to their heads can only be imagined.

34.   Myself, I like meat. I want to raise sweet fluffy rabbits and kill them with my bare hands, after their idyllic lives in a closed-system hydroponic pasture.

What makes me squeamish is to buy red slabs wrapped in cellophane at the Stupormarket. With meat-processing as with television, we try by technology to divorce ourselves from the wheel of life and death. But it goes on, indifferent to our machineries, which may in turn be used indifferently to extend our perceptions or to numb them. There is choice in the matter. And I don't believe that the alternative to buying a roast of numbness for dinner is to retreat to the purity of stone-ground wheat and stone-age technology.

What is destroying us is not our technology but the *divisions* we use it to extend. We need to be *reconnected,* not divorced from our machines too, our outered bodies. A plant has its awareness and spirit too, like a rabbit: we cannot live save by killing some principle of life. As long as that's true, good refrigeration makes sense. And so does learning how it operates, as part of the process of healing our divisions. One way for us to begin is to get straight with what we eat. Another is to reconnect with our machines as our extensions and to become involved with all aspects of our basic life-support technologies, reengineering them as necessary in the process.

35.   Many now make such designs. By a variety of tech-

nological routes and changes in disposition, the path is being explored toward dwellings that are both adequate and independent as full life-support systems: space, heat, power, water, food, the whole works; and that grace and reintegrate the lives lived within them. Taken together and with a good deal of hustling, and of course illegally, the technologies now popularly accessible give you or me the power to experiment with a first version of this Way, a light technological power-complex adaptable to home in almost any terrain and sufficiently sunny climate.

36. Image of domes and other eclectic construction spread out across the land, discrete beneath the oaks, dug-in on the prairies, sanctuaries in the badlands. Local materials, local traditions of design, adapted to place and microculture. Managed forests tended for plywoods and nth-generation plastics, manufactured in forms for consumer use and equitably distributed. Even the present technologies of skin and foam plastics and ferroconcrete are less wasteful than the structural practices of cities.

We have developed one of mankind's most magnificent machineries, the chemical industry, toward high art. Understanding the Ways of chemical form and synthesis, with increasing skill we can tailor molecules to explicit design needs. So far such powerful art has been turned to the cheek of Profit, its chiefest accomplishment the creation of miracle fabrics for shoddy uses. Were profit sufficient, this tool could equally be turned to creating a wood/cellulose-based industry of plastics, systematically biodegradable, whose range of properties would include and extend those of present-generation plastics. Who knows, such an industry might become sophisticated enough to draw its materials directly from sun, water, and air—the plants manage, and we are studying their Ways. But within this century, a first version of an ecologically sound and materially liberating housing industry is easily possible by changing our technical priorities and laws.

37.   If our society felt free to make this change, it would also feel free to let the manufacture and distribution of such an industry fall into the natural form of the local plant operating in balance with the resources of a terrain and the uses of the population that operates and is served by it. Such a model points away from centralized control systems toward a scheme of locally centralized facilitation of the needs of freedom. For such an industry, the forms of technology still leave room for many ways of co-operation more free than those of our control culture.

38.   Involvement of the community in determining the conditions of life begins in satisfaction of basic needs—in shared local decisions about the plastics plant and its relation to local housing. Universal linkage and free access to computer technology can qualitatively change the handling of social data and enable radical democratization of the information upon which decision-making is based.[9] So can extending involvement inward from the plastics plant, perhaps to the point where each citizen's training includes a period of work in local basic-support industry and practical learning from early on in such industrial arts, including their mechanical aspects. Outward from the plant, involvement extends to broader cooperations of local units, as necessary for a process of basic industrial development/manufacture, which in turn makes local sufficiency possible.

[9] See numbers 90 and 94 below.

From such a wide popular base of industrial acquaintance and self-determination, intimately linked by high communications technology, priorities and decisions can evolve through democratic systems, rather than through the Yang forms of the economy of profit and ignorance.

A HIGHLY ABSTRACT DIGRESSION

39. The present forms of our productive relationships are governed by the tendency to concentrate power and centralize control. Their development took place within a class society, guided by the interests of private power, during a period when material technologies were more limited in scope, spectrum, and amplification of human effort. Such factors contribute to the organization of our relationships of work/power/communications/control in hierarchical patterns of a general mode I will call α—in contrast to the patterns of mode β, which underlie democratic experience. (See diagram, next page.)

Work within mode α forms is more efficient than within mode β forms, in terms of material accomplishment per unit time—making them attractive and perhaps essential to a culture that must deal with human survival on the edge of material scarcity. Systems of type β are, however, less prone to make mistakes, more flexible in responding to the unexpected, pleasanter to work within, and not experienced as fundamentally oppressive.[10]

40. Like the Tao-mandala, such diagrams are devices

[10] Such generalizations start from controlled experiments with problem-solving in small groups and extend by observation up the scale of social size.

work/power/communications/control in hierarchical
patterns of a general mode I will call α --
in contrast to the patterns of mode β, which
underlie democratic experience:

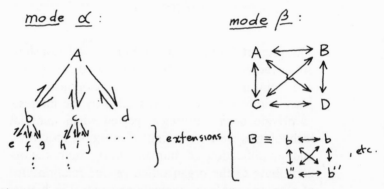

mode α:

mode β:

} extensions {

Here arrows signify relative degrees of influence; and
the letters may be taken to signify persons, groups,
organizations, etc. All real systems display some balance of these modes, constantly changing somewhat
-- for example, clerks b,c and d in A's store do talk
among themselves.
               Given our schooling, few people
find such abstract diagrams easy or natural to work
with. Yet graphics are a powerful tool of thought, a
habit worth exploring; and these particular figures
will be repeatedly referred to later in this essay.

for evoking and focusing conceptual consciousness. As α is a restricted case of β, it associates with a more limited field of concepts. The properties of these figures stem from their topology—more precisely, from their connectivity. Consider the flow of information in these differing modes, as A emits it, the others respond, B(b) emits it, the others respond:

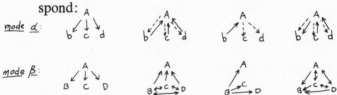

Here broken lines indicate information received and retransmitted, and thus subject to blockage, delay and distortion. *The connectivity of figure α ensures and expresses the existence of privileged positions of control and power, which vanish in the play of symmetries of figure β.*[11] On the other hand, if you count the arrows, remembering that broken lines represent weaker interactions, the totals for the two sequences reflect the common experience that democracy takes about twice as long.

41. The organization of social relationships through such modes is connected at the deepest levels with the authoritarian and democratic tendencies of a culture's psychology and politics. Yet the balance of their expression is in part constrained by material

[11] Systems of type α operate in fundamental imbalance in the tao of leading/following, of affecting/receiving, and so on. It seems clear that when concentration of power/energy/information/control becomes the permanent rather than transient condition of privileged nodes in a system —the condition I have referred to as "centralization" throughout—experience within it becomes isolated and fragmented, Divided. When the tao of accumulation/dispersion operates freely among all nodes and through time, the system operates in mode β, and experience within it feels balanced in Division and Connection. Check it out.

circumstances. Richer technology, in investing us with more than enough power to survive and multiplying the uses of our energy, enables us to shift the balance from α toward β. It does not accomplish that change, nor our choosing to attempt it. But an ample technology in harmonious use is a necessary condition of the democratization of existence.

TECHNOLOGY AND EDUCATION

42.   All real vision about technology begins in two facts: 1) Today, for the first time, we have the capacity to feed, house, etc., all mankind, adequately.[12] 2) And we aren't doing it.

Such statements have become trite, irritating, and wearisome to us, perhaps because we're the first people to live within so fully developed a social contradiction about our material circumstances. To the extent that it does not greatly oppress our minds and spirits at the dinner table, we are numbed in the deep reaches.

Until this contradiction is resolved, we cannot be said to have begun to realize the possibilities of social reconstruction opened by our technology. The direction of reconstruction is inherent in its necessary process: a moving toward full, self-determined empowerment, down to the individual level and within, in all of the basic ways necessary to human survival and flowering.

This is also the potential of our present tech-

---

[12] This fact is being extensively documented now by the players of Buckminster Fuller's *World Game*.

nology. Those who weary early of the possibilities of the Machine should remember that it has not yet been put to the service of making all people materially free, and freeing their imaginations for its furthering uses.

43. So long as there is hunger and the terror of material oppression, the basic style of our culture will be authoritarian. At this point of tension facing our revealed potentials, the cycles of exploitation that define our lives and cripple our energies depend upon the imprisonment of technology. For their survival, our systems of centralized power must limit and control technology in such a way that its potential benefits and empowerment are not realized by most people.

For this to be possible, people must be kept from not only the means but the knowledge necessary to use technology. From this imperative of exploitation spring strong forces that shape and maintain the fragmentary structure of our systems of knowledge and the processes of our specialist education, as well as the unwieldy forms of our industrial machineries. All these function to isolate people from technological power. *The demystification of technology, the propagation of knowledge and means for its use at the popular level, are essential strategies of struggle against repressive centralized power, and are key to the democratization of technological society.*

44. How degrading it is, and how bewildering, to deal with technology in a class society. The refrigerator dies, I kick it, it stays dead. Hey, the refrigerator's dead! Call the refrigerator man. The man comes; his smile is like an ice tray. I have to summon up all my casualness to ask him how a . . . relay? . . .

works, and he's not in a mood to chat. We don't learn anything from each other; our transaction is as bloodless as the brick dinner steak.

They divided our functions early, for the sake of the productive economy in its most convenient organization for profit. My sisters learned to invisibly eat their envy at the way my brother and I felt free to experiment with our hands. In high school they offered welding, but I never thought of taking it—nor did anyone I knew who was being prepped for the employment of the mind. Higher education refined the divisions further. I did my undergraduate work in theoretical physics. Our specialized texts helped us encourage each other to feel ourselves a class distinct from those physics majors interested in the experimental face of the art. So I enjoyed my ignorance of their practical skills of electronics and observation; and they refused to learn the funkier language and notation of the electrical engineers, to whom they in turn felt superior.

45.   Now, each time I successfully mess with the carburetor, diagnose the dog, or rig a transistor device to rip off long-distance phone calls, I get a surge of the peculiar freeing energy that comes from transcending the limits, and hence the condition, of my social class. The state is more than one of empowerment: it has a sharply existential edge.

In our organization around the uses of systematic knowledge, from physics to psychology each technology is divided into its aspects, and each aspect is assigned to a class of people whose identity it defines and shapes—the essence of megamachine. The profile of one's relations with the major technologies, productive and other, determines one's caste uniquely. To practice an out-caste technological skill opens one to all the qualities common to the caste(s) "owning" that skill. (A gross example of the process: you can't get on a motorcycle without experiencing a flood of images from films and advertisements.) In a culture in which people know themselves by what they can do, the inward effect is of an opening of the identity. What you know about your capacities and potential becomes unknown and broader. You enter the livening state of the Nameless.

Now Karen is helping my younger sister learn to drive. She who was always so fearful of machines, now so ripe in her changes for road-freedom, to move under her own power to visit her distant friends and follow her desire on the beaches.

46. Essential to the repression of change is our culture's great mystification about technologies. In our mythology, civilization and its technologies—physical and political—are so complex that no one can understand many of the means that determine his life-conditions or share their practice or control. Each is made mysterious, its power kept from common distribution. Nor is the mystification innocent: it functions in the service of social control. With the physical as with the social technologies, to be ignorant is to be manipulable, and to be unempowered is to be subject to control by outside and greedy forces. Because I don't know how to repair my car and "haven't the time" or capital for the right tools, the auto companies buy laws and the government to guard the waste of production and the earth in deliberate obsolescence.

47. It is essential to understand that our relationships with technology need not be as fragmentary as our culture has determined them. Anyone can learn to rebuild a car. The principles of the lightbulb, the

laser, and the sun are simple and deep, and open to view: God is not secretive. How can I put it, with the resonance of vision in these stiff words? I believe it's possible for each person to comprehend all the essential technologies of our present lives; and, given the means and need, be able to muster any in its use. And I think that any large vision of humanity's reintegration through social reconstruction must include this vision of pan-technological literacy and competence, and in fact depends on it.

48.   What hinges on this face of technology is our image of man. The mystification that the ways of the Machine are arcane and difficult and few are suited to them stands against the image of man as a creature whose impulse is toward the embracing of All, whose capacities are larger than his tools, and whose future is open. Against the backdrop of our age, this image is not a "rational" one. It requires an act of faith to project. For by the technological mystification, as by the political, your mind is left unable to grasp what has been done to it and how your imagination has been castrated.

Like the political, the technological mystification begins to break only through new experience and changed behavior. The walls are thin now, and it's possible for many individuals to transcend significant limits of their technological condition. But our culture's mystification will not be broken until each citizen's education is reformed, in content and process, to enable him to participate fully in our technologies, and their material forms are reshaped to suit this.

Such reformation is deeply political. A superficial example: the mystique about black people's lower technical capabilities will not break until the schools and the economy open to integrate them into the technical professions. (Not that black ABM technicians are to be desired per se . . .)

49. At the heart of any new technological politics must lie intimate vision. From my experience, I believe it is possible to raise a child into a new relation with technology, comprehensive, integrated, and harmonious, and that the technology we call technological education can be radically re-created for this. As yet my vision of this is too raw and new to sort out its parameters, I know only that such accomplishment must be collective. But its centering icon is for me the image of our son lying on the floor, discovering geometry with his fist and watching me build above him the butterfly of new geodesic power, while I sing him mantras about Plato and the Perfect Forms.

50. When I was seven, my mother convinced my father to move out from the urban core toward the edge of the country. I grew up in woodsy Fairfax, medium-north of San Francisco. At night the deer wandered down from the oaks to eat our tomatoes, so we pickled them green. During schooltime recess, in the freedom bought by my father's riding the growing freeways to work, I went out looking for lizards.

Dad was a jewish communist quick with his hands and his rational mind, who taught me to turn over rocks to see what was hidden beneath them. He was also a city-boy intellectual who knew from nothing about houses. We bought an absolute leaky lemon of obsolete sub-code-standard construction. And over a decade of work and family hassle rebuilt it from top to bottom. As I went to bed, I saw him hunched over the midnight dining table, studying the government pamphlet on how to do electric wiring. And over slow afternoon years helping him,

I learned how to shingle and sheetrock, plumb and stud, and care for the tools that gave us some power to change things. Then I went off to college, to be groomed for the high priesthoods of our age: after nuclear physics I did four years' graduate work in the best mathematics department. In the end, all that saved me was the coincidence of historical contradiction breaking open, and the impulses of my upbringing in a humane Marxism.

51.　Looking back, it is obvious yet astounding how my experience with housing shaped my young life, defined the broader House into whose shapes I grew during the critical years from seven to sixteen.

What was imprinted in me was less fragmentary than the practical opening of many skills, and deeper than a sense of the necessities of craft. I learned in action that I am as Man is, a tool-using animal, and that the ways of technology are open to learning and use: that I am capable, and thus basically empowered. And the process of my learning was precisely this: I watched and questioned and imitated a person who was himself good at learning, and who was learning an ordered set of things in a new context and in response to necessity. It was essential for the depth and way I was affected that he was not a specialist of skilled routine, but an amateur learning newly and rawly, in trial and failure.

The experience also developed my senses of structure, form and process, more deeply and organically than the schools ever dared attempt. For the rebuilding of a house engages productive energies in grand and minor cycles of destruction, beginning, ordering, and completion, around elemental needs of survival and grace. A grown man now, writing this I recognize how, like anyone, I have come to conceive the task of social reconstruction, the Rebuilding of our House, in terms of the child-metaphors of my most intimate learning, of leading the copper river up from the foundations to flower into light.

I was fortunate to have shared a relatively complete experience of transformation in relation to housing. I wonder how the experience of growing up in a succession of anonymous tract homes produced by unseen hands, or in the dying cities, empty-handed, shapes people's root conceptions of social reconstruction and its possibilities.

52. My experience with housing wasn't all harmonious: we carried on our culture's tortured heritage. The women did not share the building save in the customary indirect ways; so my mother hassled with the continual mess of construction and my sisters grew with their hands' powers Mandarin-bound. My parents, for all their politics and warmth, acted out the icon of conflictful division programmed into our culture: man as provider and doer, whose peace is the action of work; woman as manager of the home unit and environment, whose peace is work's termination and whose standards are shaped—even more than his, perhaps because of her relative technological impotence—by the consumer economy of overuse. Thus even within our family developed the bad politics of a scene in which users are at the mercy of technical specialists, and in which the priorities of construction aren't determined by the builders.

Nor were priorities so determined beyond the home: much of our labor to bring things up to code was functionally unnecessary. And even though

Dad was a labor journalist who covered the construction trades and well understood the politics of the codes' obsolescence, he never thought seriously of cutting more than a hidden minor corner illegally. In part, his docility came from his unsureness in a still-new sport and the inaccessible investments of capital and time that experiment in it required. But mostly it came from his being in this, as in all ways of his conduct save the political, essentially obedient to the laws and mores of our authoritarian systems, out of fear.

53.   When the impetus of collective political action freed me from the university, it was to pursue learning differently. My experience as a student and young teacher, in and out of the technological orbit, led me to study afresh how people learn what they need, and how to restructure education around this, as essential to social change. Looking back only recently over the stuff the tides of poetry bring up and leave on the beaches, I discover this image of how I learned at my old man's hands.

Even flawed, it seems to present an essential model for the way in which education—the process of learning the full wheel of our technologies, material and other—may be reconceived as a process of continual regeneration, of beginning again. Its Way is learning to learn by the light of example, of competent learners learning newly. Its medium is growing participation in a shared task, of rich form and completion and metaphorical substance, organized around real needs and broad in its human dimensions. Its working-out can begin at any point in human space, our lives, where technology faces upon major needs.

This isn't the whole recipe. But even from these

few principles, it is clear that to remake (technological) education is to remake our lives, radically
and comprehensively, into a context in which the
young grow surrounded by example of experiment
and risk in transcending our condition.

> So pick up that hammer,
> pick up that gun,
> pick up the flute,
> let's have some fun.

DOME CODA

54. Now I crouch in my outlaw dome, writing these
notes under butterfly wings that redden with the
smog-hyped sunset, while Karen builds the shed
into a craftsroom. Perhaps a shade more liberated
than our parents—if so, in part by new technology
and social conditions, in part by an effort of the will.
I bring water to the bamboo, which grows to shelter
the dome from the street and with luck will cover
the top before the city inspectors take to cruising
with the fleet of helicopters now proposed for the
police. We have given up on the government; we are
becoming guerrillas of life in an Amerika of death,
outlaws in the technological wilderness. Let me tell
you, there is nothing like standing under a heli-
copter as it swoops down to begin its gassing run to
inspire one with new vision. Most young people I
know who want to *use* technology would cheerfully
rip it off from any institution they could, and some
manage to.

55.   If the nursery survives, the ferns will grow through their cycles of frond and spore above our son's bed, refreshing his air, and generations of water dogs will pass through their larval stages in the vinyl-cupped ecology drawn from the local ponds. I'll get someone to rip me off a good microscope, strong enough to watch their sperm dance and to penetrate the nuclei of our flesh, and we'll learn some things.

And I will tell him the fairy tales of our age. How each life, plant or animal, grows from a word in a language that, within my lifetime, we've started to learn to read and to construct. And how his some-day children may live in houses written from this genetic language in a Yin script: full living creatures, exquisitely adapted to live in symbiosis with man and supply his needs of space and shelter, temperature and food, water and clothing. Taping a jury-rigged oscilloscope onto bean sprouts, we'll study how different music or anger in the room changes their electrical moods and dream about how Man and House will feel about each other.

And if the building inspector comes, that too will be a lesson our son will someday understand.

GOLEM: HIS PEDAL EXTENSION

56.   My grandmother always called the automobile "the Machine," and surely it is the problem-child of our age. There are already too many words about it. But what the hell.

What interests me is how reluctant I feel to pick up hitchhikers, despite my belief that this modest act is now one of the more important ways in which we extend a community of sharing. But my spirit is seldom free for this. Usually it is out of balance with my condition—assaulted by information and encounters, all kinds of technologically augmented stress—and seeks each scrap of privacy in time and space for equilibrium.

57.   A bicycle extends the foot. A motorcycle extends it more and extends the eyes, voice, and circulatory/metabolic/respiratory systems as well, along lines modeled more fully by "lower" life forms. A car extends all these and extends one as an integral skinned structure also. Cars (planes, trains, etc.) are thus unique in kind as pedal extensions: they have achieved a first degree of completion; they are mobile Houses.

The course of their evolution is already indicated in their popular elaboration into travel-homes. As features like skin-centered temperature systems develop, they tend toward primary functional completion. As inertial guidance systems, car stereos, and automatic headlights develop, the mobile extension of the sensory system becomes a primitive extension of the system of memoried intelligence. In war, the mobile House has already developed a step further —its present apex is ICBM/Apollo, with functions under unified control by an independent computer intelligence, directed toward externally programmed goals. From here the step to auto-reproduction is relatively small in kind; and my grandmother's Machine advances on a line of evolution that converges at some distant point with that of the Living Houses genetic technology may create.

58.   As Housing, automotive technology is subject to broad rethinking, especially in its aspects of Protection and Space.

Space is many things to us, and our needs and grasping are as intense about it as about material things. In fear of the Void we are driven to want; we strive, we acquire, and in this generate the destruction of our satisfaction, so that the substance of the object fades and leaves us to want again—not differently, but more. Likewise we armor ourselves with space, in privacies often brutalized in the moment of their achievement by the concomitants of the technologies that make them possible. And I ride invaded by shame I cannot shake off, passing the hitchhiker whose eyes and need I refuse to meet.

59. The shame is for my imbalance, not for my own need. For our dependence upon private space, or at least space alone, is a fact as well as a problem, as communes find when unbalanced communal enthusiasm and limited means pack them to choke on the poisons of living too closely together.[13] (Clearly, adequate housing technology is essential to any broad social experimenting with the family group.)

Culture-wide, our needs for space and things are frozen into our greed for their exclusive control; and the operations of profit organize our industrial technologies unrelentingly around private rather than common uses. Thus develop the car and its gross

[13] Every new work- or living-group now re-explores the tao of private/ shared as it structures architectural and social space. The first tendency generally is to overreact against the Yang, as by leaving no one private space or time. But balance takes realistic account of our animal territorial needs.

The matter of "property" is an exercise in the tao of holding/letting-go. Grasping it as personal armor against the Void, we are frozen in Yang attitude. But the children of the Bomb are coming to new terms. Raised vulnerable among radical abundance, we grow toward valuing objects for their beauty and use and being less reluctant to pass them on. An unpossessive psychology of property appeared in the Haight and spreads.

undersystem of freeways, rather than communal transportation systems. If people could ride pullman compartments on airplanes they would. The engineering to divide cars or buses reversibly into private quiet compartments is simple, cheap, and need-satisfying. Yet their design to make company feel intrusive is profitable, for it floods the bridges with stressed commuters who would rather ride alone before they suffer at the office. Breathing the smog, they complain about how technology's killing us.

60.   Most car travel, short and long, is solo.

Cars with their Housing re-engineered. A system of strategic traffic-exchanges, where lanes sort cars past pausing-places where people gather for destinations. A custom of pausing to pick up and drop off, driver or passenger each as private as he wishes, minimal effort or bother. Maybe some standard distance-fare if it comes to that. No personal sacrifices, no massive industrial revamping, all quite feasible; it could cut in half the cars needed for our present habits.

Already we see a first image of this Way of using automotive technology in the hitching habits and places of the nomad young, as these are developing around San Francisco Bay. And already the State moves to outlaw this practice. For such a transformation of a technology cannot come without broad change in values, from greedy to those that go with our needs being more satisfied by being of live service to others.

61.   I keep circling back toward Profit, and why not? In its aspect of Mobility, the car was engineered around the internal combustion engine and its poi-

sonous dependence upon dead fuels. We owe that decision to Profit. It is only natural that those who ransack tombs for gold would be careless with the old warnings that we must deal with purifying care with what comes from the world of the Dead.

In the car's early development, external-combustion steam power was as useful as gasoline, in terms of results. Steam machines were simpler of design, more easily user-maintainable, and burned unspecialized fuels more completely. For the sake of profit their development was abandoned. Interests in heavy industry and natural resources purchased the Government and the popular imagination, and forced our priorities to a power-technology more costly in all ways.

Through such perverse progresses we have become dependent upon technologies whose requirements dictate our exploitive relationships with other men and the earth. The domestic politics and foreign politics of Oil furnish a dramatic example.

Whenever the development of technology is guided by and for the uses of centralized power, rather than of people's full self-determination, the course will be similar.

62. In giving us the choice of extending our powers, cars make limiting them a matter of choice also. We are not good at this. So we use cars in ways that make walking hard and generate the need for more cars. The ecology of our motion moves in destructive spirals through unbalanced extension. At the center, choking and sedentary, the human body dies with its spirit.

In a communist society with a healthy ecology of transport, a trip by extended motion system would look like this:

Cars, collectivized to match the customs, would reside at the traffic exchanges. Around these would extend neighborhood systems of bikes and their thoroughfares, redesigned to accommodate multiple riders, babies, packages, etc., and terminating in the (unlocked) block bike-rack. The operation and distribution of bikes, cars, and their stations would be designed to satisfy not only local mobility needs, but the needs of health of the bodies using them. And custom would follow ecological suit. One's *av. daily min. req.* of cycling (or equivalent muscle activity) would be a matter of common knowledge and practice; and the spacing of houses, stores, and car-stations would in turn be designed around it.

Such a technology of person-transport would revolutionize short travel; the materials/energy it consumes would be reduced by a factor of ten. New habits plus re-engineered power could do the same for long travel. In neither case would our personal capacities be diminished in any way.

63. Our habits, mainly, make technology wasteful. The bicycles of Amerika, if collectivized, would provide for half mankind. The contradictions of a capitalist economy of abundance are amazing. Why do we laugh when we hear that tests show you can get around in most towns about as fast by bicycle as by car? Is it because car-streets are the main components of cities, occupying more space than the buildings, and we cannot imagine what we'd do with them if we banned all but delivery auto traffic, as the

Goodman brothers long ago proposed for Manhattan?

We spend $60–$80 billion a year on automotive technology (some $15 per injury). Yearly model changes account for 25 per cent of new-car price, some $6 billion of this. Common ownership and ride-sharing would reduce the remainder by one half to two-thirds. Rational speed limits and vehicle redesign for twice the life, half the weight, and simplicity of repair would reduce this in half again— that is, to 15 to 22 per cent of the present figure. (All this is without guessing in the results of conversion to a different energy-technology or to lightweight impact-oriented structural forms, more plastic than metal.) My figures may be a bit optimistic, but any serious computation will demonstrate that, given the present structure of highways, we're wasting roughly as much per year on cars as we did for the whole Vietnam war—and for much the same reasons at heart.

GOLEM: HER LOWER NERVOUS SYSTEM (DISTANCE-INDEPENDENT COMMUNICATION AND DECENTRALIZATION)

64. A higher form of public utility than transportation is the telephone, which extends the nervous system through the ear and by its electric web helps link us into a common yet highly decentralized body. By its nature, the phone network demands construction and operation as a unified whole, around local needs that are everywhere fairly evenly distributed. Once such a network is established, distance essentially

vanishes as a factor in communication through it. If it is regarded as integral, rather than as divided into arbitrary "local" and "long-distance" components, the real cost of any call depends mainly on time. Thus this technology's natural social embedding is as a free-access network maintained through the state, or in an unsocialized economy through a uniform time-use tax.

Here we have nothing of the sort: access is not a function of need, and accumulated power enjoys more of the system's benefits at a sharply preferential rate. Economically and politically, this technology is regulated by the Government for private profit. The social contradictions inherent in this scheme are so blatant that no corporate body in Amerika is so universally hated as the phone company. Thus its "property" meets the people in an interface of theft. The very codes that give business and other powers access to the network's more highly organized potentials are easily stolen, liberated for general access (as through publication in underground papers). As it becomes more sophisticated, the power of phone technology will become even less guardable, *given sufficient technical knowledge among the people at large*. (Even a visually transmitted thumbprint access code could be ripped off and spread around by photograph or videotape.)

65. If the Government didn't outlaw free use of technology, the contradictions maintained by private power would be unprotected and would diminish by our cooperation.

Consider the Wide Area Telephone Service the Phone Company offers to businesses. A WATS line costs $2,500 a month, for which you can call anywhere in Amerika twenty-four hours a day. Form a public corporation. Rent five WATS lines, run them through a storefront switchboard into cozy booths. Total cost for rent/operation/administration: $450/day for 120 hours of person-to-person calls across the nation—at three-quarters use, that's 8¢ a minute. In contrast, Bell charges you 45¢/a minute during the day, half that at night, plus $2 for person-to-person.

What matters is less finance than how we are enabled to change our ways. You won't rap for half an hour today with your brother in Detroit, it would cost you $13.50. Tomorrow the People's Phone Ripoff would charge you $2.40. Would you have a cup of tea while waiting in line for that, or sign up on a list while downtown shopping? On your left will be a room with cushions; a little black box— with $40 worth of components, some friends of mine are selling it—that lets you and five people anywhere talk with each other simultaneously; and a cheaper gadget that amplifies conversation into the whole room. At certain hours your family or group can use this room to talk in conference with groups in any five other cities, for the collective price of $24 per hour (less apiece for three hours than a movie).

Many scattered groups of people might talk together: organizers at Army bases and G.I. coffee-shops, free universities, black militants in the industrial unions, blind people and old people, Krishna chanters and musicians—all have their reasons, and would discover more if they had the chance. Or consider a media scenario: Each day reporters from the six main underground papers and radio stations in the San Francisco Bay Area meet together orally with their counterparts in five other major metropolitan areas. For an hour a day of live news-sharing and three on Sunday, each enterprise would be charged $27 a month.[14]

66. The force of this rustic example must be understood in the light of the conversion of phone technology to videophone, now a decade away if advertising and avarice hold true. This fuller medium—extending the eye, our principal information sense—will be as accessible to simple public invention (and doubtless as thoroughly guarded from it by Ma Bell and Uncle Sam).

An image for 1984. You are sitting in the People's Videophone Office with a number of others, sprawled on low cushions in a soft room, drinking and smoking. On each of the four walls you see, life-sized and in color, into another room somewhere. Your five groups are meeting together, for about $30 an hour.[15]

67. Brought within common means, such technology of group communications has revolutionary implications for the forms of political, social, and economic organization that depend upon group cooperation.

[14] With one black box, six room amplifiers, and any five-button phone, such a media cooperative could today be organized overnight for a per-hour total cost of $15 a city. Within a month it could be expanded to integrate all urban underground news media in a live news pool running three hours a night—moderated by regional switching-stations through which any group anywhere could phone in to share the electric space. In times of crisis, instant transcontinental news-sharing, picked up and rebroadcast by three hundred simultaneous transmitters, legal or illegal, linking millions—quicker than network television, and independent.

[15] To run this sub-system will cost roughly R times as much as the telephone example, where

$$R = \frac{\text{future cost of local videophone call}}{\text{present cost of local phone call}}$$

After amortization of the system's conversion and stabilization of higher operating costs—i.e., within two decades—and disregarding inflation, R will likely be less than two.

Roughly speaking, if such technology extends fully to the neighborhood level, *these forms of our organizing become distance-independent.*[16] This condition is precisely achieved when any person or group has refusable access to any other through unrestricted use of a *vivid* communications system—one in which transmitted sense impressions cannot be distinguished from present ones by the unaided senses. Vividness in eye and ear is achievable by extension of present technologies (holograms, ear-baffled microphones and speakers); the other senses will require new means, presently conceivable.

We are still at the mercy of physical distance, which forces us to abstract our broader relationships and conduct them through centralized intermediating agencies. The authoritarian forms of our educational system and our political agencies reflect this equally. To the extent that a communications technology is vivid, ample, free, and distance-canceling, it is an essential technology for enabling the democratic socialization of decision-making and learning processes. In this is reflected its nature as a collective nervous extension. And the fuller glory of our development along this technological line will be realized only as, through it, our politics, our learning, our industrial invention, etc., are transformed into fully decentralized and self-determined processes.

68.   In this transformation, our patterns of connection

[16] Even in their present crippled forms, radio and television are instrumental in the ecology of our transformation toward distance-independent social organization. The electronic impact of the early southern civil rights movement was vital to the appearance of the New Left. For a slower example: these media's economies, in harmony with the system of mass consumption, find convenient our division and segregation along lines of age, ethnic group, productive class, and so on, rather than geography. Across the nation this ghettoization by radio dial and TV program eliminates place as a factor in culture.

are transformed from the hierarchical mode α to the democratic mode β.

Our mass communications media have the potential to further either mode. Diagramming the present embedding of television technology, in the manner of page 216, we see that the forces which focus through a station operate strongly and directly upon a captive audience whose isolated reactions feed back indirectly and weakly. The α-mode of this technology operates in harmony with its politico-economic function: to manipulate individuals in the interests of centralized power. Again the pattern of Government "regulation" bought by private profit appears, shining most vividly in ATT's satellite privileges. And again on the most intimate levels of our neural networks are imprinted patterns of hierarchical control, which in turn shape our thought and action and through these are perpetuated in the world.

69. Radio offers another example of constraint of a technology's type β potentials. Here regulation "in the public interest" might have divided the airways to encourage a multitude of low-power local broadcasting units, perhaps with open local access. Instead, Government and industry worked together to make the electromagnetic spectrum a private rather than a public utility; on the whole broadcasting has become a privilege bought by high capital accumulation and sustained by its reinforcement of the consumer economy. (Some semi-open broadcasting frequencies do exist under looser regulation; but equipment costs, the general mystification of technology, and passivity inhibit their popular use.)

70. In the present operation of these mass media, the tao of affecting/being affected is frozen in imbal-

ance, almost all Yang to the central controllers of programming.

Yet, already, through the dialectic of change, counter-examples are developing. Talk-back radio appears; to the extent to which its calls are unedited and its "jockey" unobtrusive, it represents a pure type β network. (Its talk and the hiring and firing of its jockeys tend to revolve around political matters.) Now San Francisco moves to establish video cameras at neighborhood locations. Their first use would be to coordinate neighborhood "town meetings" with those of the city government through the community-supported educational TV station. To the extent that the mayor is silent and the supervisors responsive, this approaches a type β system. In such ways is expressed the straining within us for decentralized forms of political involvement and the β-mode patterns of communication that support them, as these open through technology.

71. The radical potentials of video technology are barely opened. The transformation in the perceptions of the young occasioned by growing up in contact with new sensory technology is only the first of the shock-waves of change locked up in the Tube.

Unthinking disciples of McLuhan—that cold man and political innocent—are gross materialists. They tell us it's all in Golem's body, that technology changes our heads by changing primary *quantities* like our sense ratios and mobility. They see the transformational effects of technology as implicit in its material aspect and independent of the style and politics of its use. That's bullshit: the role of video in maintaining the ecology of consumer passivity is the most immediate counter-example.

THE PERIODICITIES OF CHANGE

Before discussing the democratizing potentials of video, I want to consider the personal and social dynamics of technological impact. I'm convinced that this subject[17] is essential to understanding the process of change in technological society. Much of what I have to say relates back to Chapter IV. I say it here because collective adaptation to change proceeds, in its psychic aspect, largely through our media of communication, our outered nervous system; and new technology opens new potentials for relating individual changes coherently.

72. As ordered knowledge, whether or not embodied in mechanical devices, gives rise to new programs of behavior, a new technology becomes embedded in society. Each aspect of this embedding—political, educational, economic, etc.—is consonant with every other: the technology is a harmonious chord played on the instrument of the culture. Though its harmony may be malignant, it is always integral. Yet it is not fixed: each technology's elements can be reharmonized in many ways.

73. Like a chord plucked on a rich instrument of unexpected resonances, each new technology spreads, swells, reharmonizes others, achieves some living balance, and eventually dies. (Consider the curling iron, macrobiotics.) And the instrument itself is in constant change, transforming itself under the touch of the music played upon it. As the tempo mounts,

[17] Which we also gropingly identify as "cultural diffusion"; see below, Chapter VIII.

it lurches, trying to move in clumsy dance to the
energy coursing through it. Its keys reach back like
fingers to send the music's vibrations electric through
the hands of the Player, running in series circuit
through his mind and organizing his metamorphosis
from the cellular level up. *O Golem rise and dance,
wedded with your Maker, who for so long has
viewed you apart from his other creation and has
hidden and denied your nature under the armor of
his own false image.*

74. Each new technology spreads in a shockwave of
learning and change, a minor or major lurch of the
Instrument. The phenomenon is general; its main
features may be seen by examining the spread of
encounter groups, psychedelics, transistor radios, or
the Black Panther Party.

On the personal level, the breaking open of perception, etc., which accompanies one's initiation
into a new technology and begins the process of life-
reorganization to include it in harmony, usually
takes up to six months.[18] There follows a period
during which the self accomplishes primary reintegration—pulls order together out of the somewhat
Chaos created by the presence of new element and
new connection, the flesh of new technology as it
appears in the consciousness. Taken together, these
two phases of the "shockwave period" typically
occupy energy for sixteen to twenty-four months.
After this period, the self's work can turn to secondary integration ("polishing"); to exploring the
further possibilities of development of the new tech-

---

[18] The impact of acid is an extreme case, occurring almost instanta-
neously—a brutal but useful technology of Breakthrough. The pace of
the first impact of grass or of TV is more typical.

nology and within it; or to other technologies and their changes.[19]

75.　These phases of impact and first reorganization are easy to observe in the early interaction of many young couples. They meet, go through some months of excitement charged with opened energies. Then they seem somewhat to withdraw from their normal social space, to sort out privately their flows and conflicts and order these in some ongoing way. Late in the second year of living together comes a cusp point: either the relationship fails to engage and they split; or its *going-on* is established, and they enter a more active phase of moving out into the society of their friends.

　　These phases show up in every process in which the self is exposed to newness and tries to integrate it (the impact of new *material* technology is unremarkable as a special case). The time parameters depend of course on how adaptable the person is, and on what forces play upon his/her life. But these particular figures, say six and eighteen months, may be observed so frequently now (via new record albums, psychotherapy, etc.) that they seem to represent a present general norm for the speed of "healthy," relatively unblocked adaptation.

76.　In cross-cultural experience, e.g., the Peace Corps, "six and eighteen" months appears again. Six months is the usual breaking-point of the fever known as "culture shock," which comes from being embedded in an alien culture-organism, connected into nourishment/harmony in few of its aspects and surrounded by strange patterns. (American business-

---

[19] These phases may be studied closely in the mirror of the sciences, albeit on a different time-scale. See T. H. Kuhn, *op. cit.*

men are made twitchy because Latin Americans want to sit close enough to touch as they talk.) In six months shock-fever rises to a crisis of inward decision, in which the individual chooses to reject new order, symbolically and substantively—coming home because of homesickness, remaining an Englishman in India, failing to move on after an encounter breakthrough—or chooses to accept the benefits/costs of adapting to new order and begins to reintegrate consciousness and behavior around what has been revealed in Breakthrough. When this is complete to a first degree the individual is "at home" in the waters of a new culture; and within his skin, in osmotic balance, is a hybrid but coherent internal culture.[20]

Through this example, we can view adaptation to any new technology—be it a foreign language, a toaster, or political action—as the process of passing from one culture to another more or less distant, as this takes place inside the individual consciousness.

77.   In social bodies, the phases of adaptation to new technology are similar to those within the individual's skin. Every small group newly forming takes some months to "jell" into its first identity. After this, most self-organizing groups function for one to two years and then disperse (perhaps leaving a core that reforms to repeat these phases). In cases where the group and its enterprise persist past this cusp, they enter a third and longer phase—seven years? open-ended?—characterized by deeper commitment and institutionalization of roles.

[20] Then the Peace Corps, the Army, or the home company ships him home or transfers him somewhere else.

In larger groups—those whose members do not all know each other—the timing of these phases depends not only on the six-and-eighteen month "personal" parameter, but upon the extent to which the lower nervous system of our information media connects us into a collective consciousness. When the connection is relatively efficient, vivid, and distance-canceling, we see the shock front flash across a whole subculture with almost no "trailing lag." Broad populations open and assimilate the shock almost as a single being, and in little more time.

The history of every aspect of the counterculture has been structured by this phenomenon as it is working out in the lives of the young who have grown in electronic connection. Its rhythms are evident in the waves of different use that structure the spread of psychedelics; the explosive spread of campus demonstrations and urban counter-communities; the multiplication of free universities; the discovery of Marshall McLuhan; the way response to a Dylan album proceeds.

Some idea of the rhythms, in Berkeley and abroad, is given by the brief chronology for the white movement on the following page. Reflecting on the flavors of these signal events, their interdependence becomes clear, and some regularity in their timing appears. There seems also to be a larger cycle of four years or so, keyed partly to election times, which may surge sharply in 1972/3 and 1976.

78.   The process of social change is compounded from the impact and assimilation of new technologies. Linked as we are, many people are now going through roughly the same changes, in detail, at nearly the same time. The pace and action of change

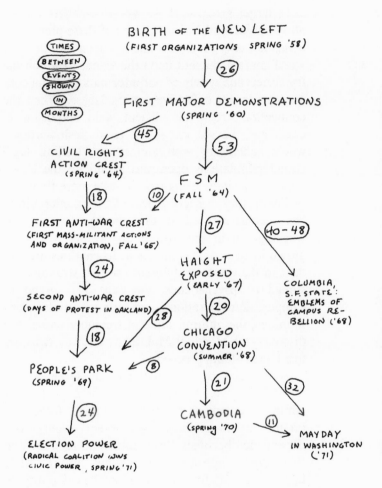

BIRTH OF THE NEW LEFT
(FIRST ORGANIZATIONS   SPRING '58)

(TIMES)
(BETWEEN)
(EVENTS)
(SHOWN)
(IN)
(MONTHS)

26

FIRST MAJOR DEMONSTRATIONS
(SPRING '60)

45

53

CIVIL RIGHTS
ACTION CREST
(SPRING '64)

18

FSM
(FALL '64)

10

40 - 48

FIRST ANTI-WAR CREST
(FIRST MASS-MILITANT ACTIONS
AND ORGANIZATION, FALL '65)

27

24

HAIGHT
EXPOSED
(EARLY '67)

COLUMBIA,
S.F. STATE:
EMBLEMS OF
CAMPUS RE-
BELLION ('68)

SECOND ANTI-WAR CREST
(DAYS OF PROTEST IN OAKLAND)

28

20

18

CHICAGO
CONVENTION
(SUMMER '68)

8

PEOPLE'S PARK
(SPRING '69)

21

32

24

CAMBODIA
(SPRING '70)

11

ELECTION POWER
(RADICAL COALITION WINS
CIVIC POWER, SPRING '71)

MAYDAY
IN WASHINGTON
('71)

BERKELEY THEATER   NATIONAL THEATER

(SPECULATION ABOUT THE LOGICS OF SOME OF THESE TRANSITIONS
RUNS THROUGH MANY PIECES IN WWW.)

become rhythmic, organized around these six-and-eighteen month periods. Together we watch the public theater that registers our reactions in the conflict of transformation—the FSM, assassinations, the Chicago Convention. And moods of feeling sweep over us in synchronous time. Traveling around the country, I'm constantly amazed at how people everywhere turn out to be going through the same trips about even their most personal lives and problems at the same time. Marcuse, McLuhan, Tolkien, Kesey, *Easy Rider:* ideas and fantasies flashing across our mind. The Haight, hair: freedom. Woodstock: joy. Chicago: terror. People's Park: mingled. Cambodia: bewildered outrage. Do you only imagine you felt a collective gasp when Jack Ruby rushed up to Oswald? The simultaneous impact of any new ordered knowledge sends us all into a collective stone, a pecular and characteristic high.[21]

79. Energy changing its organization in time is music. The music of a fast-changing society has other rhythms than the *immediacy* of communications, the *six months* of opening, the *eighteen months* of assimilation. The motif of each new technology, if of interest after first sounded and absorbed, is developed in broader phases, which repeat this basic cycle and tend to proceed in multiples of its basic

[21] It's now long enough after Cambodia to see that the knowledge of Kent State and Jackson struck us like a bullet in the brain. During the following summer, fall, and winter, word from all over was of our energy stagnant, fragmenting; our will in an often anguished confusion even in our most "private" lives. Thus we absorbed this cold benediction opening a new decade. By spring motion was renewed among us, partially but clearly, in ways whose difference will be clearer by the time this book is published than they are now. By then the second anniversary of Cambodia will be up, and if the shockwave cycle holds good we should be entering a new phase, signaled by public theater.

time units. (Perturbing factors like government control of technology make such orderly analysis impossible.) As there seems to be no upward bound to the possible extent of cultural transformation, so there seems to be no arbitrary limit on cycle length: we have been millennia in digesting, or in preparing to vomit, the knot of Yang metaphors.

But one other time length seems essential to a search for fixed parameters with which to measure and interpret the rushing of change: the length of human life. For this is the period during which—if it last so long without passing into a newer one yet —a new technology becomes a presence in the experience-since-birth of every inhabitant of an electric culture. Before this time there will be disharmony and conflict in the way its uses are received by different age-groups.

MORE VIDEO

80.   To return to video and the notion that the extent to which a technology's potentials are manifested depends on the manner of its embedding in the culture. Only when a communications technology passes into universal self-determined use does its potential as an instrument for the music of group consciousness become open to realization.

Now video power begins to pass to the people— half a century after its invention, a quarter after its introduction. Communities, city neighborhoods, and ethnic groups make bids to own their own coaxial cable systems. Already upstart corporations are pre-

paring hardware and software for semi-individual-
ized programming: the viewer will phone upstream
to a voice-operated dimwit computer, select from
its categories, and dial in to the signal riding down-
stream through the cable, tuning at will to news,
teaching films, subject-catalogued commercials, live
meetings of the city council. Or to a videotaped discussion of the contradiction involved in the real
liberation of all this taking place within monopoly
capitalism.

81. The major shock-wave will come through the sub-
technology of videotape. Already third-generation,
fully portable systems provide recorded motion-
vision (cum sound) as easy to use as good film
equipment and of roughly comparable weight and
vividness; and will shortly be superior to film in all
three respects. The mechanical systems of processing, editing, storage, reproduction, distribution, and
playback are all radically easier than film: most follow the simple models of sound-recording by mag-
netic/plastic tape and are equally simple to put on
cassettes. Conversion of the present universal TV
receiver to play videotapes is simple. By the end of
the century the technology will be able to provide
3-D color holographic images with true ear-shaped
system sound, a *vivid* medium which will open new
potentials of transformation.

Within this decade, such videotape equipment
will be brought within the means of the middle consumer. The skills of film-making are already spreading rapidly and widely among the young. The implications of this marriage are amazing. Any home or
group can be the creation or distribution nexus for
memory images complete for eye and ear. Consider

how the multiplication of music, even under essentially central control, has affected us. With videotape anyone can create our most vivid live images and feed them into the common pool, to be available in breadth limited only by our access methods. *The base for the creation and exchange of social information and art is thus radically democratized.* From this refinement of the collective nervous system great consequences will flow. I suspect these will first be expressed through the transformation of our political and sexual behavior in particular along lines of less exploitation.

82. With cheap, simple video equipment everywhere available, and cheap, simple ways to recopy and exchange individual programs, we have the material base for a pure mode β communications system. Its initial distribution-operation would be hand-to-hand and by mail, like a chain letter. Were a master-tape only ten times copyable, and its copies legible only unto the sixth generation, a program finished Sunday might multiply strictly through friendship-chains and be watched on ten million sets the following Friday. (Some prototypes now produce copies small as postage stamps.) A national interlock of cable systems, drawing on computer-coordinated memory banks open to any citizen's input (and providing an adequate indexing service) offers an alternate model for implementing the mode β potentials of video.

Some balance between these rustic and slick distribution models will be struck. And here we have what may well be an important cultural option. If technology is developed to further the rustic model, where programs are reproduced at home and passed on person-to-person, it will encourage more than simple human contact. People's tendency to depend, for their choices of what information to encounter, upon the dominant authorities of cultural interpretation will be undermined. Instead they will be enabled to turn toward each other for example. Thus freed of central guidance, cooperative groups will tend more to develop their own unique micro-cultures (many of which will grow aggressively political).

This pure acceleration of the process of *cultural divergence* is latent in the slick model also. Both models are like vats of nutrient broth, capable of harboring rich ecologies. But the slick model is more inclined to the Yang contamination: its technology enables people equally well to continue to hand their imaginations over to the arbiters of monocultural stability, dialing some masked representative of Uncle Sam for what to watch.

83. Yet with an adequate phone system in use, with this slick model a fully democratic information process can for the first time happen as *rapidly* as an authoritarian one in mass society, where hitherto throughout history the means of rapid mass communication have been controlled by an elite. For one's input anywhere into the system could multiply in generations whose length was that of one's program plus a call; and if it were sufficiently important to people could be watched by the entire nation in twelve hours.

(In considering the efficiency of these pure type β models, it's well to remember that you have a friend who has a friend who has a friend who knows me and vice versa.[22] We *are* this densely intertwined, it's not your imagination. Electronic technology for

[22] Add one friend if you are not white, aged eighteen to thirty-five, and in some vague way an activist; add two friends if you are not an Ameri-

the first time permits us to realize the strength of this connection.)

84.   Against the emergence of this popular power there is, of course, resistance. Right now a wide array of established firms are contending viciously for domination of the new, lucrative video-recording industry, with a variety of recording technologies. Overall, their research, development, and marketing are geared to establishing a passive consumer market, one as eager to be exploited in taste and pocket by mass-produced artifacts as is the rock record audience. Agglomerated as these industrial concerns are with the present industries of mass information and mass entertainment, they are not about to concentrate their priorities on developing and spreading technology that enables people to make their own movies and to get to see everyone else's almost free.

Consequently, few video systems on the open market now are compatible with one another. Some playback systems depend on technology incapable of creative home use, others can come with cameras but don't, others provide a neo-Instamatic camera; all push pre-packaging rather than user creation.

Through such soft inhibitions the authoritarian tendency struggles to reproduce itself in the further development of the collective nervous system, constraining the use of the medium to old patterns.

---

can; add three if you live in a Himalayan hermitage. I am figuring fifty independent acquaintances per person or so; the actual chains may be shorter.

GOLEM, OUR HIGHER NERVOUS SYSTEM (ENABLING THE DECENTRALIZATION OF COLLECTIVE CONSCIOUSNESS)

85. How Form moves within us! I recognize now—and have made more obvious in rewriting—that what has moved in me through this river of meditation from House to Mobility to Communications is a vision of Golem as (Hu)Man, of our technology and society as organized in our image. As of course they are, being our extension. But what drives my vision is the understanding that this image is not only mutating but is deliberately mutable. The deeper name of our species is *Homo Proteus,* and megamechanical man is only one of our possible Forms.

   We can lay hold of our being in any of its aspects to begin transformation. Few people believe this now about this one. These days the works of the Machine express ugliness so great that we cry out to deny the responsibility, to deny that their image is ours; and many of the most humane among us are misled to phrase the struggle as Man against Machine. In this and other ways we express the deep feeling of impotence that bounds most of our condition and shapes the gut belief that nothing can be done. McLuhanism likewise views us as relatively helpless in the hands of Golem, carried through pre-ordained transformations by each new device.

   I say it again: humanity, its society, and its technology are interpenetrate, change simultaneously. Machines should be no more mystifying than our mirrors, and whatever power we have to change our image is reflected equally in them. A different image of Golem is possible. It beckons in our current transformation along the lines of self-determination and reconnection to the organic World. Golem as Megamachine, the primitive, literal extension of the human body, reflects the image of the social body articulated in hierarchical class society, and centers around the individual ego inside its body House. This key metaphor is in the initial death-throes of being replaced by a new organizing metaphor, which may describe the essential entity "man" as a many-equal-personed body uniting by communication into one collective consciousness. Or, with luck and choice, it may be more subtle in its harmony, balancing the aspects of consciousness, individual and collective. (It might also take what is irreducibly "human" to include all life, and more.) Whichever new metaphor flowers in our culture, the bodies of our society and our technology will be reorganized in its image. From an image of man balanced in the tao of separate/mutual, a classless collective society with personal freedom. And corresponding to this, the image of Golem as Megamachine lumbering over a barbed-wire fense, sitting down in an empty field after the rain, going through explosive smoky changes, and turning into a flock of crows who fly away. Each under his own power, chattering in the β-tongue, and trading round all roles as they go.

86.   Change begins in the mind. Computers, which extend some of our functions of intelligence, are our most marvelous technology, and the one most awesome in its potential for our change. It opens new dimensions both for the collectivization of consciousness and for individuation as well, with radical implications for our distant evolution and our im-

mediate politics. By computer technology we extend intelligent consciousness in an outered form which can be operated on and deliberately transformed by all the gathered skills and knowledge of our persons and culture. More nearly than our attempt to reconstruct our genetic heritage of aggression, our evolution of computers displays us as the species *Homo Proteus.*

87.   Some of my friends have formed an electronics/ design company leading toward the goal of marketing a home computer bank, tied to large central facilities, for the price of a new car. Others have worked on first-generation bootstrapping programs designed for self-learning the skills of using computers as creative extensions.

In your home, the extension of a system that can connect you vividly with anyone and that gives you free access to all mankind's recorded knowledge, visual and aural, all records of all work in progress; all the day's news and the opinions of any who care to offer one, in summary or total detail; all the programmable knowledge-processes of our civilization; all everyone wants to share of his or her Story—in short, universal immediate access to all of our culture's information, the fundamental basis for both collectivization of consciousness and the full potentials of individuation. And with and beyond this, the empowerment of personal and group consciousness by the enormous multiplication of their lower ("mechanical") powers. Only the poetry of science fiction has attempted to survey the consequences; and it has been most notably deficient in attending to politics and sex.

88.   What will you do with your extension when you get it, how will you play? Learn to build a solar gen-

erator, order the parts, and ask someone to show you how to solder? Get a weekly grocery list keyed to the cheapest solutions for your nutrition and taste that tells you what to buy where when? Complete its integration into your house so that it turns off unused lights and regulates the entire house metabolism in accord with satellite weather observation? Work with five somewhere others to make and spread a videotape on government pollution, drawing on public input of muckracking videotapers who go out fresh each day in every city to follow leads? Have available to your isolated commune most of the culture's light technological resources? Research chemicals and their precautions and compute the ideal time for simultaneous demolition of Doggy Diners by a hundred highways?

Think fast. Given your socioeconomic class and habits, by 1984 you'll be linked into a first-generation system with these capacities. How timid, naive, and unimaginative our uses will be at first! But go to the poets, they know.

89.   Computers make possible a technology of vivid, direct person-to-person communication and universal information access, *assisted* rather than regulated by semi-centralized agencies which operate to refine its fidelity and connectivity and to extend the depth of its memory and low reasoning powers. The tendency of their free use is to render communication utterly decentralized and move our culture toward type β forms.

Consider the re-formation of our systems of learning through such a technology. Lacking adequate positive icons—a flock of crows will scarcely do for Golem learning—its depth is best expressed negatively. *All material need for the present centralized structures of education*—power, physical plant, de-

partment and discipline, management, whatever—
would vanish, and with it the restrictive power to
enforce them. Even within our present disgusting
customs, Martha could start study at the age of
seven or forty-seven, via her home terminal and
under the tutelage of Chemist X (who would probably bill her), and in her time and way qualify
through company knowledge tests and his endorse-
ment for employment with Dow Chemical, meanwhile practicing Tai Chi on Wednesdays with a
master in Arizona. Damn! What will become of the
classroom, the administration, professionalism,
fund-raising, face-saving and the uniform curriculum? What would they do with all those empty
buildings?

We should see instead a wild flowering of depth
experiment in the forms and processes of small-
group interaction, which forms the social foundation
of learning. For the foundation of material limitation on which the present authoritarian and fragmenting character of our educational system depends will largely disappear.

90. All this describes equally the transformation of our
systems of politics and governance. For the first
time, a full popular democracy becomes possible.
Hitherto our technological limitations in the handling of distance and of social information made
democracy necessarily *representative* in any group
of people too large to be spoken to with the unaided
voice. From this hierarchical imperative follows the
centralization of democracy and its present universal organization in forms of soft authoritarian
control.

High computer/communication technology makes
possible the abolition of representative government
and the institution of simple, direct popular-demo-

cratic government: the full realization of the classic process in which a problem is recognized, the people become informed through study, conference, debate, and then decide what to do.

A partial outline: By an open "signaling" process, problems of a local or broad scope are called to formal attention—you can tune in to a running "straw vote" program which registers what the citizenry is concerned with, and can record your own concerns, perhaps keying them to be noted by special interest-groups. You decide to take responsibility for helping to make a particular decision. You decide how much time/energy you want to put in on this one, for starters, and compute a learning program that will fill this best—perhaps drawing advice from the public market of political-decision-learning programmers. At the console, you read, see, and talk with whomever you wish, expert or study group, and extend or deepen your search if you choose. When you are ready to decide, you register your vote. When enough register, a final date is set; as it arrives the votes may be seen announcing themselves; after that the process of implementation begins.

By 1984, America could govern itself by a system of totally decentralized authority and semi-centralized agency, in which every person who wanted to share directly in any given public decision would be totally enfranchised and enabled to do so—a system of maximal political self-determination.

91.   What the actual evolution of small-and-large-group governance will be, given such a free-access system to grow with, we can only speculate. The system is rapidly coming into existence, as computers learn to read and generate programs directing the hooking-

together of their memory banks and operations[23] in the early stages of evolution toward fully conscious, self-directed life, and as blind and greedy economic processes contrive to fit our fingers to their keys. Surely the struggle central to the system's human use—and to human life itself—will be around the repressive regulation of this intelligence, the authoritarian control of its access and use. In this struggle, freedom leads us toward full symbiosis with Golem as he matures; I think that repression leads to death at his hands, and ours within them.

The demystification of technology, the propagation of knowledge and means for its use at the popular level—all ripely inherent in free use of computer technology—are essential strategies of struggle against repressive centralized power and are the key to the democratization of technological society.

GOLEM, HIS TALENT
(CYBERNATION AND THE COLLECTIVIZATION
OF INDUSTRY)

92. We are left with the basic question of our relationship with the means of production. The last few notes imply the basic empowerment of each citizen with respect to nonmaterial production—the decentralized, self-determined generation of the artifacts of art, thought, etc., which embody our nonmaterial condition. Let me deal with the management of ma-

[23] Notice the shape of computer mind that evolves: it is a highly decentralized array of intelligences, each with unique capacities, all linked to complement each other—very β, so to speak.

terial production by an example on the highest industrial level.

93.   I wanted to adapt my phone to full-room use. I went
down to the local Radio Shack outlet and bought a
kit with a printed program of assembly, which said
some things about the subtle magic of transistors.
The kit held components, simple like wire and
sophisticated like transformers. From raw materials
onward, most of the process that manufactured and
distributed the components was done by a semi-
integrated complex of machinery involving relatively little human labor or supervision—a process
that, in a greedy way, begins even to take account
automatically of my needs and changing desires, by
computerized monitoring of sales patterns.

If we reach the year 2000, when my son will be
my age, his computer will help him decide to add
new circuitry to it; help him do and understand this;
and coordinate the mechanics of component-arrival
for local pickup. The components will be sophisticated versions of the minimal-material/high-skill
integrated microcircuitry, which even now is re-
ducing the human labor of electronic technology by
a factor of ten, from production through assembly.
They will be manufactured by completely cybernated machinery with highly flexible output. The
scarce-material input to this plant will be mostly
reclaimed, for electronic technology lends itself to
this and his uses won't be wasteful; its other raw materials will be drawn from regenerative natural
sources. Its energy will derive from tidal or deep-
buried atomic sources; and the dispersal of its wastes
will be integrated with the ecology. The machinery
will be inhabited by men and women who help the
pilgrim young to understand its workings, and who
complete its capacities for self-repair. They will view

the machine as their extension—not vice versa, as is the custom now.

94. No human labor will be wasted in routine decisions about component production, provided these are made naturally, for common benefit and not for private profit—my son's order, habits, and expectations will be integrated automatically with everyone else's, and production flexibly tailored to this; or a message returned to revise these in view of production's limits. Human creation, which augments the system's capacities along its determined priorities, will feed in and be implemented as a matter of course.

When decisions about the system's priorities must be centralized in *time* rather than continuously determined by the feedback of people's changing uses, notice of this will flow to the population affected by such decisions. (In a free information system the necessity of such decisions cannot be disguised.) As with governance in general, full choice-information will be available, and those who wish to share the responsibility will be empowered to decide such matters as whether production should be organized around a different rare metal for ecological reasons; or re-engineered around a breakthrough miniaturization technology; or used to facilitate youth involvement in the use of personal weaponry.

As in the governmental domain, to thus radically democratize the decision-making process requires a radical faith in people's ultimate motives and in their ability wisely to use their powers of responsibility. Here again, what's at stake is our essential image of humanity. This faith may be unjustified. But any faith less leads us back through the Authority Complex toward fascism.

95. In this sketch of the collectivization of the manage-

ment and use of the electronics/computer industry, the details of ownership remain.[24] As with telephones, such technology opens in harmony with common ownership. Every other industrial technology is now becoming capable of such re-engineering toward cyber-integrated production and full shared control. Thus the control and decision processes of material production become fully automated in their lower reaches, are decentralized in space and time, absorbed visibly into the natural processes of daily use guided by self-determined learning and goals. In their higher reaches, as with politics, universal empowerment in the mechanical aspects of decision-making becomes possible—for example, a crude technology of forecast of the implications of decisions will soon be universally available through computers (at least to those who can pay for it).

In centrally cybernated production, as with our present industry, gross material accumulations will still be necessary to the freeing of human labor. But the accumulation of persons this now entails will be sharply reduced; and retechnologized communication will make unnecessary the centralization of decision-power which has always accompanied such accumulation.[25]

96.   The meta-technology that generates our major technologies operates through an educational system

[24] There is also the broad question of the nature of people's work in the productive process, which I'm not prepared to try to deal with. Despite the scope of this essay, it has no pretensions of completeness and passes lightly over many complex problems.

[25] The concentration of energy is a natural process, and necessary for its dispersion: consider the initial investment in the cybernated electronics plant. What is well distributed can be well put together, but to maintain this balance must be well distributed again. (This is scarcely the Way of Capitalism, where accumulated energy generates more accumulation, rather than recirculation.)

linked to industrial systems. Consider the technologies of the automobile and the encounter group. Their development involves the following sort of progression: (individual discovery) → (group invention) → (sponsorship for development) → (selection from among competing alternatives) → (full production, spread, and impact). Reconstruction of the meta-technology involves reconstruction of each of these phases.

Models for the reconstruction of the first and fourth of these are fairly clearly implicit in the discussion above. The third resembles the fourth. It is not hard to imagine correlated shifts in the more sophisticated processes of group invention. In the fifth phase, there remains the major question of how persons choose to engage their work in production itself; and how they are sustained, that is, given access to the fruits of production.

ON GRACE AND WASTE

97. The exploitive economy seems to condemn us to destructive cycles of use. We have come to look upon these as inherent in our technologies: to believe, for example, that ecological destruction is the inevitable concomitant of any massive dependence upon progressive industry, or that analysis is the death of the spirit. I have said nothing against this belief so far. In sketching a social reconstruction unashamedly ample in its use of low and high technologies, apart from banishing smog by steam, I've ignored the question of how we deal with the mess

of our uses. Nor am I fixated on the common night-mare future wherein we sit with shriveled legs, help-less as eggs, in vehicles that giant brains guide to work. In their service we are employed as compo-nents handling minute fractions of complex tasks whose ramifications we can't possibly comprehend or control. Just to make sure, Big Brother watches our every motion through Golem's omnipotent eyes.

Well, we all see technology as our projection, that's not just an intellectual's inkling. Those who believe that its furtherance is inevitably authori-tarian, or messy, are hypnotized by a few of their aspects in its mirror, and deep in the spirit do not believe we can change. Here again, we come to our core conception of Man as a being and a species.

98. I believe instead that the furthering potential and grace of our material technology is to do more with less. This grace is the grace of Mathematics, our inner language of the material world. As the world is our well for Metaphor, whose unfleshed bones are the body of Mathematics, this is the grace of Meta-phor as well. And as Metaphor is fleshed into social forms, this grace reappears as the central principle of Governance. (Its full flower as a conceptual tool is in the Tao.)

99. The internal combustion engine is a lower tech-nology than steam where both are applicable, for it does less with more: as mathematicians say, it is less elegant. Lao-tzu is quite specific about the virtues of the Way of Water. But we are greedy children with runaway power, and have no sense of taste. Still, at a sufficiently high level, technology's uses sometimes lead us toward one, willy-nilly.

Consider the handling of ephemeral information, on which our civilization is based. Currently we waste the planet's forests for our newspapers and literally a million periodicals. Video computers make possible a more sophisticated version of what the telephone network makes possible with messages: full information handling with only energy input, no materials to be wasted. True, the system's built and maintained with materials, though its operation is not: a burden shifted from the trees to the ore-bearing, oil-rich earth. But the raw-mineral base of electronics forms products that are eminently recyclable; and the technology sophisticates toward more art with less matter. When computer distribution stabilizes—a state only unbounded greed can avert—the industry can be made to depend on essentially a closed system of mineral use (given stable population) and on organic materials obtained from regenerative natural sources. These might include the managed forests that supply whatever computer printout cannot be expressed in microfilm or on recycled material. The housing industry is now the only other major predator of trees. Retechnologized construction would reduce its demands fivefold, whereupon they could also be satisfied by managed forests. (A pine tree growing forty years provides enough wood for a dome home.)

Taken together, these factors imply the total reconversion of the information industry, from resource-wasting to resource-sustaining. They also imply the possibility of reforesting literally half the continent. And again the image beckons of a radically decentralized society living in a new integration with the natural order.

100. Our present technological capacities make possible such reconstruction of every human industry, to husband the earth's resources and operate in har-

mony with the delicate ecologies of life, amply and modestly. In the cases of housing and transportation, which together involve a fifth of our G.N.P., it is easiest to see that humanity's *present* industrial capacities, if re-engineered and redistributed, could provide for all mankind the adequacy of support they do for middle Americans. It is this vision— that we can eat our technological cake and have the world too, but have never really tried—that moves the players of Bucky Fuller's World Game. But, like McLuhanism, Fullerism seems to take little account of the politics of power and our relation with the means of production; or of the deeper potentials for the freeing of our existence.

The reharmonization of industry demands two things beyond the sharing of high technology among the human family: a psychology of recycling, and bounds to our desires. Both are products of our reconnection with the organic order of the world, and of reconciliation/balance with the Yin. So long as material industry is used for armor and to fill the void inside, our empowerment condemns us to destroy.

101.   Completeness requires a remark about energy. The usual question is whether we can continue to live on our gross and escalating energy budget. We can't, at least not the way we're getting it and spilling the waste. But if we tidy up, the amount we use is the false worry of hubris. (Provided we abandon our dependence on fossil fuels, as we can choose to.)

We think we're mighty just because we can turn the sky black and threaten all earth-life. But we are gnats in an infinitesimal film of mist on a great rock ball, spinning in space alive with energy.

Each tiny shudder of earthskin releases more ergs than all our stockpiled weapons threaten. Until we come to tearing the very planet apart, our wildest uses of energy will be unnoticeable beside the sun.

Burning dead plants or leftover starmatter is kid stuff. We begin to hook into the ongoing energy sources of the universe when we harness the tides for their power—a project that may offer the easiest way of drawing energy in ecological harmony and that could begin for practical use with a year's military budget and effort.

CODA

102.   Wandering between Lao-tzu and the stars, it is difficult to grasp the immediacy of the future and the crisis of our choices about it.

Our industrial technologies are even now undergoing transformation, but in a distorted way. Already demand and manufacture are highly rationalized and integrated and labor freed. But the hallelujas are premature, for the greeds of power and profit outlaw Golem's development in ways that would mean his control by those whose production he reflects. Still, given present trends, in twenty years all but the poor of Amerika will be employing an apparatus that makes mechanically possible a system of direct participation in political decision and radically decentralized education. The struggle between the freeing and the imprisoning uses of this apparatus will be tremendous, and crucial to our further development. It will determine the uses of the cyber-automation of our industry, which will take another twenty years, and of the human energies freed by this transformation.

Twenty years; forty years. This century's examples of nations hell-bent on industrialization suggest that, if we chose, these conditions could be extended universally in forty and sixty years. At this point there will be no functional necessity for the human city—think that one over—and nonurban civilization will become possible.[26]

103. Build something; indwell in it; express the experience. An exercise in the tao of doing and resting, of creation and reception, of material and nonmaterial work, of need and art. An experiment in the technology of writing. I had a paper due for a conference, and the kid needed a nursery first. I spent most of my weeks of building just sitting around among its incomplete structure, mind as blank as the Fool on the Hill. And then sat down under the butterfly, to have this come out, umpteen struts and a thin skin pieced of individual triangles which make a common chord of colors, not built like the standard house of an essay. Dear me, how Form does move within.

And other things as well, as I realize when I ask myself why so *many* words awkwardly striving for some coherent perspective should come out from me now, on this subject, in this time. And the phenomenon of media-intervention in thought,

[26] At this point the organization of society in space is fully freed to seek new balance in the tao of accumulation/dispersion. Social-psychological needs will lead to localized densities of habitation larger than the (extended) family group. But the largest such "towns" would be modest in size, for when the ratio (group population)/(number of people a person can know) grows either too large or too small, group life becomes alienating. Such accumulations would also pass more freely through the tao of waxing and waning with time.

most familiar to acid-heads, comes in the form of a story in this morning's paper. It gives the first clear picture of upsurgent crisis in the technocratic ranks.[27] Twenty years of radical overproduction have now run head-on into the cutback in aerospace programs, etc., caused by public reaction to the Military State. Elite unemployment is 10 per cent and rapidly rising, bitterly discontented. The article predicts its energies will focus on the ecology movement and social reform, goes on to talk about how the cities are all fucked up, need change . . . On the front page of my family paper, no less.

Me myself, when I left the technological priesthood, I figured it would take at least a decade for me to seriously begin to try to recover for reuse the outer edge of the skills in which I'd been trained. I think every person who was raised inside the System and trained in specialized skills, and who has chosen to bolt role and move for freedom, faces this problem, of how to reconvert his or her portion of the skills of the old Yang culture for liberating use; rather than just abandoning them (and a large part of the self) in flight, through seeing no way of using them without being involved in their whole original context. (But first the skills we were denied must be slowly learned as foundation.) Half of my decade has passed now. In the presence of my newborn son and the dome, and at a time of trying to understand how to enter the future, through these notes my being comes together a first stage on this, and I begin the turnover for re-entry, right on schedule. I wonder where and how I will accomplish it: playing in the

[27] See note 18.

cattail ecology of some pond we know with the other children, or mixing thermite and building electronic jamming devices in a ghetto underground bunker. At the moment, both images seem pretty strong.

STUDIES

VIII.

An Organizing Strategy for the Educational Reform Movement

This study was written in late 1968, for circulation in the national infrastructure of the ed reform movement. We were at a key nexus: the first significant funds had become available for use at the regional and national levels, in the form of a $300,000 Ford Foundation grant to the National Student Association. This was a strategy paper in the debate about what to do. It is heavily dated in that higher and richer orders of organizing than those it discusses have since developed; and in the way it still deals with an elitist concept of organizer that we may be outgrowing.

I include it because, beneath these archaic particulars, it is an attempt to apply some of the thought of the previous chapters to the problems of an actual movement. The processes of growth it considers can be seen at work in any contemporary movement, and similar models and strategies are relevant—particularly to movements faced with the problem of coordinating action on a national scale.

May I be nostalgic and suggest that the public birth-cry of the educational reform movement sounded in Berkeley in the fall of 1964, as one voice in the song of hope and anguish we called the Free Speech Movement? The first of our Free Universities held its classes in the stairwells and on disaster drums in the basement of Sproul Hall, during the sit-in which climaxed the FSM. During that one evening, we tried formally to create a new style of learning in liberated territory. And to me, that scrap of our history is like the fossilized imprint of some green leaf in the mud of politics that nurtured and preserved it.

In the fallout of analysis that followed the FSM, articles about student discontent with higher education began appearing. Now, four years later, in over half of America's 2,500 colleges students are at work on their own initiative, to change the System; and in each of the others some groups of students are ready and aching to begin.

To make a panoramic description of today's ed reform landscape is a problem in itself.

* Colorado State University has just catapulted out of permanent backwoods inaction, with 2,000 kids involved in a thrust for student power built around a beer-on-campus issue. With this, the first discussions of ed reform have begun; and the first travelers from Berkeley and

Washington have arrived to bring legal resources and workshops on organizing skills.

* At the Urbana campus of U. Illinois this spring, over 500 students in semi-coordinated groups got into organizing undergraduate pressure-groups in the departments, a teacher/course evaluation project, a teaching assistant organization, curricular reform, a dormitory self-governance movement, and so on. This fall a free university of 1,000 students has formed, hippies are passing out pot brownies on the main quad, and student government and off-campus people are preparing an ed reform center to knit together regional work.

* At San Francisco State, ed reform activities passed this degree of scattered complexity two years ago, and have since become rich with interconnections and political and institutional sophistications. The teaching assistants have a union, the free university develops ambitious summer programs, the institution's mechanism of generating new courses has been restructured, already the administration has moved to clamp down on the flood of students seeking independent study.

THE MAIN SEQUENCE MODEL
OF CAMPUS EVOLUTION

So much is changing so fast, one is always behind. It makes sense not to try to take a wide-angle static photograph of the movement, but to speak in terms of the *process* of its unfolding growth. For plans made on the basis of the present state of a changing system and its needs—for one example, which only seems sophisticated, consider university planning based on statistical trend-projections—are doomed to irrelevant maturity. If we want to nourish the future, we must forget its present face and examine its social metabolism.

Anyone who travels campuses discovers their patterns of development. For me the best analogue is the Main Sequence of stellar evolution:

As diffuse, inert gases draw together, star-life condenses. Then a typical star goes through a ten-billion-year sequence of changes, consuming its substance in radiant nuclear reactions which grow, with time, progressively more intense, more complex and rich in heavy elements, hotter. As the byproducts of each reaction accumulate, another reaction begins in them before the first is played out. Now and then there are explosions, novae; perhaps a super-nova, which obliterates most of its substance and leaves it to die as a stellar ember. Different stars, with different initial masses, trace out variations on this evolutionary theme—too small, they never blow; too large, they go through all the changes very rapidly, shatter in brief bright light.

Campuses are much the same. Ed reform activity condenses out of the diffuse quickening consciousness of our generation, often out of its political turbulence: out of people coming together to work. It starts with a free speech issue, a reform committee, a free university. Sooner or later it moves, in a fairly predictable way, through the spectrum of what I will call "first-order activity," most of whose elements are visible at Urbana. Eventually more sophisticated "second-order" activities are generated—I will get to them presently.

There are similar evolutionary sequences in other sectors of the campus *ecology of change:* the black sector, the cultural sector, and so on. Tutorial programs mature to community action groups. Free U's give rise to underground newspapers and black student unions. Film societies and rock groups nourish political organizations. Black and white organizers make community theaters and colleges. In the campus, as in a star, all processes connect, and each change feeds back into all. Ultimate brothers should not bicker so among themselves as we do.

Within the campus and our lives—if I may flourish the metaphor—the "ultimate stellar heat" that is being approached is not an institutional form or condition but the perfect heat of free individuals living in harmony with their desires and rhetoric. For this is the goal of "educational change," is it not: that we manage to live the lives of learning that we believe and say are possible.

This vision suggests a strategy for campus organizing: to stimulate all the accessible varieties of first-order activity, perhaps with deliberate indifference as to whether they be "political," "educational," "cultural," etc.; and, when appropriate, to catalyze second-order activities.

CULTURAL DIFFUSION

This campus model differs from its stellar cognate in that the main evolutionary track is not fixed but evolving. A simple example: the student power/beer issue at CSU was in many respects similar to the free speech eruption at Urbana two and a half years earlier that triggered the politicization of that campus' consciousness. But the change in subject reflects the national shift from student movement-consciousness being phrased largely in political terms to its being phrased in broader cultural terms. And the CSU outbreak, while still resulting in a traditional first "cops on campus and arrests" scene, was accompanied by chalk-ins on the quad, a body paint-in, a temporary liberation of the student center, and massive sensitivity training by imported organizers. So, in short, the base from which beginnings are made has become much richer and more sophisticated. And so on up the line; the whole evolutionary track is drifting westward, so to speak.

This drift is one aspect of the phenomenon we've been calling *cultural diffusion,* roughly phrased as: "the kids in the boondocks are as hip at thirteen as we were in the City at sixteen, and it's all the telly's fault." In this case, the traveling of organizers is partly responsible for the drift— that is, for *the self-acceleration of our change.* In other cases, the media are more strongly involved. But in the ed reform movement's rapid evolution, the media—even campus papers or the Xeroxes circulating in the national infrastructure—lag behind the word and training borne by travelers, who go out from or around to the campuses, moving through conferences and crash pads and nascent regional centers. In part, the leading edge of change spreads through travel because we don't have a sufficiently flexible and responsive communications network. In part it is unavoidable, for, increasingly, training is of a complexity and sophistication that our present media cannot adequately convey.

By and large, people are more effective than paper or videotape as spreaders of social knowledge. And I think that *cultural diffusion—the increasingly simultaneous propagation of our social and cultural forms, almost as they are created—is the most accessible accelerator pedal on the motor of our change.* This premise is a strong motivation for the organizing strategy I am working up to propose for the national level of the ed reform movement. Its basic theme is to facilitate the travel, training, and interaction of organizers, via a decentralized institution designed as a network to create and circulate, not information but social knowledge: organizing skills, analytic techniques, training games, information with action consequences.

THE FREE UNIVERSITY,
A DECENTRALIZED FORM

Let me sketch some other features of the process from which this strategy derives and which it's intended to nourish. One trace is in the visible institutional shell the ed reform movement has grown, which, with the flesh beneath, expands section by section, building in some organic symmetry whose prognosis is by now almost apparent. The free universities are the movement's most concrete institution—characteristically, a decentralized form.

San Francisco State's Experimental College, the first one really to flourish, sprouted in a primitive form in spring 1965. By 1968 there were some 250 to 300, appearing weekly at places like Nazareth Normal Teachers College. No one person had visited more than a minor fraction of those now in existence. Only two conferences had brought more than a handful of them together; yet they were already beginning to intercommunicate heavily by interchanging travelers and organizers.

Whether defiantly autonomous or partially subsumed in the structure of the parent institution, all free universities are variations on one basic primitive model of a decentralized arena for educational experiment. (On how many campuses is their motto, "Anyone Can Give/Take a Course"?) The main feature of this model is: (*decentralized editorial control*) + (*centralized administrative facilitation*).

AN HISTORICAL EXAMPLE OF THIS FORM

Before 1958, student political activity was splintered in traditional, inflexible sectarian political groups. On many campuses, the New Activism began with the formation of an "umbrella organization," a nonsectarian left/liberal coalition of those who wanted to organize new political activity. Such umbrella organizations sheltered and nourished special-interest groups—in peace work, civil rights, education, etc. —until they were strong enough to make a go of it independently. Berkeley's SLATE, formed in 1958, was the Western prototype; by 1960 there were at least seventeen umbrella groups on West Coast campuses. As late as 1969, this function was being served on many campuses further back on the Main Sequence by SDS chapters.

Within the domain of political organizing, umbrella groups fit roughly the same model: (*decentralized editorial control*) + (*centralized administrative facilitation*). And, like the free universities, they are rich breeding grounds for new groups to form in. This decentralized form facilitates new growth.[1]

SOCIAL FORMS AND THEIR PRODUCTS

Free universities have spread by a social organizing process of the form: (*organize a real example*) + (*propagate by media and contact*) over (*people ready to move*). Proc-

---

[1] Notice that this model may be translated from campus space to group space. There it describes the operation of a learning group whose members have not bound themselves to a central focus, but coordinate their independent activities and share common resources. Another example appears at the end of Chapter IX.

esses of this form catalyze growth that is independent and spontaneous, spreads rapidly, and is deeply decentralized in that its forms and standards are under no central control, not even an aesthetic one.[2] Other examples are to be found in the proliferation of echo-communities of the Haight after her media exposure; and in the rash of campus sit-ins and movements that followed the FSM. I think it significant that we see here decentralized institutions and organizing forms being propagated in a decentralized fashion. This harmony between nature and growth may be characteristic of, or at least achievable by, reflexive institutions.[3]

Some of our organizing games, like the Totalitarian Classroom, come naturally to commenting upon themselves; they are inherently reflexive. They are generated by an un-centered network of organizers, and are spreading by a process of the form: (*involvement in an example*) + (*training*). Such a process, in our lush days of conferences and mobility, is sufficiently rumor-quick that it rapidly escapes control: nobody knows who's playing these games now, or in what form. Our games aren't the only ones spreading in this way: think of the touchy/feely technologies. What all games spread by such a process have in common is that, like folksongs, they inspire ingenious local adaptations.

[2] Other forms yield other products. For example, the political organizing process of Mississippi Summer (1964) and Vietnam Summer (1967) took the form: (*develop a theoretical model*) + (*implement it in simultaneous locations by cadre and contact*), again over (*people ready to move*).

[3] See Chapter IV.

SECOND-ORDER ACTIVITY

A crucial question is whether the present decentralized forms and process of the ed reform movement can generate and sustain activities more sophisticated than those mentioned so far. Evidence suggests they can. Within themselves, free universities are evolving beyond their initial spontaneous model, devising self-funding procedures and experimenting with ongoing series of programs. Among themselves, they are beginning to link up in regional cooperations and establish regional news networks. Their early organizers have done their shots and departed and are now coming together to learn how to work toward change in ways that build on what they've learned already.

Such activities I call "second-order" because there seems to be a clear distinction in perspective, commitment, complexity, and skills between such activities (and their organizers) and those classed earlier as "first-order." Among other institutional marks of second-order activity are these: The movement has begun to support trainers and critics drawn from its own ranks. General cooperation between campuses is evolving in quite a few regions. (Some regional alliances are condensing more rapidly because traveling organizers have been put in the field to encourage them.) Those who have done local first-order organizing are beginning to form *intentional learning communities,* which seem to represent the leading edge of our institutional experiments.

SECOND-ORDER ORGANIZERS

First-order organizing skills are those involved in a typical first-order activity, like a free speech movement or the founding of a free university. They include power-structure research, primary charisma, contingency planning, running a communications center, and so on.

Second-order skills have only recently begun to develop and are more wildly various. They range from grant-getting and the teaching of self-funding skills, through training in sensitivity techniques and social technologies, to coordinating and consoling organizers. Their common denominator is that they are used to help first-order organizers start doing their thing, or do it better.

In this function, second-order organizers are powerful agents of cultural diffusion, for the edge of our collective knowledge is in their persons and not otherwise accessible. This is because at present overviews of such knowledge can accumulate only among those who travel.[4] Second-order organizers are already responsible for most of the new strategies and social artifacts (games, institutions, etc.) now appearing in the ed reform movement. They not only spread change but are increasingly its laboratory. And this will probably be truer as they form learning communities to work together more intensely.

[4] One political consequence is that almost all the real power for decisions on the national level—aside from the major chunk that gets lost somewhere in trying to satisfy the NSA bureaucratic structure—is in the hands of a relatively few traveling second-order organizers. Local control of national policy is remote. And organizing strategies that centralize the future institutional growth of the ed reform movement—by, say, pumping the available national money into an Ed Reform Center in Washington—are not likely to make the problem of local control and flexibility any easier. But the strategy I'm proposing points at tying in second-order organizers more intimately to the specific regions they work with.

Second-order organizers began to appear as a recognizable class in 1966. By 1969 there were fifty to one hundred of them working in the ed reform movement (not all full-time). The critical factor in their development and training is travel. A person does a first-order organizing shot: say he leads a student government power trip. Maybe he begins to travel then, or—equivalently—maybe travelers drop in on him, attracted by the fire. He graduates or drops out of school, wants to make more change, doesn't know how, begins wandering to find people to learn and work with. In the intense education of the mobility net, he begins to learn a new order of business.

INAPPROPRIATE STRATEGIES

Given this perspective, what is an appropriate strategy for helping the ed reform movement grow in the near future?

Each of America's motions—assassination, election, rising expectation—stirs up more available energy for social change among the young. The high schools shake with more (and more sophisticated) action now than the colleges did in the mid-sixties. On every campus there are groups of people ready to come together in first-order activity. So *strategies for the liberation of energy are redundant:* there is free energy aplenty and more on the way; the problem is to help it learn how to express itself.

"The soil of energy is abundant," you would say, if you were a Taoist gardener in this springtime of change, "and everywhere first green appears. What use have I for sowing?" Similarly, *strategies aimed primarily at stimulating first-order activity are redundant.* There is already so much first-order activity that only a few of its special facets are even catalogued. If you plot the growth-in-time of the numbers of free universities, dope-smoking fraternities, student curriculum committees, demonstration arrests, and so on, you will find their graphs to be logistic curves: exponential growth curves *which have not yet begun to level out*. That is to say, concretely, that by 1972 there will be as many campus underground papers, free universities, teacher/course evaluation groups, and so on, as there are presently tutorial projects.[5] The present processes of the ed reform movement—unenhanced, and with no additional institutional structure—are spreading these activities adequately.

Granted, we would like them to spread more rapidly and become more sophisticated and of higher quality. But in fact the only strategies we know for stimulating first-order activity involve sending second-order organizers to campuses, or having campus people travel for interaction and training with second-order people. And this, from another perspective, is second-order apprentice training.

THE TAC/SGIC STRATEGY

In short, the circumstances of our process lead us necessarily to strategies that concentrate on second-order organizers and activity. There is one intermediate strategy—centralized administrative media facilitation of decentralized first-order activity. (The free-university strategy of centralized facilitation and decentralized control has a crucial quality that cannot be reproduced on a national scale: all the interaction involved is face-to-face, between people who generally are involved in the facilitated activities.) An example is NSA's Tutorial Assistance Center, which tries to service a thousand tutorials with directories, contacts, studies and reprints, advice about grant-getting, etc.

[5] This estimate proved roughly true.

Such administrative facilitation might be useful in the ed reform movement. But there are better ways to invest our limited resources on the national level than in producing, coordinating, and shipping paper. NSA's Student Government Information Center is another example of this model in operation over a landscape of concerns much more similar to that of the ed reform movement than is the tutorial landscape, and it has been an inert entity. The main aim of TAC's strategy has been to *upgrade* the tutorials, and in this its success has been at best very limited.

So there isn't much evidence that this strategy genuinely aids change; and no one suggests that it accelerates change. Its main virtue seems to be that funding agencies can recognize programs based on it as plausible and safe. But the time for taking on projects because they are fundable rather than because we believe they are efficacious—as NSA did with its teacher/course evaluation program—is past: there is real work to be done.

(Many in the movement feel the need for better circulation of working studies, contact lists, inventories of our human resources and skills, and so on. But this can be equally well served by regional circulation centers. And I think it is possible to move by a strategy that generates this circulation as a byproduct: a strategy in which whatever central administration there is services second-order organizers traveling and building in regions where one of their functions is to make sure this circulation happens.)

THE REAL TAOIST McCOY STRATEGY

The best strategy for furthering the movement seems to me to be to multiply the second-order organizers and to aid them in using their skills and developing new ones. That is, to put our national resources into the leading edge of the movement's change, accelerating and extending its development. Considering it as an institution, we should nourish its most advanced, tender, and tentative parts—like the intentional learning communities now forming—rather than its established features, like the free universities.

How can this best be done? By following the Tao of Transformation. Let me illustrate with a tale from Chuang-tzu, Lao-tzu's chief exponent:

While watching a great cataract whose pool was so turbulent not even a fish could play in it, Confucius noticed an old man swimming. He hurried to the rescue; but when he got there, the old man was walking on the bank with his hair tousled, singing. "I thought you were a water sprite," said Confucius, "but when I see you close, you're a man. Do you have a special way of swimming?" "No, no special way," said the man, "I began swimming here in my earliest days, I grew up happy at swimming, and it has become my nature to swim here. I enter and go down with the water in the very center of its whirl and come up again with it when it whirls the other way. I follow the way of the water and do nothing contrary to it by myself: this is how I swim."[6]

To move in accord with the nature of the medium. Maoist guerrilla strategy is one adaptation of this metaphysic to a social organizing process. I am suggesting another. There is a process of growth and change now at work in the ed reform movement whose product pleases us. We should facilitate this *process* as unobtrusively and naturally as possible, "following the way of the water." All we know of how second-order organizers come to be and do their thing is the present developing structure of their training and activities: a structure of human play in a network of travel

[6] This is my paraphrase of Chuang-tzu's Book XIX, Chapter 9. Book III, Chapter 2, the tale of how the ruler Wan-hui's cook cut up oxen for nineteen years without needing to sharpen his knife, is a better illustration; but it is longer and more elliptical.

and mobility. *To further the movement, enhance this network and its play.*

A MODEL FOR A NATIONAL STRATEGY

Let me suggest an organizing model our present resources could bring into being.

Begin with the *stubs*. These are work-oriented intentional learning communities whose main product is change in the system of higher education (usually in some geographic region). Stubs are beginning to form naturally as second-order organizers come together to invent ways of working on a continuing basis. In late 1968 some stubs were:

* The Pennsylvania Project: five organizers fielded by NSA under an OEO grant, to service rural Pennsylvania colleges, who set up base in York, Pennsylvania.

* The Institute for Educational Development: a self-supporting group of seven organizers who originally worked together in the Catholic College Circuit, and who set up in Philadelphia on an ongoing basis.

* The New Learning Community: a group of nineteen who began regional ed reform activities from their base on Manhattan's lower West Side (Four were second-order organizers; most of the rest, Antioch work-study students.)

* Dragon's Eye: a motley group of self-supporting organizers who tried to build a work center in Berkeley.

Other stubs were then forming in Washington, Minnesota, Urbana, and so on: they had only begun to appear in the previous half year.

Intentional learning communities will spread by the same process model as did the free universities. Their number will multiply with the natural increase in second-order organizers and as more and more of us spend enough time in the distinctively cold and stressful climates of organizing to feel our need for some new basis of warmth and community to sustain our selves and our work.

The stubs are important, not only because they hold an increasing number of our most highly skilled people, but because they are already becoming regional nexuses, ganglia where organizers meet and rest and base themselves during travel. Such nexuses are the main structural feature of the mobility network we are developing.

CAPPING THE STUBS

To *cap a stub* is to provide it with resources for:

* Crash-space and food for several days, for a fairly large number of people (ten to twenty), once or twice a month.

* Private apartment and shared office space for several people for longer periods (up to four months).

* Open space adequate for large meetings and training sessions.

* Adequate transportation for whoever comes needing it (perhaps several cheap cars).

* A mimeograph and supplies; electric typewriters; an adequate phone budget; secretarial services.

In addition—anticipating the function of the capped stubs—some freeing of the time and skills of the resident organizers will be necessary; and thought should be given to this when planning or budgeting for the capping operation. (It is difficult to estimate a typical capping budget at the time of this writing; but $8,000 per year per stub, give or take 50 per cent, seems reasonable.)

The stubs, like the Free U, are *open space* for the ed reform movement: particularly because they are just sprouting and are mostly undifferentiated functionally. The capping operation is designed to open more space for things to happen and grow in: unused or multi-use architectural space, social space in the rich interactions of a diverse stream of people. Indeed, the stubs will probably be more open to change and growth, to the extent that they bring together people working in related but diverse areas of change—like politics, media, the arts—not just educational reform.

THE ORGANIZER GAME

The main aim of this strategy is to train and field second-order organizers. Given a national network of capped stubs, or some equivalent structure, we have a board for a *decentralized organizer training game*. An organizer moving on from first-order activity enters the network at some nexus. It confronts him as an extended library of information, skills, social technologies, experiments-in-progress. He must learn how to learn from it: this is a game, at which he develops his own style of play as he moves along.

He moves between stubs, visiting few or many. He learns to solve the problems of travel on limited resources by hitching, sharing rides, bargaining for his transportation costs. Some stubs are cold, unfriendly; others are warm; at some he lingers until someone kindly tells him, "You should move on, you're not learning anything here." From one stub, he surveys the ed reform activity in the campuses of its region. From another, some campus-action circumstance beckons, and he enters it for the duration at whatever level of skills—mimeograph cranker, political theorist—he has. He meets the heavies and others resident and transient at stubs: learns from them, dislikes some, works closely with others, goes out with them on team campus visits, learns what he can do on a campus. Always he is enmeshed in the constant circulation of information, strategies, skills, and interaction that are the life of the movement and its training medium; and his travel makes him a natural agent for this circulation.

He is free to devise his own learning strategy; or he may seek those in the network who will help him "map out a program." In return, the network and its people are open to him. That is, there are the open space and resources to accommodate his travels, and the people of the network are receptive to his presence and role—even, or especially, if he has not yet developed his capacity for work—and take on his companionship and training as a brotherly duty. The success of such a strategy, of course, depends as much on the cultivation of a group ethic as it does on the development of an institutional structure. But what else can I say about that here?

(Another description of this model is that it establishes a network of multi-function experimental laboratories, independent but intercommunicating. The parallel to models for scientific and technological research-and-development is obvious.)

FUNDING

Assume that funds are available, from a Ford grant or otherwise. Define an apprentice (second-order) organizer as one who does not yet generate his support from his work skills. The game will involve the number of apprentices proper to the network's capacity (which will expand as the capped stubs grow and multiply). Each apprentice will receive a partial travel allowance; a subsistence allowance for personal spending; and an allowance for room and board at the stubs, plus office space and use of facilities. (Exclusive of travel, the cost could probably be kept to $150 per apprentice per month. We have as yet no useful data on how long it takes apprentices to become self-supporting.)

Rather than have apprentices bargaining with stubs for their keep, it would probably be best to have a central administrative facility make periodic payments to each stub, on the basis of actual apprentice residence and use of facilities. (Yes, I am suggesting sort of an F.T.E.* for the ed reform movement, though rates would vary from stub to stub.) Fully developed, this system would provide a significant fraction of the ongoing capping budget of each stub. The main problem would be to keep the central facility from exercising control over the process. This could be done by making sure that the selection of apprentices was a decentralized function of the second-order organizer network, and that the apprentices were free to choose their own itineraries.

What real approach to this ideal is possible? Most stubs come into existence as already self-supporting and more or less headed toward the goal of drawing this support directly from their skills. But their budgets for space and facilities are pitched to basic subsistence; from their perspective, cap-

* Full Time Equivalent.

ping is a luxury operation. It is too early to tell if their work will free enough money for capping (though in some regions student governments might be persuaded to join in providing a capping budget). If this turns out to be possible, apprentices could actually use the network for not much more than the price of their food.

ENTRANCE AND BROTHER/SISTERHOOD

In this time of available energy and people ready to move (but unskilled), each of our beginnings runs the danger of being overloaded and swamped as soon as it becomes known.*

The organizer game, however fully it is played, needs some form of *entrance criteria,* some way of determining who gets funded and who gets to stick around to learn and work. The problem can be approached in a number of ways; all have their thorniness. What is essential, I think, is that control over the criteria and their application be decentralized: that is, be in the hands of those who inhabit the network and do the work and training. (Though the ed reform movement began to develop national funding from monied institutions, it had no trace of a mechanism to insure decentralized control of the planning for and disposition of these funds.)

Let me suggest an extreme model for decentralized control of the organizer game, one whose elements go beyond the narrowly political. Change happens so fast, even when we anticipate it we come out behind. There are growing among us not only new skills and new forms but new mo-

---

* Within six months of this writing, travel between uncapped stubs swelled to the point of straining their resources and internal community.

dalities of work. The vocation of social change involves more and more intimate parts of our selves; and we are finding that we must work together and hang together in new and deeper ways in order to be able to continue working and learning. For this reason, and because the new social forms we are building are designed ultimately for ourselves, we are beginning to come together in what I have called intentional learning communities, which might better be described as young *work-families*.

The stubs were the first institutional trace of this mood. Around them, one senses strongly another mood which has been growing: there is a brother/sisterhood of change in which we are mutually involved. Perhaps we are ready to make this mood more explicit, and in establishing the training game to further not only a developing institution, but a social psychology and an ethic.

Suppose the stubs, as they form, were to constitute themselves explicitly as work-oriented families with the additional commitment and learning that this entails. There would then be a simple model for cooperation and interchange between them; and for the recruitment of apprentices and their entrance into the network as travelers.

That is, the stubs would form a coalition of families, a decentralized craft-guild for educational change. Members of one family would be welcomed in any other and have priority for accommodations, etc. Apprentices would be chosen, with a seriousness appropriate to the act, by the families independently; and their access to the network (and whatever central funding) legitimized by this selection. This would solve the problem of entrance in a full social form; though there are stronger and less institutional reasons for proposing this crystallization of our growing mood.

IX.

Activism at Mainstream U; the Organizing of Counter-Community

THE FOLLOWING DIAGRAMS describe typical patterns of evolution of new social energy as it appears in youth communities and is manifested in organized group action.

The campus sequence sketches five phases—covering some five to ten years—in the spread of activism at Mainstream U, a large state university (upper middle class). The sequence is idealized and might include many more groups; the phases are not sharply defined, and the typical groups of any phase change from year to year. By Phase 5, the range of activities is appropriate to a small live city, and the thrust of evolution passes into the development of the institutional structure of counter-community (merging with Phase 5 of that developmental sequence). Every campus demonstrates some version of this model, modified by circumstance and size. By 1972 perhaps a hundred major campuses had evolved beyond an (updated) version of Phase 3, and most urban counter-communities could trace their origin to such roots.

PHASE O:

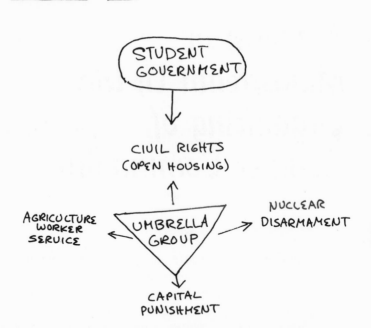

(SUCH "UMBRELLA GROUPS" -- NONIDEOLOGICAL RADICAL
COALITIONS SHELTERING WORK ON SEVERAL ISSUES --
ARE TYPICAL WOMBS FOR CAMPUS ACTIVISM.
IN THE LATE 60's MANY SDS CHAPTERS SERVED AS
UMBRELLA GROUPS. SEE CHAPTER TEN.)

PHASE 1:

AD-HOC COMMITTEE AGAINST SPEAKER BAN

WOMEN'S DORM RULES CHANGE COMMITTEE

STUDENT GOVERNMENT

STUDENT PEACE COMMITTEE

YOUNG DEMOCRATS

SDS

CORE

SNCC

PHASE 2:

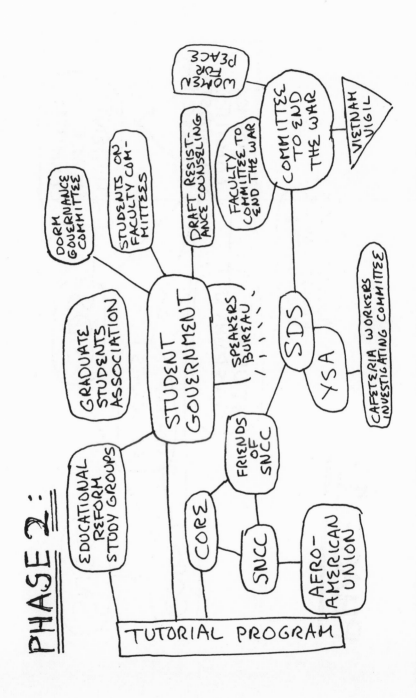

TUTORIAL PROGRAM

EDUCATIONAL REFORM STUDY GROUPS

GRADUATE STUDENTS ASSOCIATION

STUDENT GOVERNMENT

DORM GOVERNANCE COMMITTEE

STUDENTS ON FACULTY COMMITTEES

DRAFT RESISTANCE COUNSELING

SPEAKERS BUREAU

FACULTY COMMITTEE TO END THE WAR

WOMEN FOR PEACE

COMMITTEE TO END THE WAR

VIETNAM VIGIL

SDS

YSA

CAFETERIA WORKERS INVESTIGATING COMMITTEE

FRIENDS OF SNCC

CORE

SNCC

AFRO-AMERICAN UNION

PHASE 3:

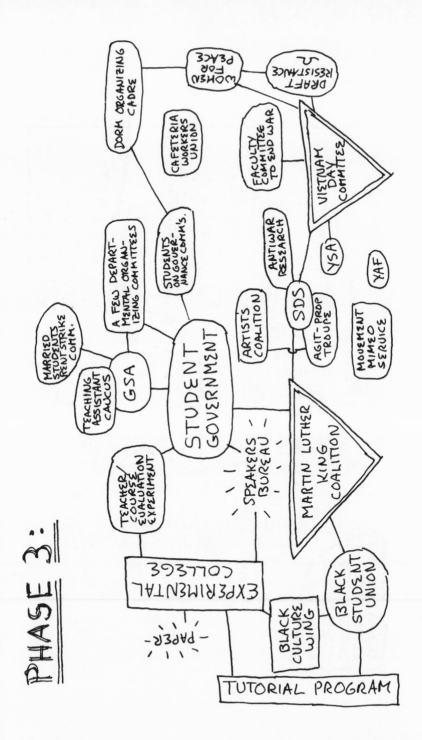

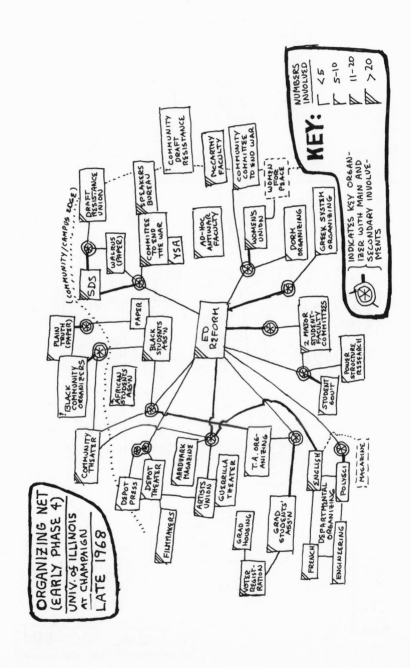

PHASE 4:

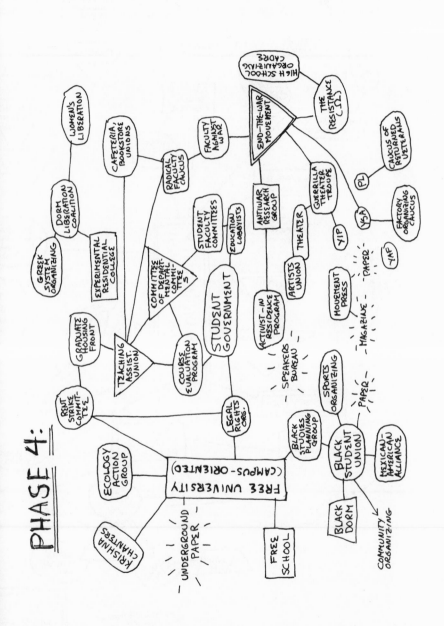

FREE UNIVERSITY (CAMPUS-ORIENTED)

KRISHNA CHANTERS

ECOLOGY ACTION GROUP

UNDERGROUND PAPER

FREE SCHOOL

RENT STRIKE COMMITTEE

GRADUATE HOUSING FRONT

LEGAL RIGHTS ORG.

STUDENT GOVERNMENT

BLACK STUDIES PLANNING GROUP

BLACK STUDENT UNION

BLACK DORM

MEXICAN-AMERICAN ALLIANCE

COMMUNITY ORGANIZING

SPORTS ORGANIZING

PAPER

TEACHING ASSIST. UNION

COURSE EVALUATION PROGRAM

COMMITTEE OF DEPARTMENTAL COMMITTEES

STUDENT-FACULTY COMMITTEES

EDUCATION LOBBYISTS

EXPERIMENTAL RESIDENTIAL COLLEGE

GREEK SYSTEM ORGANIZING

DORM LIBERATION COALITION

WOMEN'S LIBERATION

CAFETERIA, BOOKSTORE UNIONS

RADICAL FACULTY CAUCUS

FACULTY AGAINST WAR

END-THE-WAR MOVEMENT

HIGH SCHOOL ORGANIZING CADRE

THE RESISTANCE (CO)

CAUCUS OF RETURNED VETERANS

FACTORY ORGANIZING CAUCUS

YAF

PL

YSA

YIP

GUERRILLA THEATER TROUPE

THEATER

ARTISTS UNION

MOVEMENT PRESS

PAPER

MAGAZINE

ANTIWAR RESEARCH GROUP

ACTIVIST-IN-RESIDENCE PROGRAM

SPEAKERS BUREAU

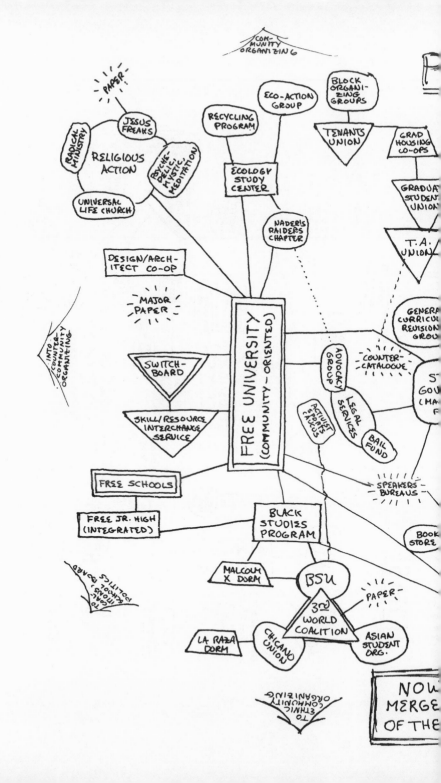

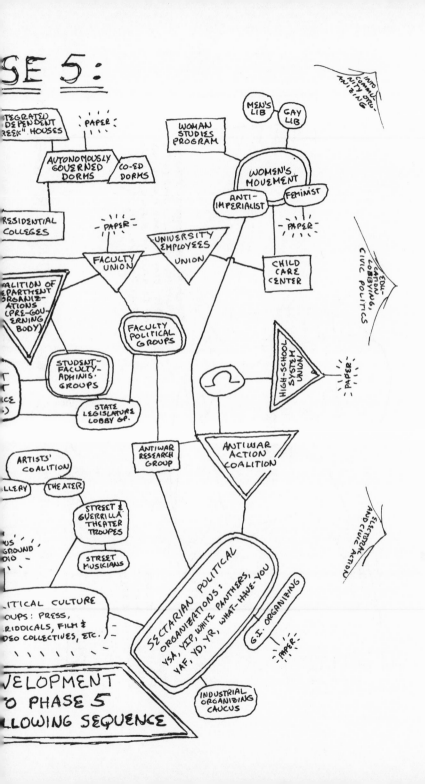

SE 5:

INTO COMMUNITY ORGANIZING

INTEGRATED "INDEPENDENT GREEK" HOUSES
PAPER

MEN'S LIB GAY LIB

WOMAN STUDIES PROGRAM

AUTONOMOUSLY GOVERNED DORMS
CO-ED DORMS

WOMEN'S MOVEMENT
ANTI-IMPERIALIST FEMINIST

RESIDENTIAL COLLEGES

PAPER

EDUCATION LOBBYING CIVIC POLITICS

UNIVERSITY EMPLOYEES UNION

PAPER

FACULTY UNION

CHILD CARE CENTER

COALITION OF DEPARTMENT ORGANIZATIONS (PRE-GOVERNING BODY)

FACULTY POLITICAL GROUPS

T ... CE)

STUDENT-FACULTY-ADMINIS. GROUPS

HIGH-SCHOOL SYSTEM UNION

PAPER

STATE LEGISLATURE LOBBY GP.

ARTISTS' COALITION

LLERY THEATER

ANTIWAR RESEARCH GROUP

ANTIWAR ACTION COALITION

ELECTORAL AND CIVIC ACTION

STREET & GUERRILLA THEATER TROUPES

US GROUND DIO

STREET MUSICIANS

LITICAL CULTURE OUPS: PRESS, RIODICALS, FILM & DEO COLLECTIVES, ETC.

SECTARIAN POLITICAL ORGANIZATIONS: YSA, YIP, WHITE PANTHERS, YAF, YD, YR, WHAT-HAVE-YOU

G.I. ORGANIZING

PAPER

VELOPMENT O PHASE 5 LLOWING SEQUENCE

INDUSTRIAL ORGANIZING CAUCUS

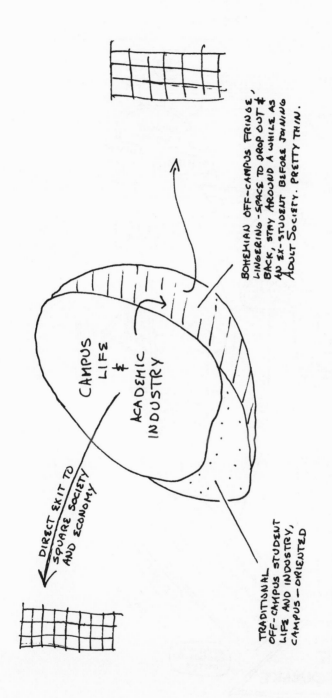

CAMPUS
LIFE
&
ACADEMIC
INDUSTRY

DIRECT EXIT TO
SQUARE SOCIETY
AND ECONOMY

TRADITIONAL
OFF-CAMPUS STUDENT
LIFE AND INDUSTRY,
CAMPUS-ORIENTED

BOHEMIAN OFF-CAMPUS FRINGE,
LINGERING-SPACE TO DROP OUT &
BACK, STAY AROUND A WHILE AS
AN EX-STUDENT BEFORE JOINING
ADULT SOCIETY. PRETTY THIN.

PHASE 0 : STEADY STATE :
GROUNDPLAN & THE IVORY TOWER (circa 1955-65)

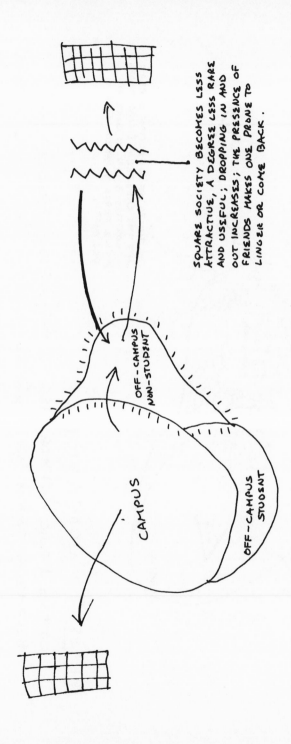

SQUARE SOCIETY BECOMES LESS ATTRACTIVE, A DEGREE LESS RARE AND USEFUL; DROPPING IN AND OUT INCREASES; THE PRESENCE OF FRIENDS MAKES ONE PRONE TO LINGER OR COME BACK.

OFF-CAMPUS NON-STUDENT

OFF-CAMPUS STUDENT

CAMPUS

PHASE 1 : THE FRINGE SWELLS, STARTS GROWING FREAKY

(A BIT OF CORROSION. FLOW RATIOS CHANGE, NO MORE STEADY STATE)

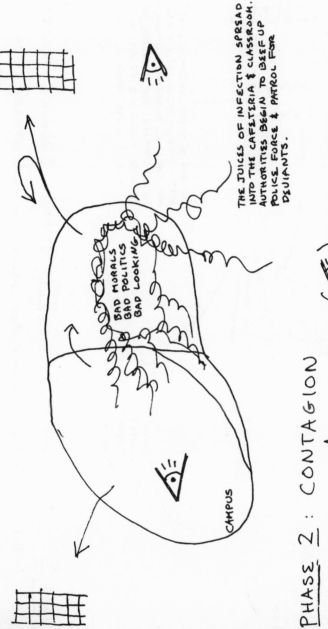

CAMPUS

BAD MORALS
BAD POLITICS
BAD LOOKING

THE JUICES OF INFECTION SPREAD
INTO THE CAFETERIA & CLASSROOM.
AUTHORITIES BEGIN TO BEEF UP
POLICE FORCE & PATROL FOR
DEVIANTS.

PHASE 2 : CONTAGION

CAMPUS & CIVIC AUTHORITIES (👁) WATCH FRINGE

BECOME A SOURCE OF DIS EASE.

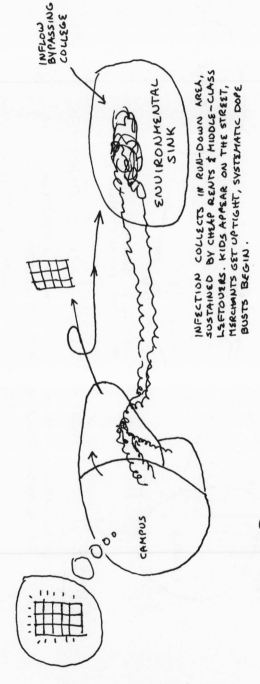

INFLOW BYPASSING COLLEGE

ENVIRONMENTAL SINK

CAMPUS

INFECTION COLLECTS IN RUN-DOWN AREA, SUSTAINED BY CHEAP RENTS & MIDDLE-CLASS LEFTOVERS. KIDS APPEAR ON THE STREET, MERCHANTS GET UPTIGHT, SYSTEMATIC DOPE BUSTS BEGIN.

PHASE 3: VOLUNTARY YOUTH GHETTO FORMS

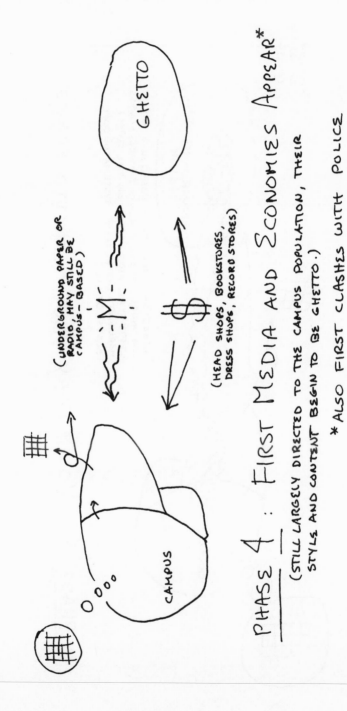

PHASE 4 : FIRST MEDIA AND ECONOMIES APPEAR*

(STILL LARGELY DIRECTED TO THE CAMPUS POPULATION, THEIR STYLE AND CONTENT BEGIN TO BE GHETTO.)

* ALSO FIRST CLASHES WITH POLICE

GHETTO

(UNDERGROUND PAPER OR RADIO, MAY STILL BE CAMPUS-BASED)

(HEAD SHOPS, BOOKSTORES, DRESS SHOPS, RECORD STORES)

CAMPUS

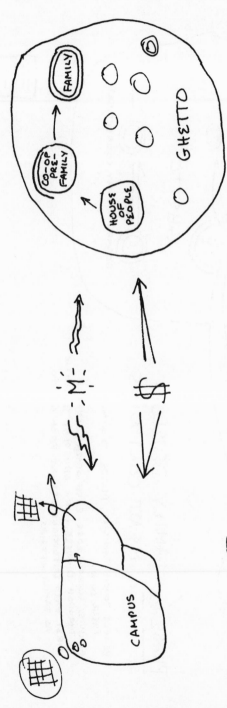

PHASE 5: EXTENDED FAMILIES DEVELOP IN

GHETTO. (IN HOUSE CRUCIBLES, HEAT AND PRESSURE
-- FROM ACID, YEARNING, ECONOMIC & SEXUAL COOPERATION,
POLITICAL & CULTURAL REPRESSION -- BRING PEOPLE TOGETHER
INTO NEW COMPOUNDS.)

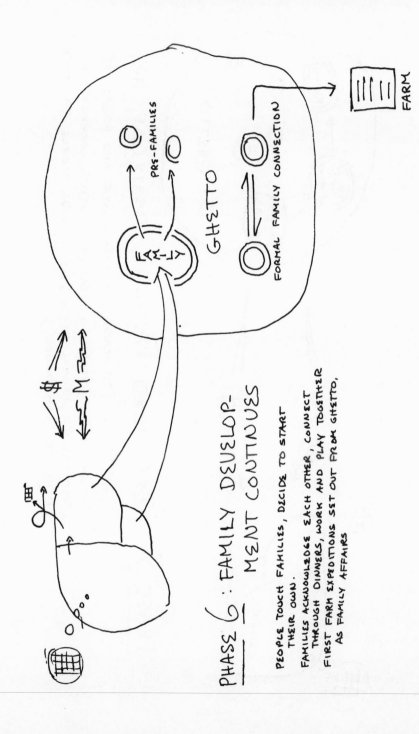

PHASE 6 : FAMILY DEVELOP-
MENT CONTINUES

PEOPLE TOUCH FAMILIES, DECIDE TO START
    THEIR OWN.

FAMILIES ACKNOWLEDGE EACH OTHER, CONNECT
    THROUGH DINNERS, WORK AND PLAY TOGETHER

FIRST FARM EXPEDITIONS SET OUT FROM GHETTO,
    AS FAMILY AFFAIRS

PRE-FAMILIES

GHETTO

FORMAL FAMILY CONNECTION

FARM

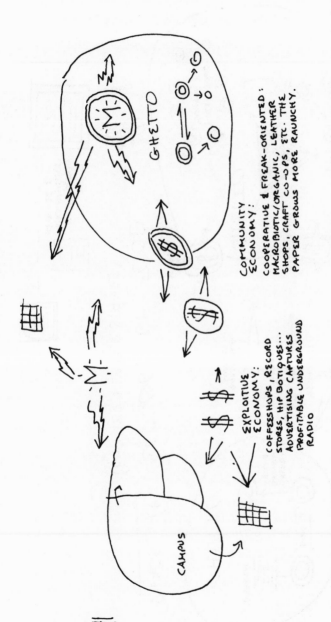

GHETTO

COMMUNITY
ECONOMY:

COOPERATIVE & FREAK-ORIENTED:
MACROBIOTIC/ORGANIC, LEATHER
SHOPS, CRAFT CO-OPS, ETC. THE
PAPER GROWS MORE RAUNCHY.

EXPLOITIVE
ECONOMY:

COFFEESHOPS, RECORD
STORES, HIP BOTIQUES....
ADVERTISING CAPTURES
PROFITABLE UNDERGROUND
RADIO

CAMPUS

PHASE 7 : ECONOMY & MEDIA DIVERSIFY, DIVIDE

WORK-FAMILIES FORM TO BASE THEM.
SELECTIVE TRASHING OF EXPLOITIVE BUSINESSES.

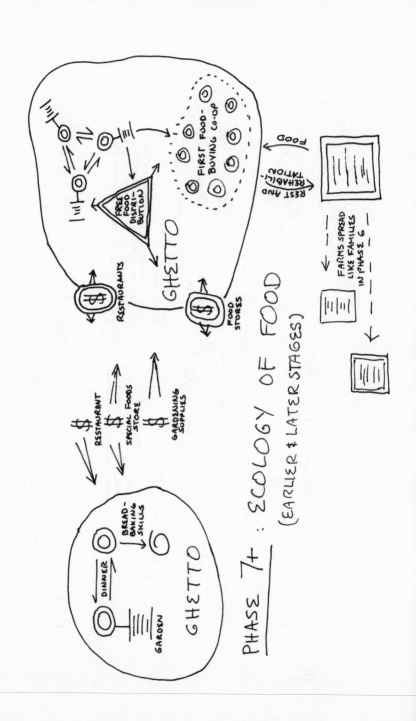

PHASE 7+ : ECOLOGY OF FOOD
(EARLIER & LATER STAGES)

PHASE 7⁺ : FURTHER DEVELOPMENT

HEREAFTER, THE NETWORK OF ACTION GROUPS AND THE INSTI-
TUTIONAL SUBSTRUCTURE OF THE COUNTERCULTURE GROW
RAPIDLY MORE SOPHISTICATED.

IN EVERY SECTOR OF THE SOCIAL WHEEL
OCCUR SUCCESSIVE WAVES OF
DEVELOPMENT. THESE SKETCHES
ILLUSTRATE SEQUENCES AND CONNEC-
TIONS VISIBLE BY 1971. (THEY ARE
BY NO MEANS COMPREHENSIVE, EVEN
WITHIN THE SEVEN SECTORS CONSIDERED.
NOR DO THEY BEGIN TO SHOW THE WEALTH
OF COOPERATIONS POSSIBLE WITHIN THEIR
TOTAL ARRAY OF GROUPS.) EVERY URBAN
COUNTERCULTURAL GHETTO MAY BE EXPECTED TO DEVELOP IN
THIS FASHION. ANTICIPATING THE RICH, SEQUENTIAL CHARACTER
OF THIS DEVELOPMENT MAY BE USEFUL IN PROVIDING FOR IT.

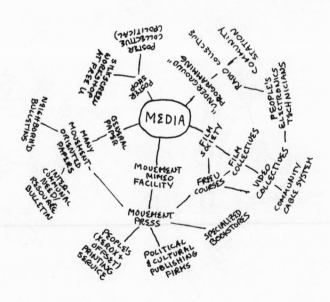

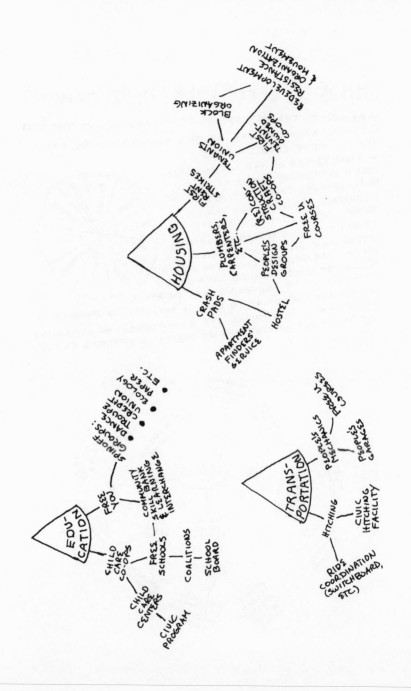

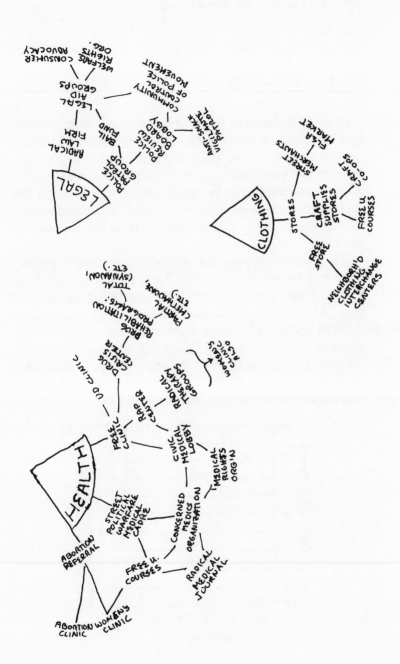

SOME OBSERVATIONS, DEPENDING
ON THE DIAGRAMS

• In the fifth diagram, the school considered is the second-best campus of a better state university system, quartering 30,000 students in an isolated town five times that size. Here its activism is shown, as completely as I could survey it, early in Phase 4 (*à la* 1968), about a year before the student ghetto became conscious of itself as a counter-community and began to turn its energies from the campus into the town.

The diagram on page 300 shows the numbers of persons actively involved in the various foci of campus organizing energy. Some 400 altogether, they constituted the *activist core*. At this time, about one student in eight was an occasional activist, and one in eight of these was continuously active in the organizing net, i.e., in this activist core. Related proportional figures apply to the other phases; I think they are fairly independent of what particular forms a phase displays in any particular year. Very roughly:

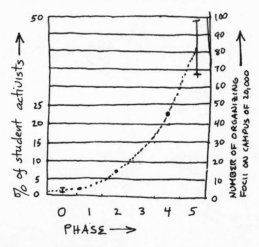

In any phase, the activist core involves roughly one-tenth of the activist population. (What deep constancy is being acted out in this?) This core is a nervous tissue in the campus body, composed of excitable cells connected by overlap or mutual contact. (At any time this tissue also includes several times as many unnamed cells that are more ephemeral and not organizationally visible.) As in animal evolution, raw increase in the number of cells not only permits them to assume more specialized functions but leads them, in the changing environment, to develop into a more complex system capable of more sophisticated functions—a higher brain directing the organizing of social energy.

• A cell of the activist core generally involves from five to twenty people, and connects some ten times as many occasional activists. When a cell grows larger, its tendency is to divide into interlinked cells of this size. Thus the total number of cells in a campus is about 1 per cent of the number of activists, give or take a factor of two. Hence the "organizing brain" of a small campus in Phase 5 (3,000 students; 1,200 activists) will have about as many cells as that of a large campus in Phase 2 (20,000 students; 1,200 activists), though it will probably be more sophisticated through being better connected within itself. On the other hand, even a very active small campus cannot generate enough core cells to permit the higher orders of brain complexity now visible at some large campuses.

Antioch appears to be an exception to this rule. But for unique historical reasons it is more nearly a self-governing community than a college. As communities develop, the unnamed cells become organizationally visible and less ephemeral (as in communes). As all social functions come to be organized by this brain, the number of cells, exclusive of simple living groups, approaches 10 per cent of the total population (a hundred or so typical cells are shown in Phase 7+ of the sequence of community diagrams above).

• All this suggests the following bizarre speculation. When a certain "critical density" of organizing cells is reached in a population, counter-community consciousness emerges.

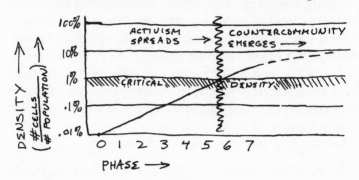

While the density is sub-critical, say less than 0.5 per cent, organizing proceeds mostly horizontally, drawing more and more people into activist consciousness. By the time the density reaches 1.0 per cent, one person in ten is in the active core, engaged in building new social form; and the lives of the other nine are directly affected (at least by having friends so engaged). At this point activist consciousness has spread through essentially the whole population, and collective consciousnes begins a different order of evolution. Though cells continue to proliferate, approaching their limiting density, the edge of organizing energy turns to the vertical, concentrates on generating higher orders of connection among the cells, and the evolution of a comprehensive and integral society commences in earnest.

• Within each organizing cell there is again—even in the best of our cooperations—a key organizing core, generally involving from one person in three (in small cells) to one in fifteen (in larger ones). Call it the nucleus,[1] for it contains the main elements shaping the character and action of the cell and moderates most communication within the cell and

---

[1] Or better the "nuclear material"; for science is coming to a broader understanding of how these functions are served in the cellular ecology.

with other cells. Then a crude portrait of the structure and
embedding of the organizing brain begins to emerge:

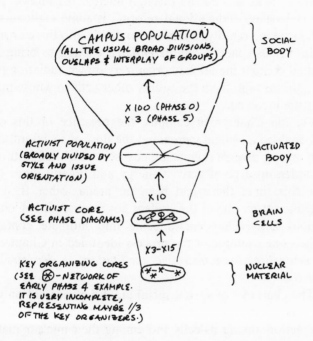

Following this, we can understand three stages in the evolution of new social order: *A,* during which the social body
becomes activated; *B,* during which all its members become
involved in cells organizing energy; and *C,* during which all
the cells become fully democratic, and each person a full
member of the nuclear material.

(Of course, these stages are not so strictly sequential as they
are pictured here.)

• The "real example" diagram on p. 300 begins to display the interconnection of cells in a campus organizing core ("brain"), as this occurs through nuclear organizers. Here the cell called "educational reform" is some eight months old. Growing rapidly, it is about to divide into three or more cells. Yet its space is *undifferentiated enough* to bring into mutual contact the ten key organizers shown radiating from it—and through them the twenty other cells in whose nuclei they are involved.

On the Champaign campus, the presence of this open cell enabled a radical increase in the flow of social information among diverse organizing nexuses, which led in turn to a sudden upsurge of activist energy and organization. (Before this time, there had been no arena, other than the bureaucratized one of the student government, in which the various activist tendencies came into intimate contact.) This is one example of the process identified in Chapter IX as *centralized administrative facilitation of decentralized activity.*

The character of such a social brain depends not only on its size but on the topology of connection and modes of interaction among its cells and among their nuclear matter. A proper academic study would proceed by analyzing these exhaustively for a number of particular case studies. But for us groundlings, involved in building real movements and real communities, diagrams such as these have immediate practical usefulness.

In a number of campuses and counter-communities, I have had this experience: We gather in one room a good number of people from the activist core, including as many nuclear organizers as possible. Setting up a large blackboard and someone to tend it, we conduct a two-stage *fishbowl.*

In the first stage, a fisherman fishes out what the people know about the developmental history of the organizing they are continuing, and it is assembled on the blackboard, bit by bit. We see the first organizations form, grow, divide, change their names and focus, disappear, diversify. We watch the broad flow of activist energy surface in mass events—teacher-firing protests, festivals—and give rise to organization, then subside while a resurgence is prepared; we see how antiwar energy, frustrated, expresses itself through ecology for a time; and so on. As key people's names are mentioned repeatedly, we identify successive waves of organizers, see how broadly and long they worked and how they moved on, and whether they helped train others to carry on and transcend their work. When we are fished out, the blackboard records an historical perspective on the present state of the local movement—a perspective now shared by all those present, enabling all the cells they represent to understand themselves as articulations of a common motion.

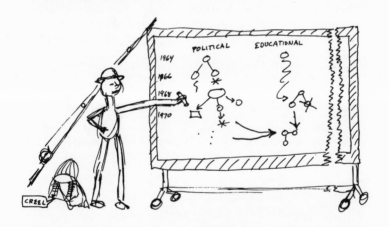

In the second stage, the blackboard is reversed, and we concentrate on the present state of the movement. One representative from each cell describes the size and internal organization of the cell and its connections and interactions with other cells. As the information comes out, it is diagrammed; together we watch a sketch of the present brain unfolding. When we're done, we have a rough power-structure analysis of the movement and its communications net. The authoritarian or democratic balance of its system may be understood in the terms of Chapter VII. Usually the actual sketch shows clearly what parts of the brain are unnecessarily isolated from or subordinate to other parts, and suggests how new cells can be created to decentralize or coordinate the functions of present ones.

Each of these stages takes a long afternoon on a large campus not beyond Phase 3, or in any other organizing pool where the total number of cells is still small enough for almost all to be represented in one room. A richer context requires a group working together for a while—i.e., the creation of a reflexive cell—and organized dissemination of its investigation.

X.

Speculations on the Free Schools Movement

1. IS IT A MOVEMENT?

FOR DECADES THERE was a handful of radically progressive schools in America. In the sixties new consciousness emerged, began many kinds of experiment, turned inevitably to "lower" education. By '66 *Summerhill* was already popular, giving people common rhetoric to work with, and new schools began to multiply. This was also the year of the first one I know to have been evolved from a political context (SDS/REP), the Ann Arbor Children's Community. By late '71 there were some 400 "free" schools. It's hard to say what they have in common, besides some tendency to dethrone old Authorities and foster self-directed learning, and a lot of problems. Though all are reacting against the official system of education, as yet they share no clear vision, let alone mutual allegiance.

Are they a movement? What is a movement? Facing common need, people come together to try to puzzle out a way of doing things differently. In the beginning they share no clear understanding of their situation and mutual interest, or of where and how to move to build what they need. Always when mass will bursts out, it stands at first confused and divided, shaking off old mystifications, before it goes on to develop common ideology and practice; or fails in this. The free schools movement, like any other, will flourish to the extent that it develops a collective consciousness that works to extend and deepen itself in the society. Only this can keep it, school by school and as a whole, from being blunted, moving off into dead ends, or being reabsorbed into the dominant system.

Each free school must understand itself as part of a movement, and the movement as a force among counterforces in a culture in which great currents of liberation and repression contend in history. This is hard; we are taught to understand what we do, as well as how we suffer, only in private, isolated, and a-historical terms. People are still trying to describe the philosophy and practice of free schooling in such terms, stripped of their broad social and political consequences and obligations, following the pastoral *Summerhill* archetype. That's not enough.

2. HOW FAST IS IT GROWING?
HOW LARGE WILL IT GROW?

Consider a parallel movement in higher education. The first campus-based free university appeared in '65; by '69 there were 500. They are a *population,* spreading through a new niche in the social ecology, and are subject to the laws of ecology. One law is that a population cannot multiply indefinitely: its numbers approach some *upper limit* in time. Moreover, in general, a population increases in a specific way toward its upper limit. Plotting its numbers on a graph against time,[1] we get a *logistic growth curve*. (See diagram next page.)

As the environment becomes favorable, a small, stable population begins to multiply. This is described by the "toe" of the curve. The curve then rises as a straight line, describing a period of geometric (exponential) multiplication— here increasing tenfold per unit of time. Finally some limiting factor causes growth to level out, in a reverse "toe," approaching its upper limit. (For free universities, the upper limit cannot exceed the number of campuses; the curve has no "toe" because the organism is new.)

Now take the main curve for free schools. It has a legitimate "toe"; some have been around for a long time. We are now in the straight-line period. They are doubling in number yearly, and will for some time, approaching one of the limits indicated, unless the environment changes radically. What would stunt free-school multiplication? *Radical reform of the public schools.* Unlikely within this decade. *Economic depression, political repression.* Not to be expected on a major scale before '76 (though, like the aerospace elite, many who now feed on affluence are beginning to feel the pinch). By then the initial multiplication of free schools will be already cresting.

Thus these figures seem plausible now:

	FALL 1973	FALL 1975	FALL 1977
Schools	1,600	6,500	25,000
Students	50,000	200,000	800,000
Staff	10,000	40,000	160,000
Parents	70,000	300,000	1,200,000

[1] Such graphs are most convenient with the population-axis increasing geometrically, and the time-axis only arithmetically.

for **PROJECTED GROWTH**
of **F.S.M.**

theoretical limit, all children in small free schools — 4

limiting value: one school per 4,000 people, or 6-8% of students — 3

limiting value drawn from present reservoir of predisposed parents & kids — 5

1,000,000
300,000
100,000
30,000
10,000
3,000
1,000
300
100
30 OR LESS
10

Numbers →
Time →

'62 '64 '66 '68 '70 '72 '74 '76 '78 '80

< NOW >

PAST GROWTH
for **OF FREE SCHOOLS MOVEMENT** — 3

AN IDEAL LOGISTIC CURVE

10^6
10^5
10^4
1000
100
10
1

limit: capacity of population

upper "toe"

straight-line (geometric) growth

lower "toe"

Numbers →

Time →

SPREAD OF EXPERIMENTAL COLLEGES

10,000
1,000
100
10
1
2

2500 COLLEGES = LIMIT (ACTUALLY LESS)

the first ones began in '65, hence no lower "toe"

'64 '66 '68 '70 '72 '74 '76 '78 '80

3. ARE THESE FIGURES REALISTIC?
PARALLELS WITH FREE UNIVERSITIES

The movements for free schools and for free universities have many similarities. Both are concerned with reforming the educational system by creating alternate institutions. The values and directions of change both try to embody are similar. So are their deficiencies—e.g., they're as yet unable to re-create the learning of our more technical skills, like the sciences. Each movement spreads by a process of personal contact and media exposure—which does not so much convince new people as motivate those already prone to make their own examples. As schools multiply and people seek information, *newsletters* appear, *conferences* are called, the potential for the *internal education* of a movement appears. As the density of schools increases, *urban and regional cooperations* grow among them. After several years of local work, *speakers* and *traveling organizers* appear, drawn from experience in the movement itself, to help it build and circulate its understandings. (Upon the careful cultivation of such italicized agencies depends the movement's further development, beyond its first flush of intuitive expression.)

Higher education is everywhere pretty much the same, so each campus is the potential host of a free U. Free U members seem mainly to select themselves by psychological predisposition: by their need and readiness for freer ways of learning. Their proportion in any college, plain or fancy, seems remarkably constant: some 6 to 10 per cent of the students.

If the parallel holds, consider the 44 million kids aged six to sixteen. Figuring only for nonreactionary, white, middle-class families, some 40 per cent of the total, 6 to 10 per cent predisposed works out to 1 million to 1.5 million white, mildly liberal kids, as a first base for free schools to spread through in the next few years. (This estimate points up the racist/elitist character of the present movement, one of its principal problems.) More broadly: each town, each school district of over 500 students, each ethnic group or neighborhood of over 4,000 persons, has enough predisposed/receptive parents and students to spawn a small free school. A vision of 50,000 free schools is not unreasonable.

4.   TEACHERS AND PARENTS

There are now battalions of frustrated teachers, mostly young, looking for something better to do than teach in the System. More and more put in a few years, find it unbearable, drift unengaged. Forecast for the decade: the public schools will grow worse. An unstable economy will refuse their rehabilitation; they will continue their development as battlegrounds for the society's racism; as the political climate grows ugly the reins of control will tighten within them. Meanwhile deep trends continue, moving many from technological to human-oriented jobs; from detached to socially relevant work; from "straight" jobs in bureaucratic hierarchies at work determined by others to work of their own choice and making. All in all, the seventies will see no shortage of people ready to staff a first great wave of free schools.

In general, these people will be making heavy changes in their own lives toward more integral ways of relating— sexually, emotionally, communally, ecologically, politically. The nature and difficulties of these changes will strongly influence what they can or want to do in free schools, and how they will go about teaching.

The same will be increasingly true of free school parents.

We must see them not only as individual people in change, but as a changing *class*. It's hard to measure the more intimate aspects of their change. But some social aspects are clear enough to warn us that the present crop of some 20,000 free school parents gives us only a limited idea of what to expect and plan for in the future. The great majority of them are over thirty, and almost all ended their undergraduate college experience by '63, or at the latest by '65. That is to say, before the first campus sit-ins, hippies and the Haight, Vietnam-as-issue, the Beatles, grass and acid, Panthers and Women's Lib—back in the palmy days of civil rights, when Amerika and her institutions still seemed open to liberal change.

Some were relatively radical once, or since. But the college experience and the growing up of all of them were qualitatively different than these were for the generation coming to adulthood in the late sixties, from whom will come most of the parents who will build the free school movement to massive proportions during the seventies. Consider a member of the Class of '68, who has a child in '70, who is school-age in '76. In '68 about 4 per cent of college students participated in experimental colleges, and 5 per cent tutored "disadvantaged" children—that is, involved themselves personally in experimental education; 20 per cent took part in demonstrations against some aspect of the authority of the State and/or the Educational System; 20 per cent smoked grass, one in twenty did acid, *Fortune* estimated 40 per cent were in basic sympathy with the "goals of the New Left."

By '80 there will be over 30 million parents of school-aged children in the twenty-seven to thirty-five age range. Of these, more than 2 million will have been directly involved in counter-education; 6 million in organized demonstrations against illegitimate authority; 10 million in psychedelic drugs. These estimates are *low;* they take no account of the way all the curves of involvement are soaring—2 million turned out for Cambodia/Kent alone, the year the Weather-people went underground and the newspapers blanked out eight bombings a day nationwide. There is less sign now than a decade ago that our institutions are open to the changes we want. Surely many parents will commit their kids to free schools if the form continues to be viable.

5.   OUT OF A CHANGING SUBSTANCE; IN A CHANGING CLIMATE

At each college now the incoming freshmen are markedly more life-radical than the seniors. Change piles upon itself that rapidly nowadays, and will do so in the free schools movement as well. The movement will expand through the seventies on a wave of people who have been through confrontation politics, psychedelic drugs, encounter and hip culture. We plan for the future by studying the changes of the present, and any projection for the movement must take into account such radical shifts in experience and perception, the suddenness with which they happen, the sharpness of their later echoes.

The gamut we must deal with runs from sex to politics. Presently the edge, in the broad domain of sex, is like this for people in their twenties: women's liberation spreading, gays coming out and straights investigating their bisexuality, group marriages, public nudity, legitimate abortion, open sexual liaisons and non-private-property attitudes about lovers' bodies. All this will show up integrally in the curriculum/process of free schools. For in live contact with students the forces of change running through people's lives cannot fail to be expressed. And in this matter of sex, as in many others, the free schools will be ideal experimental vehicles—small, highly flexible and various, more or less removed from larger social control—for testing out the integration of new cultural knowledge/experience into basic education. Well in advance of this wave of sexual opening, the movement should begin to discuss its nature and impact, more thoroughly than Neill has done. But we probably won't, and each school will be left to understand and struggle with sexual matters mostly by itself.

All the openings of the sexual edge have their political aspect, and politics will follow after any opening of sexuality in education—think about nudity, and getting permits from the county building inspector. More broadly: the free schools movement will grow and be shaped in the political climates of this decade, conflicting thermals will feed it and stunt it. Any projection must predict the weather during the season of growth. You don't need a Weatherman to know which way the wind blows. For most of the decade, the polarizations of Amerika will increase; there will be more violence, especially of a semi-organized kind, and a coldening climate of political repression, directed at all forms of liberated behavior or doctrine. For this is the decade when it begins to get hard, after the easy dreams of the sixties: when Amerika's true resistance to change, and for each of us our own, begins to come into the open.

6. TENSION, CO-OPTATION, CONTAINMENT, REPRESSION

Free schools will quickly become a major alternative to the public system and will drain from it more and more of its innovative teachers, responsive kids, and certain classes of parents. To this extent, the mainstream system will grow even less adaptable, and polarization between the two will deepen and grow bitter, in style and politics.

But there will also be a blurring of the lines between them. The presence of an alternate system, covering all levels of education, will cause the mainstream system to adapt competitively, in the classic way—by modifying and adopting the lesser pieces of the radical program, as fragments stripped of their broader implications. Thus we see already some loosening of curriculum, schedule, learning-group size; some fuzzing of the grading system; expansion of teaching into affective domains; and so on. For the next five years we can expect a deluge of articles in national magazines boasting the modernization of the suburban junior high.

But some lines cannot be crossed. So long as schools serve to prepare the young for the present industrial machinery, they must teach them to defer to experts, obey bureaucratic authority, work unwillingly, specialize narrowly, and maintain the chauvinisms of class, race, sex, and age. Whether or not the mainstream schools seem to come more under parent control, and no matter how much ecstatic new technology is used to "enrich" them, they must continue to be staffed by a corps of teachers trained to pass on the ruling orthodoxies of mainstream culture—consumerism, sexual repression, nationalism, idol-worship, etc.

Enough people will not be satisfied with this to cause a further adaptation—an attempted "encysting" of the alternate system within the mainstream one, to neutralize its effect. Within many urban and suburban schools will grow "free" sub-schools; and many local school systems will sponsor experimental campuses. Together these will constitute a sophisticated addition to the tracking system, and, whatever their "freeing" of the kids, will preserve the principle of elitism. Unless students and parents make something else happen, the effect will be to isolate change-energy and protect the larger system from transformation.

A cautionary tale, from an earlier movement: By now the campus free U's have grown somewhat stale. College administrators welcome them as "constructive," i.e., nonthreatening. And they are right. Such groups have needed space, resources, legitimacy, accreditation, and have sought these mostly from the established institution and in its terms. To be tolerated they damp their potential thrust for change in their host institutions and in social structures, instead orienting themselves to personal change and private experience. Where they do not, as at San Francisco State, multiple forces attack them.

Independently founded free schools will face the same pressures, the same blunting of their thrust. Powerful undertows of need will pull them to depend on cooperation with the great urban bureaucracies. The price of support will be a soft repression, a biasing of goals, standards, and processes. Only the development of sharp collective consciousness and community-based independence from the mainstream system can keep open the possibilities of social reconstruction inherent in root educational change.

Here's a paranoid scenario for the next few years, as free schools pass their founding flush and begin grappling with the problems of how to move on:

A network of periodicals from the educational underground will arise to testify to a dozen regional cooperations. (First versions of these cooperations are evident already in Berkeley and New York, and prototype journals include *NSEN, Ed-Centric,* and *Outside the Net.*)

As individual free schools are doing now, soon many local and regional cooperations will work hard on grant proposals to foundations and Federal agencies. Most of this work will be wasted. Only a few small family funds will respond well, in nonconstraining ways. The giant foundations that deal in education, like Ford and Carnegie, will perform like the Government agencies (OE, NIMH, OEO) to implement official social policy, funding what's "safe" and encouraging its dominance in the movement, judging in a sanitized style who and what programs are "responsible" enough to support and what constitutes "results."

As it becomes clear what massive discontent and radical

potential are represented in the free schools movement, both private and Federal agencies will bestow demonstration grants in the $200,000 to $2 million class upon local or national cooperations that are taken to represent the most "promising" features of the (anarchic, disorganized) movement. If the parallel with the higher ed reform movement holds, these grants will be badly administered, politically crippling, sexist, and racist; and the major part of the funds will be absorbed in administrative unwork. Agencies already cooperative with the private and Federal funding structure —like the Antioch-centered Establishment of experimental higher education and the Berkeley city schools—will be chosen as the conduits through which funds will flow to satellite "independent" free schools programs.

This Establishment-sponsored "vanguard" will be rendered larger than life by the selective attention of the mass media. Thirsty for official recognition and support, the mass of free schools will come to shape their philosophies and practices in accordance with this amplified image of what succeeds. In polarized opposition, we will see a "small, hard-core radical minority," most defiantly countercultural, some with hard left politics, probably fairly isolated from each other. Most free schools whose spirit is that of Summerhill will be readily absorbed as ancillaries to the public schools, as most private schools have always been, and will see no clear reason to resist this. (In this lack of oppositional spine will appear the consequence of the incompleteness of Neill's philosophy, which deals only with community that frees the individual, and not also with the general re-formation of society.)

In the same way that Young Americans for Freedom are now multiplying on the campuses, so soon, in city and country, right-wing groups will form and act more openly in lower education. They will advise and be advised by local and Washington politicians, not all Republican, who will also be their avenues of access to FBI and other "subversive" files. Such groups will mount campaigns, locally and nationally, against free schools of all kinds and levels. Their viciousness will rise in direct proportion to that of the hardhat/racist backlash as it continues to unfold. Thus hand-in-hand with liberal "encouragement" of the free schools movement, we shall see its attack by a broad spectrum of overtly repressive forces—a powerful combination of push/pull to bring it into line.

As it becomes recognized as a massive leading edge, the free schools movement, like ecology, will be courted by politicians and made the subject of Presidential rhetoric and some legislation. By 1976 the threat of its unregulated growth will lead to major state or Federal programs for redistributing education tax money for parents' "free" use, in the form of tuition vouchers. At best, this could open an enormous freedom for experiment (at the cost of allowing much of Amerika to continue at will in racist education). But there will be conditions, of course—beyond the powerful conservative effect of giving control of the vouchers to parents rather than to children. Free schools will have to conform to certain regulations, not only of plumbing, but of practice, to be eligible for voucher redemption. The tame will flourish, the wild starve.

Those that will not be domesticated, that deal openly and deviantly enough with, say, sex-drugs-and-politics, will be harassed by inspectors and closed after arrests, or dynamited in the night.

7.   BEYOND FREE SCHOOLS

So far I've spoken of the free schools movement in terms of its being a growing collection of small, relatively autonomous experimental schools. As such, it has material needs, a political identity, philosophical and political problems, etc., all of which we are only beginning to grapple with.

Yet this institutional façade, the domain of our immediate necessities and decisions, is also an illusion. For I think that free schools, however we now conceive them, are a transitional institution, and that the movement whose present frontier they represent is in its essence trans-institutional. In concert with other current group experiments, they mark an early stage in a revolution of social forms that will transcend our present understanding of what institutions are and how they function.

We are engaged in a profound transition—old news, but it hasn't really penetrated our consciousness. All of the great divisions articulated into our lives—work/play, rich/poor, body/mind, male/female, subject/object, religious/secular, and of course, teacher/student, learning/action, school/world—all these and more shall be broken, melted and reconfigured in a more integral harmony, if Man is to survive.

Though we live from day to day on the level of hassling with the building inspector, we must seek such terms as these to make sense out of what we are doing, out of the changes we go through in our parts in the Change that is acting through us. There are no two ways about it: no terms less broad will do. We would be mistaken, for example, to go by our past experience with new educational forms—the fraternity, the public school, the land-grant college, the kindergarten—and expect that free schools too will simply multiply to saturate their niche in the American institutional ecology and then persist for a century or so as a stable, well-defined institutional form.

Rather, I think, we shall come to see them as a dew in the meadow of change, each drop dispersing again into new forms as the sun cycles. Already free schools are noted for being short-lived. Universally, such May-fly life is taken for failure. But I think it may equally mark success. For, to the extent that a school is a free space for change, its operations transform its members, carrying them to new consciousness of what is and new conceptions of what is to be done. Such transformations cycle in the periods described in Chapter VIII. That the average life-span of a free school is now eighteen months is no accident.

So, if we are not overeager to recognize a form in which we can rest our action, we should expect to see people found free schools or work in them, continue transformation, migrate alone or as whole groups into other cooperations, which may no longer be called "schools." From this perspective, whether individual free schools persist or disappear is not important, as long as each provides an integral period of experience for all its participants. Free schools are probably best seen as Kleenex institutions, to be made, used, and discarded (unless we escape our old notions about, and commitments to, institutional permanence, we will be in for much agony in such decisions).

Yet though their flesh change fast, free schools will be with us for some time. The estimates above for the spread of free schools presume nothing about the endurance of individual schools, much about the multiplication of a consciousness against a uniform background of need. Overall, these free schools will function as transition valves, arenas of experience leading their participants into new adventures. Many may be decade-stable as continuous loci of transition for rapid generations of learners.

The Law that says *making change changes,* leads us, alone and together, through clear sequences of evolution in consciousness and action. These sequences, still developing, are common and beginning to pass into folklore, though they have not been written about much. They are compounded from successions of experience on the major learning frontiers of our time and seem on the whole to be leading people toward the undifferentiated seed of a new form —a group at once family and pride, cooperative work unit, playgroup and mutual school, doctor and priest of its members: a flexible intimate society that supports and frees its people to assume and reconfigure all the necessary human roles, and that is itself protean in its manifestations in the larger society, appearing, in our present terms, for a while as a school, as a sexual consortium, as a laboratory, as a dispersed collection of friends.

Toward this seed form communes, political action groups, media collectives, and other new cooperations are now mutating. We should expect each free school also to mutate in this direction as experience enlarges its perspective. Indeed, if one critical imperative of our change is to re-create so deeply the nature of the groups in which people are embedded, a free school which focuses on relevant learning for all its participants (not just the kids) may proceed on this metamorphosis quickest of all.

8.   AGEISM, FREE SCHOOLS, AND CONFERENCES

One evening, at an early conference of free schools, Jackie Perez Motion started talking about youth collectives. Already ten-year-olds are gathering in them in preference to home, she said, and soon we shall see children much younger choosing to develop in environments not dominated by adults.

She didn't get much chance to draw out her argument. Umpteen people jumped her verbally. Their evident passion indicated that she had touched a raw nerve, the key psychosis (in the strict sense) of the free school movement— the belief that kids are uniquely dependent upon our efforts as "adults" to *construct* the circumstances of their education for them.

There's no point arguing whether younger people "need" older ones: the unfondled infant grows up cold. The deeper truth is that we are present in their world, and they will learn essential things from us whatever we do. In free schools, as in any others, we will be conscious only of fragmentary and superficial aspects of what it is we are teaching them by the ways we live. This is no argument against being purposeful about the educational process, as best we can. But it is a dangerous narrowness of vision to mistake the school we construct for their actual School.

In its altruistic focus upon providing for the needs of others, the free schools movement threatens to become the ultimate liberal trip. You will recall: we started out Doing Good for the oppressed Negro and others of color; went on to Do Good for the Vietnamese, as best we were able; and then turned to Doing Good for the poor whites, the culturally oppressed straights, etc. Now we are Doing Good for our own oppressed children. God forbid they should reject our attentions—we might have to face the prospect of doing ourselves some radical Good.

I don't know how many people have told me that the problems of free schools are more with the parents and teachers than with the children—that free schools are generated as much in response to their needs as to those of the kids, and serve as vehicles for the acting-out of adult fantasies and therapies. This is to be expected; it testifies to objective social conditions. There should be no need to rehearse again the circumstances of our own oppression: we each are discovering them, and every open space calls on us to make the changes we have held back from.

Adult needs must be openly recognized, and their learning co-equally focused upon, rather than acted out covertly or vicariously. Only thus can the space of children's learning be freed from that oppressive control that comes from living our lives through them. Children need not only the contexts we create, but also freedom from them—the more so since much of our learning these days is remedial, addressed to destructive ways into which they have not yet been fully acculturated.

Their ultimate school is our own lives, plus what else they discover. In seeking to benefit them we would do well to tend to ourselves. If we are involved in creating conditions and ways that fulfill us as humans in a web of life, I daresay their education will be fairly well provided for, whatever institutional arrangements we may make. Surely the most profound teaching we can exhibit to the young of an age of Transformation is our own example as persons actively engaged in the struggle to re-create our own lives—internally, in groups, and in the larger social order. (In the politics of change, all the skills customarily thought of as being taught in school, from mathematics to welding to emotional control, fall into the perspective of this struggle, and will be learned in terms of their use or misuse in it.)

But see—again, and so easily, I fall back toward the terms of ageism, speaking only of adults as a key to children's learning, rather than equally of the converse truth. It's only natural: I'm much more conscious of the things I have to teach my son than of what I might learn from him.

My lopsided consciousness is shared by many. At a conference of some 300 people, there were a few mid-teens and maybe a dozen children from two to seven, plus an eleven-year-old. From the age-distribution you'd never have known that it represented a frontier movement of education, in which the young were to be newly and integrally involved. It was like any movement conference—say, the antiwar movement, or black liberation, save that in these young teens would be better represented.

I want to look at this conference as at a school, and in terms of its ageism, for it was a learning-exchange among people trying to make new sorts of schools. Yet young people neither shared in its planning nor were consulted— though it was brought off by people in their twenties who are intimately involved in free schools. The presence of minors wasn't actively discouraged, but invitations circulated mostly among adults, and the fee structure was inhibiting. Nor were there, in the conference program, topics of interest as the young would define them, nor space for these to be generated, let alone actual free-school students whose presentations were featured.

Such political analysis may seem a parody. But it is necessary in some form to discuss responsibly the workings of a movement of many people whose lives are conjoined in experiment—a movement whose development is still entirely in the control of a minority, one distinctly political in having vested interests of power and limitations of consciousness which it cannot transcend alone. Be forewarned: this is the sort of analysis we shall shortly have to contend with from children themselves, who will take its terms with deadly seriousness.

It's not just a cute coincidence that 1971's Berkeley elections, which brought radicals fractional power for the first time, and the first school board campaign by a representative of a regional coalition of free schools, also brought the first Children's Liberation platform, equally conjoined with the others to form the broad program of the April Coalition. The Kid's Lib platform was written by a ten-year-old. I felt this uneasy chill, listening to him rap down the same kinds of terms I am rephrasing here. But maybe he's a freak, maybe he'll go away; as long as there's only one of him, there's no real problem. Listen: write me, will you, if you spot any more?

Back to the conference. As usual, we acted it out mostly in terms of old visions of what our schooling together should be like. Had it not been exclusively adult-centered, would it have been so dense with schedule, having neither recess for intimate interaction (save at meals) nor playground (save for two small body workshops)? Mostly people gathered in crowds to hear a few Names hold forth and to quiz them. I was one, I guess, and found I couldn't help but contribute to the hierarchies-of-wisdom game, running on in the same old male rapping style—so retrograde to find it entrenched in a movement this rich in together women.

As conferences go, this one had a fair amount of open space and several strong workshops formed around freer processes to deal with practical matters relating to a mass democratic base (like regional cooperations of free schools and communes). Most important was the ad-hoc radical caucus that formed to tackle survival strategies. As the first manifestation of its sort (that I know of) in the free schools movement, it initiated the first protest against the present authority structure of the movement, already well developed and powerful in its influence. In the main session the second day, the caucus presented the problem of a few authorities speaking for the many involved in important work, and demanded that personal profits made through connection with the movement be plowed back into it in substantive ways. A new stage of movement consciousness was perhaps beginning.

But this spontaneous political drama, and the body workshops, were the only "classes" in this school that were not of a long familiar sort. The dominant mode was argumentative; only rarely did group energy flare in the intensity of the circle of testimony in which experience is shared and distilled. If free schools are developing new consciousness about educational process, it has so far shown up in conferences only in their looser structuring, and not in organized effort to bring people together around newer modes of action and interchange.

There are newer modes aplenty, and reason to use them. Any frontier movement ought to be reflexive, ought to turn the full force of the understandings about educational process now available to us upon its own operations and serve as the laboratory for its own best experiments, making possible a different order of business.

For there was a different order of business, I am convinced, that we came there for but found unlisted in the program— some business of the spirit, increasingly urgent, but only vaguely and imperfectly transacted through our actual categories of conference-dealing plus that one flash of political consciousness. I don't know how to name it. It has to do with being involved together, interdependent on the edge of an uncertain future; and with levels of consciousness, allegiance, and commitment. (Secretly I think it is the birth of a people's spirit; but I am trying to be sober here.)

This business of the spirit reveals itself to us in shared experience, in group ritual. But it is not much furthered through the group forms of the conference—purely verbal interchanges, passive attendance to art, and dinner in the cafeteria. Better vehicles would be: campfires, rainstorms, building something together, making music together, playing with an ample video feedback net, centering the occasion on the actual birth of a child, reverencing some change in the natural or human season—almost any collective action not in the male tradition of harsh light, utilitarian discussion, and rhetorical argument.

Or we might bring in the younger people, and work with them in learning new forms and new ways. I keep coming back toward their perspective, to see how far we are yet from an integral advance. By the second afternoon of the conference, after nearly having a breakdown the night before when it came my turn to sit in the Authority chair and try to keynote some humane version of the old drama, I had had it with words; I couldn't get it together to go hear Kozol talk. I'm still somewhat sorry, for I've never seen him, and I heard he was fine that session. But I was obsessed by this notion that what people learn, in schools, conferences, etc., is not only the cognitive content of their transactions, but also the continuous social lesson of its forms. A bit freaked by seeing the old lessons endlessly relearned, and weary of the proliferation of worldly words among people coming to care deeply for each other, I let Beth, a gentle lady not given to rapping, lead me off to play with the children.

And there they were, the dozen or so youngs of this free schools conference, off by themselves, away from the meetings in which they'd be indifferent nuisances. Usually some relevant mother was nearby, doing the standard duty. But for the most part they were being attended by an eleven-year-old, who had taken their care upon himself and all con-

ference long was shepherding them in games (while in another room Jackie's remarks, about growing consciousness
among youngs, were being greeted with consternation).

We settled in and made a little music. Then somehow,
quicker than a wink, I became the ferocious Nose-Kissing
Monster, and the Shepherd organized great monster-hunts
among his flock, for an hour of squeals, chases, and kissing
tumbles. My first monster, I'd thought him up only a week
ago, while snuffling Lorca; this was his first tryout, and a
grand success. I had never before realized how eager children
are for a little monstrosity—not just any monstrosity, but
one with some grace and control, funky and real enough to
test themselves against, yet with the intelligence to be tamed,
and not immune to reconciliation.

Aren't we all the children of a monstrous fantastical age,
needing to grow together by our versions of such ritual? I
remembered daring the National Guard in Chicago, running
from the shotguns in Berkeley, an endless rain of bombs over
Indochina. Where are our monsters with the wisdom to
yield; where the tribes against whom we test our bravery yet
with whom we are united in the festivals of the Great Spirit?
And what of the meeting rooms of this conference—in what
thin way were such collective needs met by our exchanges
of opinion there? Were the political theater or the sharp
questioning of Name speakers our ways of organizing a
monster-hunt? And where was the kiss?

Crawling on the floor, my clothes instantly filthy, I saw
the conference as a school from the children's perspective.
Here they were learning again that to be a child and to be an
adult are pretty unrelated occupations. To be an adult and
meet about schools is to crowd into a stuffy room and talk
talk talk for long hours at a time, not moving your body at
all or shouting or whispering or eating or touching anyone
else (but maybe laughing a bit and a few hugs at the end).
This is what growing up and becoming serious means. They
would get the same image if our business were real estate.
Why should they be interested? But what they *would* dig

doing all together would be something more emotional and active; and so would I.

See, I don't think this business of learning from children is just a romantic fancy; nor is what we have to learn from them just some humane redecoration of the rooms of our consciousness. That marvelous person Margaret Mead has described one cultural transformation that is upon us as the passage from *post-figurative* to *pre-figurative* learning—that is, from a condition in which adults transmit the entire body of each child's knowledge, through our present stage of increasing age-democratization of the learning process for the young, to what will be necessary for the dynamic stability of a culture of continual change: adults learning major life-lessons from their children, who will lead them in adapting to changing conditions of the material world and of human reality.

Well, that change goes *deep,* I don't have to tell you. (The youth catalyzation of the civil rights and antiwar movements, and kids turning their parents on to grass and encounter, are only quaint first expressions.) In its fullness, our conception of the nature and function of an educational system will be overturned. And in transition, each of us will constantly be confronted by opportunities of learning—for growth or for survival—for which our culture never prepared us.

So we should prepare to meet with our children in strange ways, not least because for some time to come much of our relevant learning must proceed along lines which were dropped or repressed during our own childhoods. The free schools are a laboratory to work out the forms of these meetings and through them will evolve toward fully democratized and pre-figurative learning communities. But that is a long way off. For now, I could stand to attend a conference designed as much by the younger members of free schools as by the older, integrally, for our mutual learning. Though the kids might get us to do something weird, like make up flags or ceremonies.

XI.

A Communications Network for Change in Higher Education

A REAL MODEL OF A SPECIALIZED COMMUNICATION NETWORK

IN THE MID-FIFTIES, when I knew its world, science fiction/ fantasy (s-f) was a young literature with an audience of perhaps 200,000 in America. This population was rich in scientists and in intellectual and social deviants—or freaks, as they're called now. Within it was a subgroup, largely of freaks, who formed a loose nucleus held together by friend-ships, avocational bonds, and a specialized communication network.

S-f is rich with esoteric references to this nuclear society. Its members were writers and magazine people, collectors of magazines, specialists of the literature and its writers' lives, people who functioned as social links in this diffuse hamlet society, young followers and devotees and romantics of the field, and so on: an odd genre's fauna. Collectively, they called themselves Science-Fiction Fandom; individually, fans.

Fandom began taking shape in the late twenties, following the proliferation of magazines touched off by Gernsback's pioneering *Amazing Stories*. It is thus deeply a communications phenomenon. This may account for the sophistication of its communication network, which—like Fandom's structure, its social and professional functioning, and the circus spectrum of its population—had more or less stabilized by the late forties.

In size, structure, and the general topography of its communications, Fandom closely resembles the "floating colleges" that Derek J. De Solla Price[1] posits as the fundamental intracommunicating intellectual groupings throughout much of science. Price's model particularly describes professional/social groups operating in frontier fields of scientific and technical innovation; so to find it applicable to the generating group of an innovative literature may not be surprising.

Like a floating college, Fandom was a system in dynamic equilibrium, with a relatively high rate of turnover among its thousand or so members. Of these, some 10 per cent were central, being both more densely connected with each other and more prolific and influential. Like a floating college, Fandom's population was relatively mobile (though as a result of personal life-style, rather than of government grants). And like a floating college, Fandom had three levels of communication: personal interchange of visits and letters;

[1] D. J. De S. Price, *Little Science, Big Science*. Columbia University Press, 1963. (See pp. 70–90.) Price calls them "invisible colleges," but the term "floating" is both more appropriate and already in use in our field. I interpret his model slightly differently than he sets it forth.

local, regional, and national meetings; and published communications.

In this last respect, Fandom differs from Price's model, though in each case publication is the only uniform currency of communication. The publications network of a floating college generally consists of one or several professional journals—e.g., *The Worm-Runners' Digest*—to which several hundred members contribute more or less actively. The domain of uniform circulation of these journals defines the floating college's territory. Within it an informal mechanism arranges for individual distribution of reprinted articles. (Xeroxes of work-in-progress also circulate, among quite small subgroups.)

Fandom's publications' network was much more complex, partly because it was an amateur, second-order system. Fandom had a first-order, centralized system already: the s-f magazines themselves, which are essentially a professional literature, uniformly subscribed to, with no arrangement for reprints. But Fandom publications formed a sophisticated information network not only because they were an auxiliary amateur system free of rigid professional necessities, but also because they serviced the needs of an unusual population.

One index to this is the range of subjects an important fanzine[2] might deal with—e.g., analyses of the literature, personal memoirs of fanfolk, deviant psychotherapeutic theories, archaeology and mythology, rocket fuels, the history of printing, gun lore, and bad jokes. S-f fans, as a class, had a bewildering array of interests. They were diverse in other respects as well, autonomous, and as prone to cliques as artists. Their publications system had to deal with this, and deal also with their urge and need to be bound together by more than professional and intellectual concerns: actively to be a society.

---

[2] The "fanzine," from "fan magazine," is the staple unit of publication.

FANZINES, CIRCA 1955

Against this background, an indigenous medium evolved: the fanzine and its distribution system. In form, the fanzine was mutable. Some were "one-shots"—on a single sheet, tossed off by a beery group for fun one evening, or of many pages, celebrating a person or an event.

Most fanzines were periodical. In a constant flux new ones appeared, to flourish or limp for a few issues and disappear. Some specialized in neophyte literature of the field; others were periodicals of debate. Some represented the interests of an intracommunicating subgroup of Fandom; others, one person's thought and writing. Some followed jagged editorial policies; a few set standards of excellence for a decade.

Fanzines had a fairly standard physical form. Most had circulations of between 50 and 200 and were indifferently mimeographed on hand-cranked machines in basements somewhere, or at the office after-hours. Some were jobs of excellent craftsmanship done in hand-set type, or by the Gestetner mimeo, which at the time was the highest-quality cheap mass-reproduction system available for amateur use.

Most "one-shots" were distributed to a specialized extension of some standard mailing list. Some periodicals had their individual lists, and were also sent to anyone requesting them. (Constant and intimate reference to each other among fanzines kept this system of requests functioning fluidly and actively.)

Other periodicals were organized into more elaborate distribution pools—e.g., the Fantasy Amateur Press Association. FAPA had about 120 members, of whom maybe 40 contributed regularly to the quarterly mailings, each of which included say 30 more fanzines on an ad-hoc basis. Every three months or so, your FAPA dues would bring you this thick motley bundle of multipapered fanzines, mailed from some central assembly point (which rotated regularly among various clusters of members in the country).

Faced with maybe a thousand pages of mailing, you would sort out the fanzines you followed regularly and respected, the one-shoters of friends, and whatever else looked interesting. Some reference might turn you on to something you missed last round. And you in turn might write in reaction to something in the mailing and distribute it the next mailing in some friendly fanzine or as a one-shoter.

So, by the mutable medium of the fanzine, several thousand people, organized in depth around an open-ended subject field, were joined in a loose active communications system. They were connected, not by a central publication, but by a delicate shifting network of overlapping information spheres. Within this network, the specialized common language of Fandom evolved, without wiping out local dialects, assimilating new components naturally from the network's variegated inputs. Since the network was generated by many autonomous centers, it formed a public free economy, in which standards of taste, relevance, and competence were highly individual and competed on an open market. And the decentralized quality of the network also provided the space and freedom for the development of intracommunicating social and intellectual subgroupings.

REFINEMENT OF THE MODEL:
A COMPUTERIZED FANZINE

Consider the problem of constructing a useful communication network for the domain of educational innovation, which needs to be defining itself constantly in new directions. The members and groups of this floating college of change tend to be young, autonomous, and highly individual. Many can tie in to institutional resources and have access to mimeo or Xerox facilities and sometimes mailing funds. They generate a multicentered conversation with strong inputs from diverse sources—computer technology, existential psychology, social action, and so on—that needs to be peculiarly free.

The principles of the fanzine network need only be married to computer technology to form the basis for a real experiment. Here is the hybrid model in its extreme form; most of its essential features are realizable (somewhat differently) with current technology and budgets.

The system's heart is a big black box that accepts inputs in the form: TYPED MANUSCRIPT + DISTRIBUTION LIST. (They may be punched in directly from peripheral consoles.) Their form is perfectly free. Individuals and groups may publish once, sporadically, regularly. Essays, notes, reports, computer-transmittable pictures, monographs, dinner invitations, recruitments, whole journals with an open variety of editorial policies and functions. There is no central and limiting sense of what is appropriate to the conversation. (It may be expected to become recognizably deformalized, personalized, and more flexible.)

You—an individual or a group—draw information from the system at your console, or as print-out mailed to you at convenient intervals by the central computer. What you receive is completely personalized. You have a list of small periodicals you follow and you ask to be sent the work of your friends and some others, whenever it appears. Any inputs on some subjects are to be sent to you automatically; and summaries or notices of inputs on some other subjects. You also receive what friends and strangers choose to send you. But every item you get is marked with a priority—you can set the categories up to your own taste—and so you're free to ignore unsolicited junk.

You are free to select the distribution of what you produce: this is an art, which you can let some editor in the network handle for you. As a receiver of information, you encounter the network as a flexible instrument or game, at which, as at the game of the Sunday *Times,* you must develop skill to learn what you need out of what's available. (In this and other respects, the network encourages participation.) Constant cross-referencing to articles, themes, and sources will be an important feature of the network—even more than in present floating colleges—and you will have to learn what combination of journals and intellectual gossips is your best guide to the multiplex literature. (The fanzine network generates such specialized guides.)

The central feature of this hybrid system is the freedom it permits and encourages. Needs for information can be defined and satisfied on an individual (rather than mass) basis. Though the conversation has no central government, a common vocabulary of change can still grow, and will: ideas get around, especially in such a rumor-quick system. Unlike the relatively closed conversations that heavily centralized professional journals seem to generate, the structure of this network encourages a conversation quickly open to new components and directions, one that keeps a constant diversity of themes in rolling contact. (Some editors will become specialized channels for new terms without closing off others, filling that niche in the ecology of conversants.) And, perhaps most importantly, the network also facilitates the nucleation and development of subgroups organized on any basis of work, ideas, or friendship.

At the end of Chapter VII, I sketched a few aspects of change in social process as our civilization comes to extend itself through high computer/communications technology. Here we have a more detailed (though overly print-oriented) model of the freer processes of information that become possible. It will be seen that they lead toward true *publics,* rather than to masses of individuals; and toward radical cultural diversity.

IS IT PRACTICAL?

How could a real experiment along these lines begin? Take the several thousand people working at the edge of change in higher education, in programmed instruction, community action, affective education, counseling, sociology of education, video, etc. They already communicate informally and partially, by Xeroxes and reprints and through ancillary specialized journals.

They would *assess, centralize, rationalize,* and *extend* this present distribution system. Most inputs would be distributed to only several hundred people, and a central facility could compensate for authors who can't take advantage of the growing availability of high-speed Xerox and cheap offset. Inputs for systemwide distribution could be mimeographed or offset. Distribution assignments and requests could easily be correlated and prioritized by computer, as in the fully computerized network. At worst, individual periodic issues of this diffuse "magazine" could be assembled by hand according to computer list. Funding for this information network could come in the form of a graduated support-fee.[3]

A NOTE ON EXPERIMENT

A group that attempts such an experiment might make a simultaneous self-study of the way the creation and use of this network affects the character of correspondence, both

[3] Perhaps depending on input/receipt use. See G. Pask and H. Von Foerster, "A Predictive Model for Self-Organizing Systems," *Cybernetica,* Vol. III, No. 4, 1960. Their models of self-organizing data-interchange systems might aid description of the change process which this network's creation would comprise.

printed and written. Perhaps only an impressionistic account can be had of the difference in the way public ideas grow. But hard quantitative data should be obtainable on some aspects of the conversation's change.

For example, the distribution and mean of audience-size for papers should shift, perhaps in this manner:

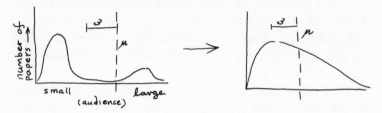

There should be kindred shifts in the distributions of papers (information) received by individuals, along variables like size, shared audience, recentness, informality, use-resultant cross-referencing, and so on.

All such factors relate intimately to the ease and power with which a massive group can think together. For surely the topology—the connectivity, directionality, etc.—and the technology of the group's communications net largely determine the way ideas are formed and exert their influence. By such quantifiable factors one trace of this can be followed.

XII.

Transcending the Totalitarian Classroom: The Day They Purged Maurice Stein

WHEN THE GREAT LOS ANGELES earthquake of early '71 cracked open a third of the California Institute of the Arts buildings, I figured it was merely divine retribution for the ugly way Maurie Stein had been fired. By then the dismemberment of the School of Critical Studies was well under way, and the only thing I could do that was useful was give people backrubs to ease the pain. But before everything got too chaotic and demoralizing to deal with, back in the first term, when the space of our school still seemed open, I tried to conduct a regular "class," for the first time in years.

Tuesday and Thursday of every other week, we met on the lawn in the afternoon, moved indoors when it grew cold. My friend Paul organized the group when he was with Liz, a gregarious dance major, so five of the seven students turned out to be from her school, the most discipline-heavy of C.I.A.'s six divisions.

We needed a title to satisfy the Accreditors, so I called it "On Learning and Social Change," and listed my papers as bibliography. But the real name of our course was "Learning from Our Experience." I had in mind no curriculum— only to make a small space where we would be free to help each other figure out what was happening to us, and what to do.

By our sixth meeting, things began to get interesting. The previous ones were mostly about getting to know each other and creating the trust that enabled people to bring up the things that concerned them. In that process we talked a lot about learning, the arts, the politics of the school, drugs, and so on. After this, and five twilight odysseys across campus in search of a room to continue talking in, the customary magic happened, and we began to function as a group.

Sixth meeting, we were sitting on the lawn, beginning, when Paul came up, tumbled a bit with Liz, and said, "Mary Ann ran off a thousand catalogues for Critical Studies, and she has to stay until they're assembled. Why don't we go help her?" Class, schmass: the idea was to be open, and we trooped off to the office. We jockeyed around a while until we fell into a mutual rhythm, each person walking around the long table with its twenty neat stacks, pausing at the end to staple and stack a catalogue and walking back to begin again.

Pursuing our slow rotation, after half an hour we began to talk again. I'd been trying to lay off rapping, for obvious reasons. But something I said casually to Richard caught his attention; his energy flared, centering the group. I found myself talking to all, as he pressed me for detail on how Amerika and the landscapes of possibility had appeared fifteen years ago, when I entered college. I went on for a bit about what it was like to grow up as a freaky member of the Silent Generation in a time that held no hint of real options, and how it felt to have the FBI at our door during the McCarthy years. And then I fell silent, amazed by the well of memory opened in me by their attention and embarrassed by Richard's avid interest. As we went on gathering papers and talk swirled off, I realized how hungry they were to understand the past of this troubling present and to have a sense of human connection with it.[1]

Opening up like that left me with too much energy to handle in slow routine, and after a while I dropped out of rotation and stood at the end of the line, assembling the last four sheets and handing them to people as they came up. Soon someone stood next to me, assembling the penultimate four sheets, and then others ceased their circulation to extend the static line. We were acting out spontaneously the formation of an enzyme: within two minutes our molecule was functioning as an integral unit, assembling the precursor pages into organic form at twice the rate of anarchist production. After we were through, we talked a while about what this efficiency had cost our process, and how the more complicated cooperations required by this linear teamwork had taken enough attention to destroy our conversation, and the function of various modes of production in a capitalist state; and then we dispersed to dinner.

When we met again, the atmosphere was charged and complex: the clampdown at C.I.A. had begun. From the start the president and provost were upset by the eclectic sprawl of courses offered by the faculty Maurie had assembled—fifty freaky scholars, mostly young, life-radical

---

[1] Now that I think of it, this incident helped push me into pulling together *The Wedding Within the War*.

and high-powered—and that he left us free to teach what we would was intolerable. Neither they nor most of the deans were charmed by 5 A.M. *Mantra Chanting* or *The Aesthetics of Rock;* they wanted a few Art History courses to satisfy the State Accrediting Commission. And they just couldn't deal with walking into the Critical Studies office and being unable to tell the teachers from the students.

It's true that our school was chaotic. The governing council we had chosen by lot, one from each sign of the Zodiac, was just coming to face the real problems involved in taking over the functions of the deanship from Maurie (who still somewhat clung to them), integrating the work of our school, and coordinating with the needs of the other schools. But no one in the administration had the patience to wait for results, beset as they were by all the frustrations of founding a new (and badly planned) institution, plus a certain need for control. Barely two months into our experiment in self-structuring, the word came down at a deans' conference luncheon: Maurie should shape up his school, or be relieved of his duties.

Rumor is quick on a campus that small. By the time we met on the lawn at 4:30, everyone knew. Paul and Beth had seen it coming since school started, and we'd talked about it in class; but the others were still shocked when the discord became formal and public. Richard was asputter with the indignation of the innocent. "But they can't do that," he said, "this is the only class I have where people aren't always telling me what to do. If they try to take it away . . . I'll fight 'em, that's what I'll do, I'll fight." In the end, neither students nor faculty could manage any effective resistance to the school's reorganization. Still, we spent half an hour going over the institution's power politics, and our paranoia.

When we went inside, prepared by the moment's emotion and our last meeting's experience of teamwork, some level of reserve gave way, and talk for the first time moved to a certain deeper level. For weeks Beth had been advancing her uneasy feelings about the contradiction between a professional career in a classical art and the kind of life and person she wanted to be. Now, following her lead, one by one they began to confess their versions of her tensions and doubts—even Larry, the graduate student, already well into his work as a teacher. I lay back and just listened. For a long time they struggled to bring out their feelings about what they wanted and needed; about what sort of artist it was worth becoming in this time, and with what relation to society; about the examples of their teachers' lives; and so on. It was dark when we broke up, many unsettling questions opened, none resolved.

When we came together again, the atmosphere of crisis had subsided some, though our school was feverish with committee caucuses. The group formed without the usual horseplay and kidding around. I waited for someone to pick up the threads of our last meeting. No one ventured to. Laurie asked when their experience reports would be due; we talked listlessly about the technical details. Someone made a joke about bureaucratic function. It didn't sound funny. Winter was coming to Los Angeles, the lawn was chill, we went inside early. Same scene. Troubled, I started talking about something or other; found myself rapping on; shut up. We sat there in paralyzed silence for a solid hour. We were miserable, we couldn't even manage to talk about what was happening to us; it was like one of those awfuller hours with your shrink. Charlie stood up and left abruptly. Finally Paul grunted in dull brain-flash, got up and turned off the light, revealing the darkness outside, sat down again. As late twilight swirled around us, a slight sigh escaped. He took out his guitar and played softly. Charlie came back, with a half-gallon of wine. We moved closer together on the linoleum floor, heads came to rest on laps or legs. Liz rubbed Laurie's shoulders; the bottle passed around. When nightfall was complete, we left, still in silence.

Looking back, I see that this interlude of paralysis came after we made a breakthrough of sorts. We had talked together, worked together, and confessed; and had reached a level, perhaps of honesty, that we needed to go on from. Yet we were not together enough as a group to do this at will. And so we sat silent, because no one wanted to go back. I was too preoccupied with the governance crisis and futile strategies of resistance to prepare for our next meeting. But drifting there I ran into Beth, and we wound up going to the supermarket to pick up some food.

When we got back a party had already started. Charlie had come into some champagne, had been at it since three, and brought the rest along. His blond pigtails floated like wings as he waved us in to the bottle circle, where we tore open the bags. Bread, cheese, apples, wine. No one felt like saying anything to remind us we were a "class." Paul fell to his guitar, I had my flute, people started singing something current. The door was open, friends dropped in from late rehearsals, there was food enough. Singing went on, changed to clapping and chanting, tribal harmonies rising and falling, passing through one frantic crescendo. Somewhere in there we got into a back-rubbing thing and wound up in a working circle. I forget how it all fell out in detail, but those hours were pretty mellow.

Meanwhile C.I.A.'s power-play went on, our committees bumbled along trying to delay the inevitable, and the Managers' patience ran out. One day Maurie got a memo from President Corrigan, relieving him of his duties and appointing the provost as interim dean. A meeting was set at Corrigan's house that night, to explain the matter to the "senior faculty" of Critical Studies. By the time it began, some fifty of Maurie's sympathizers, faculty and student, had found their way across the freeways to crowd into Corrigan's living room. In that space, formal as a museum and as chockful of modern graphics on display, we sat, an angry tribe, but too academic and disorganized to be dangerous. Still, the president was careful to bring us ashtrays.

For hours we went round—it was impossible to get a straight answer—about what the president and provost felt was wrong with our school and what plans they had for revising it. They kept telling us that no one's job was in danger (and, to be fair, they wound up firing only eight); that it was a case of personal incompatibility, Maurie being unfit to be a dean. Politics reduced to personality. They were outraged because he couldn't keep secrets and had allowed confidential memos from the administration to be circulated. I remembered how my class had reacted to them, to the attitudes and plans they revealed—the brass had reason to be upset.

But what they kept harping on most was Maurie's paranoia, which made him, they said, intractable and uncooperative. The deans adduced examples of his crazy behavior. There was no ventilation; we were sweating. By the time the Noted Elder Journalist started pontificating about how paranoid the school's governance meetings had been, I couldn't stand it any more. "They're all paranoid," he declaimed, waving an arm vaguely in my direction. "Who, me?" I said, standing up, "Me? I'm not paranoid. No, me, I'm not paranoid," my voice rising out of control into a very real shriek that propelled me backwards, twitching and gibbering, to fall two casual inches away from the huge picture window, twined around some *objet d'art* and still crying, "No, no, nobody's paranoid."

I didn't break reality. After a moment the provost went on explaining, in a slow, controlled voice, precisely how paranoid Maurie was. But why shouldn't he have been paranoid? Since before school opened, when they suppressed the brilliant student handbook that Michael Bell labored for a month to cast into a concrete poem, they had threatened Maurie's firing, reminding him weekly by more and more open displeasure and diminishing cooperation. We protested: we all had felt apprehensive for months, with good reason. The provost hinted at dark matters he chose not to reveal, "for Maurie's good"; spoke again of paranoia.

Meanwhile the tableau is like this: facing the president and consort of deans, across the little open circle remaining in the room, is Maurie, seated. And standing behind him is the provost. You can see his hands in the lamplight; they rest on the chair above Maurie's shoulders, now and again touching him for emphasis in the course of speech. But the rest of the provost is in shadow. For an hour now his features have been invisible, his voice coming from the darkness above Maurie's head. I wonder again what irony led the Disney money to pick as C.I.A.'s campus boss a man so dedicated to the theater, and to the traditional vision of the director's tyranny as being essential for group art. Suddenly Maurie understands what is happening, or perhaps he has borne it and now breaks. He spins out of his seat, yelling, "Goddamn you, Herb, come out of the shadows! Let me see you when you talk to me! You've been doing this all the time, you've got to stop it!" And for a moment it seems that Maurice is going to grab him, wrestle him into the light. Then the provost steps out and continues talking, quite calmly and reasonably. The hostile deans, behind him now, nod their heads significantly: have we not just seen an example of paranoid irrationality?

After that, the theater was downhill all the way, a six-month series of rear-guard actions to protect what jobs we could. The student protest meeting the next day was energetic but indecisive, and was not repeated. It is too distressing and commonplace for me to go into the details of why even Maurie's friends were unable to muster organization and spine—suffice it to say that the situation was fucked from the start. Only the earthquake cheered us.

It was about that time, perhaps on the very afternoon of Maurie's firing, that our class met again, in the room we had come to think of as our home. Again the atmosphere was turbulent with weird energy. We spent some time sharing bread, fruit, wine, and a joint. I started talking more about my first experiences in the years of purge and paranoia: what it was like to be a child of Commie parents, to babysit at twelve, alone at night waiting for the knock on the door; the incredible pressures to conform in school; and so on. And something opened up between us—at first with Larry.

I knew Dance students were, on the whole, the straightest and most sheltered at C.I.A. But Larry's early description of the dance-based learning games he'd developed with children had so entranced me that I didn't realize how distant our worlds were until he gave me his Experience Report to sign. In the awkward script and run-on speechy sentences of one long unaccustomed to writing, he described our class, adding: ". . . and though I had never worked with a hairy & freaky person like Mr. Rossman before, I learned that he is like me in many ways . . ." Or something like that. "Gee," I said, handing it back to him, somewhat at a loss for words.

This time, after the wine went around again, he started talking about his draft physical. He was trying to get a C.O. but thought they might let him out because of his eye thing. I couldn't quite grasp the shift from the McCarthy years. His eye thing? Yes, sometimes he saw the world reversed, light for dark and vice-versa, for some minutes. Far out! We started talking about color-blindness, wearing prisms to see things upside down, and so on. Then he said, "And I used to see things that weren't there."

Like what?

"When I was a child, every night after they put me in bed, when they closed the door. People would come out from the closet, walk across the room, go out the window. A whole line of them. I called for my parents to come see them. They came, they couldn't see anything. After a while they wouldn't come, they just told me to go to sleep, there was nobody there. After a while I started seeing them less and less often, eventually it just stopped. That's funny. I'd forgotten about that for a long time."

And then others started to trot them out; I think five of us confessed to strangeness. Richard, the brilliant mime and extrovert—it turned out he did automatic handwriting. Every now and then he'd be sitting, and his hand and fingers would start to move, just like that. Paper and pen translated the motion into strange words, scrawled for page after page. "Oh, is that what it is? I didn't know it had a name." "There are books about it," I said, "check the library. How come no one ever told you the name?" "I never told anyone before, only a couple of close friends my age, and they didn't know anything." "How come?" "Huh," he snorted, in adolescent scorn, "think I'm crazy? The way I figured, it was something so weird, it might have military value. I didn't want them locking me up in some room, with armed guards around it and scientists poking me. So I just kept quiet."

"Well," I said weakly, "lots of people do it. Besides, the pigs don't care about that sort of thing." Recovering, I said a bit about the experiences of telepathy and teleportation I'd shared with Karen. I am only now realizing that the pigs may indeed care.

I think the last to testify in this vein was Liz, our triple-Ares churn of positive energy. I used to tease her about the songs she wrote and sang so well—wholesome and uplifting, packed with mid-sixties Baez optimism. Now, as twilight swept over our close circle, she told us of her summer on the northern coast, in a large technological commune; and described how they used to sit in the living room at night, around the fire, and conjure forth large violet balls of energy, drift them around the room with their minds, bumping from person to person. "They said a spaceship was buried in the hill," she said, "but I didn't see it." When she was done, we were quiet for a while, and then went off to dinner.

I don't think I came down to L.A. again before Christmas vacation; and after that the general air of demoralization at

C.I.A. was so heavy that most cooperations, including ours, fragmented lingeringly. When I saw Maurie again, in a brief space of peace, I told him how our class had gone and what it had come to. He was delighted by the clear progression it revealed in the midst of turmoil, and observed, "When the social fabric is tearing apart, the fabric of individual consciousness begins to tear too." I thought this applied more to the whole experience of the sixties than to our brief stay at C.I.A., but I still savored his insight.

EIN INDEX

A

B

F

G

H

I

J

jobs, 49
Joyce, James, 120*n*

K

Keniston, Kenneth, 87, 117*n*
Kesey, Ken, 120*n*
Kleinman, Neil, 11
KMPX, 79–81
knowledge, 47, 59, 161–3, 165–6, 173–4,
        191, 254–61; the way of a man of,
        132–4
KPFA, *see* Pacifica
Kuhn, T. H., 146

L

Lao-tzu, 153, 177–8, 183, 264, 287
leadership, *see* authority
learning: conjugate levels of, 45–6; field
        theory of 61–3; cyclic model of, 69,
        138–44; as death and birth, 69, 146,
        155; and participation, 66, 87; by
        imitation, 12; soft forms of, 122–8;
        as problem-solving cycle, 129; the
        way of a man of knowledge, 132–4;
        in the university, 160–1, 170–1; as
        sequential process, 172–4; as de-
        centralized cultural process, 250,
        255–7, 267; hybrid forms of, 20,

R

S

T

U

V

About the Author

A veteran activist, MICHAEL ROSSMAN was a leader of the Berkeley Free Speech Movement. In 1966 he left school, where he had been a graduate student and teaching assistant, to become a traveling organizer of educational change. Since then he has worked with students on more than seventy campuses throughout the country in seminars and workshops, helping to create a significant new body of experiment and thought about education.